HENRY BENNET, EARL OF ARLINGTON, SECRETARY OF STATE TO CHARLES II

HENRY BENNET, EARL OF ARLINGTON, SECRETARY OF STATE TO CHARLES II

Violet Barbour

General Books

A General Books LLC Publication.

Published by General Books LLC.

CONTENTS

1

SECTION 1

PREFACE.

The Ministers of Charles II were not chosen for their honesty, nor were they retained in office for services rendered the state. Yet, as the King himself was far from dull-witted, so the men whom he advanced were always intelligent and sometimes exceptionally able. If they accomplished little to their credit, it is not because they were sunk in frivolity and vice, as is commonly assumed, but because they served a lazy, venal, and capricious master, whose government was perpetually on the edgeland frequently over the edgelof bankruptcy. The errors of the Cabal Ministry, in particular, have been more cordially recognized than its difficulties, and the five men who composed it have been execrated without being sufficiently known. Least known of the five, save by the testimony of his bitterest enemies, is Arlington. Yet, during the twelve years in which he was Secretary of State, no measure of importance was contemplated by the government without his participation, and in questions of foreign policy his knowledge and experience gave him the deciding voice. For five years, from the fall of Clarendon in 1667 to the outbreak of the Second Dutch War in 1672, his influence with the King made him the greatest personage in England.

To deal with any part of the social history of this reign whichlas only Mr. Chesterton could sayl" attracts us morally ", is not the intention of this essay. Its purpose is rather to determine the extent of Arlington's political activity, the measure of his responsibility in the resolutions of the government, and in the success of those resolutions, particularly in the field of foreign affairs.

The materials for such a study are greater in bulk than in content. Arlington's private letterslif he ever wrote anylhave vanished. His letters to the Duke of Ormonde, half-friendly, half-official, form the most intimate and interesting part of his extant correspondence. Some of these letters have been published by the Historical Manuscripts Commission;1 a large number which have not been printed are among the Carte MSS. in the Bodleian Library. The Clarendon MSS., also in the Bodleian, furnish in practically complete sequence the despatches written by Bennet in his capacity of resident in Spain, previous to the Restoration. Certain of the letters which he addressed in the course of his secretaryship to the English ambassadors at Madrid and the Hague were published by Thomas Bebington in 1701. A small fraction of the correspondence emanating from his office may be found in abstract in the *Calendars of State Papers, Domestic* and *Colonial.* In general Arlington's official letters are little better than no letters at all for the information they afford, since it was his rule never to trust any one. To compensate in some sort for this deficiency we have the minute and voluble commentaries of the French ambassadors in England on the secretary's official conduct, as well as on all other persons and occurrences that met their observation. Many of their despatches have been published in Mig- net's *Negotiations relatives a la Succession d'Espagne,*but the bulk of the correspondence must still be consulted at the Archives des Affaires Etrangeres at Paris. Of quite as much human interest are the rough notes of debates in the Committee of Foreign Affairs, jotted down by Sir Joseph Williamson and preserved in the Public Record Office at London.2 Much information in regard to the foreign situation during Arlington's secretaryship is to be found under the headings " France ", " Holland ", and " Spain " in the State Papers at the Record Office.

1 *Calendar of the Manuscripts of the Marquis of Ormonde, preserved at Kilkenny Castle,* new series, 7 vols.

Of letters to Bennet there is no end. Those of Charles II and of Abraham Cowley in Brown's *Miscellanea Aulica,* those of Sir William Temple published in his *Works,* those of Ralph Montagu, written while he was ambassador to France,8 and those of the Prince of Orange,' are the most interesting.

The memoirs and diaries of this period contain a great deal of information about Arlington of varying degrees of reliability: Pepys, Clarendon, James II, Sir William Temple, Bishop Burnet, Sir John Evelyn, the Earl of Ailesbury, the Count de Gramont, and the Duke of Buckinghamlall have an opinion of the Secretary of State. Equally rich in information are such collections of letters as the *Nicholas Papers, Essex Papers, Correspondence of the Family of Hatton,* and *Letters addressed to Sir Joseph Williamson.*

The dates given in the text of this essay are all according to the Old Style or Julian calendar. In the footnotes, letters and documents cited are dated as in theoriginal, but when such dates are New Style, or Gregorian, that fact is indicated by the letters N. S. In the spelling of proper names, the practice of the *Dictionary of National Biography* has been followed.

a Foreign Entry Books, 176-177.

8 Hist. MSS. Comm., *Manuscripts of the Duke of Buccleuch and Queens- berry, preserved at Montagu House, Whitehall, 2* vols.

Original Letters from King William III, then Prince of Orange, to King Charles II, Lord Arlington, etc., London, 1704.

The generosity of Wellesley College in awarding the Alice Freeman Palmer Fellowship to the graduate of another institution, and the award by Cornell University of the President White Fellowship in European History, made possible the accomplishment of the research necessary to this study. The writer is glad to express her indebtedness to Professor C. H. Firth of Oxford for advice as to sources of material; to Doctor N. Japikse, who facilitated a search in the Rijksarchief at the Hague; to the Reverend Herbert Wilson, Rector of Harlington, for permission to examine the registers of that parish; and to the Reverend H. I. Kilner for the same privilege in respect to the registers of Little Sax- ham. In the work of revision, the suggestions of Professor G. L. Burr of Cornell University have been most helpful. The subject of the essay was suggested by Professor Ralph C. H. Catterall, also of Cornell, to whom the writer is particularly grateful for his kindly interest in the progress of the work, and for much valuable advice and criticism.

V. B.

Ithaca, New York,
January, 1914.

2

SECTION 2

CHAPTER I.
Youth Of Henry Bennet.

The family of Bennet has ramified widely through the counties of England, and, while generally well-to- do, is seldom illustrious. In the sixteenth century the Bennets of Berkshire were undistinguished gentry living in Wallingford and making undistinguished marriages in Oxford and Buckinghamshire.1 From this obscurity one John Bennet emerged brilliantly at the beginning of the seventeenth century as a lawyer, politician, and courtier. Under the patronage of James I he rose to be judge of the prerogative court of Canterbury, member of Parliament and of the Council of the North, and chancellor to the Queen, Anne of Denmark. The fortune he accumulated in these places of trust was reported to be fabulous, but for all its glamour, Sir John figures rather humorously in the letters of that time as a shrewd, pushing man of business, well under thethumb of his termagant wife.2 The fine airs of Lady Bennet were the joy of the Court, and so huge were the farthingales she wore that neither coach nor chair could hold them, but she must go afoot amid the cheers of street-urchins."

1 There *is* a partial genealogy of the Bennets of Berkshire among the Rawlinson MSS., A 429, f. 3. Other particulars, given in connection with Thomas Bennet

(brother of the John Bennet noticed above), who was a wealthy alderman, and became Lord Mayor of London in 16o3, are to be found in the *Remembrancia,* 2o8, footnote r. Richard Bennet, greatgrandfather to Henry Bennet, married Elizabeth Tesdale, sister of the founder of Pembroke College (Oxon.), Thomas Tesdale, a prosperous trader in malt of Abingdon. (See Wood's *History and Antiquities of the Colleges and Halls in the University of Oxford,* 616-628.) Many of the family were educated at Oxford (see the notices of Bennets of this connection in Foster's *Alumni Oxonienses),* and I find one of the sons of the above-mentioned Richard Bennet referred to as ' Richard Bennet, Gentleman " (Little, *A Monument of Christian Munificence,* 63-65), which would indicate that the family stood higher in the social scale than tradesmen or yeomen.

When the Lord Chancellor Ellesmere surrendered the seals, Sir John Bennet was one of the competitors for his place, and offered the astounding sum of thirty thousand pounds for it, but was justly refused in favor of the learned Sir Francis Bacon.4 With similar inducements Bennet besought the King to appoint him Secretary of State, and again his offer was ignored.5 In 1617 he had the consolation of a diplomatic mission to Flanders, of such trifling consequence that it would never have suggested itself to any one except the trifler then reigning over England.5 Sir John accomplished nothing in it, and was glad to return to his legal responsibilities. He was a powerful and a courted man in 1621, when, without warning, the whole structure of his fortunes collapsed. While the impeachment of the Lord Chancellor Bacon held the attention of the House of Lords, another impeachment, brought into the Commons where Sir John was member for Oxford, discovered the fact that during the nineteen years in which he had been judge of the Prerogative Court he had received countless bribesloften from both parties to a suitland had appropriated vast sums bequeathed to charity. The Court of Star Chamber took over the case, and sentenced Sir John to a fine of twenty thousand pounds and imprisonment in the Fleet. In 1624 he was pardoned and released, but his career was ended. He died unnoticed three years later.7

1 Leonora Vierendeels, daughter of a citizen of Antwerp. She was the third wife of Sir John Bennet. The first, Anne, daughter of Christopher Weekes, Gentleman, of Salisbury, died in 16o1; the second, Elizabeth, daughter of Sir Thomas Lowe, alderman of London, died in 1614.

8 Birch, *The Court and Times of James I,* II, 14, June 3/13, 1617, Sir Dudley Carleton to John Chamberlain, Esq.

4 *Cal. St. P., Dom., 1611-1618,* p. 449.

Ibid., p. 498.

He was sent to demand of the Archduke Albert, governor-general of the Spanish Netherlands, the punishment of Hendrik van der Putte, or Henricus Puteanus, a Jesuit lecturer in the University of Louvain, who in a book entitled *Corona Regia* had satirized James and his Court. Bennet's reports to the Secretary of State, Sir Ralph Winwood, and to the English ambassador at the Hague, Sir Dudley Carleton, are in the Record Office, State Papers, Flanders, 12, *passim.*

The eldest son of Sir John Bennet, also named John, shared his father's ill fortune as he had shared his prosperity. He had received an education at Oxford, studied the law at Gray's Inn, and thereafter traveled on the Continent as it was fashionable for young gentlemen to do.' In 1616 the King knighted him at Theobald's,' and in the following year he was sworn of the privy chamber of Charles, prince of Wales.10 The report of his father's wealth made him a very eligible young man, so that the elder Sir John had no difficulty in arranging a match for him with a young lady of quality, Dorothy, daughter of Sir John Crofts, knight, of Saxham in Suffolk. The Crofts were well received at Court and related to several noble families," considerations which were doubtless attractive to the head of the House of Bennet. King James was wont to stopat Saxham on his way to Newmarket, and had professed himself an admirer of his host's pretty daughters," but as Crofts was blessed with nine, it is impossible to infer with certainty anything as to the appearance of Dorothy in particular. In fact we know nothing about her at all.

7 There is an excellent sketch of Sir John Bennet, in the *Dictionary of National Biography,* by J. M. Rigg.

'Alumni Oxonienses; Cal. St. P., Dom., 1611-1618, pp. 59, 11o.

Shaw's *Knights,* II, 158, June 15, 1616.

10 Hist. MSS. Comm., *MSS. of the Duke of Buccleuch,* I, 195, April 17, 1617, Sir John Bennet to Secretary Winwood.

a See the extensive notice of the Crofts family in the *Little Saxham Parish Registers;* also a statement by Sir Edward Walker, Garter King- at-Arms, that Secretary Bennet, being most nobly descended, on the mother's side, from several earls' families, might take the name of one of them, as Bradston, or Ingoldsthorp. *(Cal. St. P., Dom., 1664-1665,* p. 246.)

For a few years after their marriage the young couple lived in Saxham when they were not with the Court. The register of the church of St. Nicholas at Saxham records the baptism of their sons: John, the eldest, was born in 1616, and his brother Henry, the future Secretary of State, two years later." After his father's disgrace young Sir John Bennet retired with his wife and children to the quiet and beautiful village of Harling- ton in Middlesex, twenty miles from London, where the elder Sir John had acquired the manor of Dawley in 1607." He had not the abilitylor, perhaps, not the ambitionlto restore the family prestige, and so, dropping out of the society that once knew him, lived in seclusion, a country gentleman of moderate fortune.1" Many children were born to him, of whom five reached maturity. Besides the eldest sons already mentioned, there were two boys, Edward and Charles, and a daughter, Elizabeth."

12 *Little Saxham Parish Registers,* 169.

18 *Ibid.,* 7. The date of Henry Bennet's baptism is Sept. 6, 1618.

14 Lysons, *Historical Account of those Parishes which are not described in the Environs of London,* 127.

18 Sir John Bennet, when endeavoring to escape assessment by Parliament in 1643, valued his real estate at $300 a year, and his personal property at $500 (State Papers, Interregnum, 497, f. 120). In the order book of the committee for assessing the tax of the twentieth part of personal property *(ibid.,* A. 61, p. 26), Sir John's tax is $120, which would make his personal property worth $2400. According to the value of money at that time, he would not be accounted a poor man.

1' Parish Registers of Harlington, Middlesex (not printed).

At Harlington Harry Bennet's childhood was passed. Being a younger son, he was early destined for the Church," and probably for the living of Harlington, the advowson of which was attached to the manor of Daw- ley. He attended the Westminster School; thence, at the age of seventeen, he matriculated at Christ Church, Oxford, the college of his father and grandfather." The following year he was presented to a studentship." His brother John was entered at the same time as a gentleman commoner of Pembroke College, of whose founder the Bennets were collateral descendants.20

Oxford was then undergoing a purification and chastening under the direction of its new chancellor, William Laud, bishop of London. Gambling was forbidden, ale-houses were few, students were expected not to disturb the peace. Harry Bennet must have participated in the last celebrations of the Westminster Supper, which Christ Church men from Westminster School were wont to hold annually in joyous drunkenness until Laud abolished it in 1638. He must have witnessed the pageantry of the royal visit to Oxford in 1636, for the King and Queen were entertained in his own college, and sadly bored, no doubt, by the lucubrations of Christ Church dramatists.

The lure of a parsonage in Harlington with forty pounds a year did not arouse in Harry Bennet an enthusiasm for theology. He did not take orders as divinity students were expected to do. It was recalledlong afterwards in his defense that at this time he was entirely orthodox,21 but the orthodoxy of complete indifference is often indistinguishable from the orthodoxy of conviction, and in Bennet's case the former is more probable. He became, however, an eager student of classical literature and developed a just taste and a pleasing style. " He was a better scholar ", says John Sheffield, duke of Buckingham, " than commonly Courtiers are; and so well versed in the Classick Poets, that I never knew any man apply them so properly on any subject whatsoever, and without any pedantic affectation." Straying still further in the pleasant ways of secular reading, he fell in love with the memoirs of Philippe de Commines, and with Davila's history of the Huguenot wars, both of which he recommended later to the attention of Charles II with the advice to burn.all other books."

"Wood *(Fasti,* Sept. 2&, 1663), Sheffield *(Works,* II, 86), and Evelyn *(Diary,* Sept. 10, 1677) all state that Bennet was educated for the Church.

18 *Alumni Oxonienses.*

"The one hundred and one fellows of Christ Church are called Students. They were entitled to a stipend of from forty to sixty pounds a year.

20 *Alumni Oxonienses.* See p. 1, footnote 1, of this biography.

In the university world Bennet passed for something of a poet, and was a regular contributor to the little volumes of Latin odes and English pastorals with which Oxford celebrated births and marriages in the royal family." Trite and flavorless verse as it is, some of the poet's opinions and aspirations have crept into it and show what he was thinking in the perplexed years preceding the Civil War. In the following couplet wefind him asserting the divine right of kings with all the emphasis and whole-heartedness of youth:

M Grey's *Debates,* II, 3o7.

22 Sheffield, *Works,* II, 86.

28 Clarendon MSS., 58, f. 362, Sept. 25, 1658, N. S., Sir Henry Bennet to Charles II.

24 The volumes of verse to which Bennet contributed are as follows: *Flos Britannicus,* Oxford, 1637; *Coronae Carolinae Quadratura,* Oxford, 1638; *Death Repeal'd,* Oxford, 1638; *Musarum Oxoniensium Charisteria,* Oxford, 1638; *Horti Carolina Rosa Altera,* Oxford, 164o; HPOTEAEIA Oxford, 1641. I was able to trace Bennet's poems through the index of the second volume of Madan's *Oxford Books, a Bibliography of Printed Works relating to the University and City of Oxford, or Printed or Published there.*

" We must not Question: What Gods and Kings doe Silence commands t'our Actions, and Thoughts too."

This was a theory of some significance in 1638, when all Scotland was signing a Covenant of resistance and Charles I was equipping an army by methods that did not recommend themselves to lovers of English liberty. In 1640, when the Second Bishops' War was drawing to its humiliating close, Bennet sternly condemned the Scottish cause, not because it was unreasonable, but because it meant rebellion:

" May all our Kings Designes succeed
And yet no loyall Subject bleed,
But, in their stead, let Rebels feele
The sharpest anger of his steele;
Or, like to Cadmus ofspring bred,
Their blood by one another shed.""

The last of Bennet's poems to appear in print was a prefatory eulogy of two dramas by Thomas Killigrew, the courtier and wit. Killigrew had married Bennet's aunt, the beautiful Cecilia Crofts, a maid of honor to Queen Henrietta Maria, and it was therefore natural that the young scholar should undertake the friendly office of extolling his relative's work to prospective readers. The verses begin with an expression of wonder that genius has attained such heights without university nurture:

" But why in vaine doe I urge this, when You Have gain'd those helps which learned men n'ere knew And greater too than Theirs ? your thoughts have reade

28 *Musarum Oxoniensium Charisteria. Horti Carolini Rosa Altera.*

Men that are living Rules, whiles bookes are dead.
Y'have liv'd in Court, where wit and language flow,
Where ludgements thrive, and where true maners grow;
Where great and good are scene in their first springs,
The breasts of Princes, and the minds of Kings:
Where beauty shines cloath'd in her brightest rayes,
To gaine all loves, all wonder, and all praise." "

This Arcadian view of court life was not adopted in the heat of versification, nor was it outgrown with Bennet's callow years. He carried through lifelthrough thirty years' experience in the Court of Charles IIlthe illusion that wisdom, beauty, and worth flourish best in the presence chamber.

From Bennet's attitude in regard to the Scottish wars it is not difficult to infer on which side he would be found in the greater conflict impending between King and Parliament. The University, as was natural under Laud's chancellorship, was

Royalist by a great majority, and in Christ Church, whose Dean, Samuel Fell, owed his elevation to Laud, loyalty to the King was very strong. When Bennet received the degree of master of arts on the twenty-sixth of May, 1642, civil war was inevitable and both parties were preparing for it. London and the surrounding parishes were in the grip of Parliament, which may have been the reason why a young man of Royalist inclinations would prefer to linger at Oxford rather than return to his home in Harlington. Probably he drilled with the other students in the great quad of Christ Church, while the King's commissioners of array watched them from a window, and he may have been one of the " many proper young gentlemen " who " skirmished together in a very decent manner " the Saturday afternoons of August and September." His brother John joined the King's army at the very beginning of the war, and in November his father became so elate as the royal forces bore down on London, that he left the quiet of Harlington and rode forth to meet the King, taking with him all the horses that his stables afforded. If a much-garbled " information " is to be trusted, he had the honor of dining with Charles at Colnbrook, and the next day, November 12, rode with Rupert's horse in the cavalry skirmish at Brentford, wearing a knotted handkerchief, the King's token, in his hat.a No doubt Sir John, following his venture yet further, saw the royal army turn back before the citizens of London lined up on Turnham Green, and having seen it, returned soberly to Harlington and the ways of peace.

21 The Prisoners and Claracilla: Two Tragae-Comedies by Tho. Killi- grew, Gent., London, 1641.

Harry Bennet, though as staunch a Royalist as his father and brother, lacked the militant temperament. It is probable that, during the first year of the war, he remained at Oxford, which city after the failure of the march on London became the King's headquarters and was therefore an environment much to Bennet's liking. We hear nothing of him, however, until, in the lattermonths of 1643, he entered the service of the junior Secretary of State, George, lord Digby.

K Wood, *The History and Antiquities of the University of Oxford,* II, 438-455.

20 " A Charge of Delinquency exhibited against Sir John Bennett of

before the Commissioners for Advance by Leiut. Colonell

John Biscoe. That the said Sir John Bennett did ayde and assist the late King against the Parliament by sending horses unto the said late King and that he furnished the late King with horses when he came to Col- brooke and soe to the fight att Brandford and that he rode with the King to Brandford fight against the Parliament and that he dyned with the King att Auditor Poweirs howse, wore the Kings signall att the fight att Brandford which was a handkercheife in his hatt and rode with the King there with his Armes and sent the King after two Coach horses." (State Papers, Interregnum, A. 22, p. 276, Informations received by the Commissioners for Advance of Money, Sept. 23, 1651.) It is possible that " Auditor Powell's howse " where Sir John dined with the King was at Brentford, and not at Colnbrook, but the latter seems more probable.

This nobleman, the heir of the Earl of Bristol, had a stormy career behind him, though he was but thirty years old when the Civil War broke out. He had been a youth of brilliant promisela promise which his manhood repeated but never fulfilled. Courage, wit, exceptional beauty, and a winning manner enabled him always to make an enviable first impression.'0 But he had none of the qualities that should have lent weight to these advantages. His shallow resourcefulness never dealt with more than the immediate difficulty; his eloquence evaporated leaving no residuum of common sense; his intelligence raced off on fool's errands in astrology and alchemy. He was a mischievous egotist. The King had made him Secretary of State, not because he was fitted for such a post, but because Charles could not serve two military masters, and Prince Rupert had already established himself in that capacity. How Ben- net attracted the notice of Lord Digby one can only surmiselprobably by his scholarly tastes and pleasant manners; and perhaps there is truth as well as malice in Clarendon's explanation: " He had address enough to make himself acceptable to any man who loved to hear himself commended and admired."81 Nominally he was Lord Digby's secretary but, by his own admission, had little to do,82 Digby being already supplied with a secretary who transacted the routine business of his office. Nevertheless Bennet's duties, however honorary, kept him at Oxford and nourished his ambition for a more prominent part in affairs.

80 When Digby first appeared at the French Court, one panegyrist declared : " He was the discourse of the whole Court, and had drawn the eyes of all men to him. His quality, his education and the handsomeness of his person, his alacrity and courage of action against the enemy, the softness and civility of his manners, his knowledge of all kinds of learning and languages, rendered him universally acceptable." (H. M. Digby, " George Digby, Earl of Bristol ", in the *Ancestor,* XI, 83.)

" *Clarendon Stale Papers,* III, Supplement, Ixxxii, Character of Sir Henry Bennet.

In the summer of 1644 Bennet for the first time witnessed a campaign at close range, for Digby attended the King on his march through the West and South, and Bennet followed Digby. After Charles had forced the Parliamentary infantry to capitulate at Lostwithiel in Cornwall, he led his army eastward, and Sir William Waller, unable to risk a battle until he should be reinforced, fell back before him. An attempt to surprise Waller at Andover, which barely failed of success, was the occasion of Bennet's one military exploit. The enemy, warned of the attack, had made good their escape, but George Goring, one of the most reckless and popular of Charles's officers, hurriedly raised a volunteer corps of horse consisting of about two hundred gentlemen, and with them dashed after Waller's straggling rear-guard. There followed a running fight, in the course of which Bennet, who was one of the volunteers, received a sabre-cut over the nose, which bit deep into the bone and left a scar that he carried all his life. This ended his volunteering, though he continued with the army until it returned to Oxford in November, 1644, and so must have seenlacross a swollen noselsomething of the second battle of New- bury."

88 See p. *12.*

33 Bennet's participation in the skirmish at Andover is attested by Wood *(Fasti,* Sept. 28, 1663) and by Sir Edward Walker, who says that Bennet received his " honourable scar " (misprinted *star)* there. *(Cal. St. P., Dam., 1664-166),* p. 246.) Wood writes as if Bennet's military career extended over a considerable period of the war, but I believe that is guessed. The Duke of Ormonde, writing long afterwards to Arlington of an escapade of the Earl of Ossory during the Dutch War, said: " I wish he knew as much of these sallyes as you though it cost him such a cut over the nose, then there might be hope his head would settle." (Carte MSS., 51, f. 180, June 9, 1666.

Copy.) This leads one to infer that Bennet's experience of the war was limited to a sally, and that thereafter his head did settle. Accounts of the skirmish are in the *Diary of Richard Symonds,* 141; in Walker's *Historical Discourses,* 106; and in a letter from Lord Digby to Prince Rupert of Oct. 20, 1644 (Additional MSS., 18981, f. 297). In none of these is Bennet's name mentioned.

In the winter that followed, Digby found employment for Bennet that took him out of England, whither he was not to return until after the Restoration. He carried letters from the King to the Queen at Paris, and from there journeyed to Rome in the train of Sir Kenelm Digby, the secretary's cousin, whose errand was to seek the Pope's assistance for Charles I. Sir Kenelm treated Bennet with the utmost kindness, but the young man was unhappy over the prolongation of his absence from England, and over the silence of his patron there, to whom he appealed very humbly: " I presum'd in my last letter to begge new Orders from your lordship, for, not having had the honour to receive any of your commands since my coming over, I am now at a fault for want of them, since the advantages which I receive from waiting upon Sir Kenelme Digby in his emploiment here, are, with it, upon the point to cease ... I cannot tell how to entreate leave of your lordship to returne into Englande, when I call to minde how use- lesse, and yett how burthensome a servant I was to youthere; Nor to continue any longer abroade, because I cannot pretende to those fiers (which quicken other men to search out wayes of improvement) when I am left to my owne lazy and weake conduct, but since I have wholly resign'd my will to your lordship and that you are pleas'd to take a care of mee, it would ill become mee to have an appetite to any but what you shall thinke fitt to appoint mee." "

" Henrietta Maria in a letter to the King, dated from Paris, Feb. 10, 1645, N. S. (?), refers to the expected arrival of " Digby's secretary". (Green, *Letters of Queen Henrietta Maria,* 288.) In her next letter, of Feb. 28, she says: " I have received at the same time three of your letters, by Bennet, Leg [and] Talbot." *(Ibid.,* 289.) Sir Kenelm arrived in Rome about the last week of May. (Carte, *Life of Ormonde,* bk. IV, par. 218.)

But the decline of the royal cause after the battle of Naseby made the situation of the King's followers so uncertain that Digby would not summon him, and Ben- net remained in Rome until January, 1646, when he accompanied Sir Kenelm to Paris.

He had not been long there before his former master claimed him again. Lord Digby had come to Paris from Ireland, where the Lord Lieutenant, the Marquis of Ormonde, was holding out for the King. Finding Bennet eager to attach himself once more to his service, the secretary hurried him off to Ireland with letters to Ormonde which included the following cordial recommendation of the bearer: " I have divers things to have added, which would have swelled this letter to too vast a bulke; and therefore I have comitted them to this bearer Bennett, the young Gentleman whom I have spoaken to you of before, who is now returned to mee out of Italy, whither I had sent him, and is one whose discretion and fidellity I doe infinitely trust."

This was the first of many journeys which Bennet made between Ireland and France in 1646 and 1647, as secret messenger, carrying letters from Ormonde and Digby to Queen Henrietta Maria at Paris, and return-

K Clarendon MSS., 25, f. 113, Aug. 28, 1645, N. S. (?). " Carte, *Life of Ormonde* (Collection of Letters), CCCCLVI, June 17, 1646, N. S.

ing with her replies. He is usually mentioned by them as being newly arrived or on the point of departure." Though it was a humble period of his career, it nevertheless served him well by bringing him to the notice of the Queen and the Prince of Wales, and by acquainting him with all the men who could pretend to importance in their counsels.

When the Lord Lieutenant was finally obliged to surrender his office to the commissioners of Parliament, Digby saw that nothing more was to be hoped from Ireland for the present, and in September, 1647, went off to France taking Bennet with him. They joined the other English exiles at the Court of St. Germain, where the charm of Digby's personality gained for him many friends and as many enemies in a surprisingly short time. Queen Henrietta Maria made much of the handsome Secretary of State, and as his devoted follower Bennet, too, found favor in her eyes. Therefore, near the end of 1648, he was preferred to the post of secretary to the young Duke of York, second son of Charles I, who had recently escaped the guardianship of Parliament, and had fled to the Continent.28 It is probable that Digby was glad to facilitate this arrangement, for he was planning to join the French army in quest of further adventures and renown, and he knew that Bennet had no mind for further soldiering.

27 Carte, *Life of Ormonde* (Collection of Letters), CCCCXCVI, DI, DII, DIII, DXXVI, DXL.

M The appointment seems to have been made before James reached Paris after his escape from England, for Bennet's name appears on a list of the " Servants which are to attend his Highness at Sea ", dated Nov. 12, 1648, N. S. (Co/. *Clarendon State Papers,* I, 445.)

3

SECTION 3

CHAPTER II.
Secretary To The Duke Of York.

The change of masters gave Bennet an improved standing socially and attached him more closely than before to the service of the exiled Stuarts. Also, it made final his separation from his family. After the execution of Charles I, Sir John Bennet accepted the authority of the Commonwealth and in 1652 made his peace with that government according to the Act of Oblivion.1 Edward Bennet had followed the Duke of York abroad, and later served in his French regiment,2 but he and his brother Harry saw little of each other and apparently cared still less. To his mother Harry wrote rarely and perfunctorily, assuring her of his safety and letting himself off with that.' Probably he had not seen his home since the outbreak of the war.

At the time when Bennet entered his service, the Duke of York was a sober-minded boy of sixteen, conscientious, stubborn, and rather dull. He was easilygoverned through his affections, but Bennet was never able to lay hold of them, partly by natural incompatibility and partly because the Queen, by her liking for the young man, had prejudiced her son against him. Bennet had no lack of opportunity to cultivate his master's good-will, for in September, 1649, he accompanied Charles II and his brother to the island of Jersey, whence the King expected to be summoned by Ormonde, who was again in Ireland. But the winter passed and the summons did not come, for Cromwell's Irish campaign ruined the calculations of the Royalists. The King left Jersey in the spring of 1650 to try his fortunes in Scotland, but Bennet remained with the Duke of York, passing the time drearily enough until the autumn, when they rejoined the Queen at Paris.

1State Papers, Interregnum, A. 155, f. 164-167. Cases coming before the Committee for the Advance of Money; *ibid.,* A. 12, p. 4. Order Book of the Committee for Advance of Money.

Carte, *Life of Ormonde,* bk. VI, par. 126-127.

8 A copy of a portion of one of Bennet's letters to his mother, written from Paris, July *22,* 1656, N. S., is among the Rawlinson MSS. (A. 40, f. 263): " The uncertainty of my removes from Germanic into Flanders and from thence into these parts, hath hindered mee from writing this long while to your Ladyship. I have heard nothing from my brother but conclude him very well because I am assured hee was not in this action wherein this side have lately susteyned so great a losse, his Regiment lyes in Conde which it is here feard the Spanyards will besiege."

The bickerings of his suite and the hectoring of his mother soon made James so unhappy that in October he ran away to Brussels, where the Duke of Lorraine received him as the spider welcomes the fly. He began to arrange a marriage between James and his daughter, with the condition that he be allowed to reconquer Ireland and make of it a protectorate for himself. When rumors of the Duke's negotiation reached Paris, " the Lord Byron his governor, and Mr. Bennet his secretary, both well liked by the queen, and of great confidence in each other, thought it their duty to attend upon him."" But James had very little joy of their dutifulness, for, acting on the Queen's instructions, they convinced the Duke of Lorraine that Charles II would not be bound by his brother's pledges, and behind their young master's back they turned the whole affair into ridicule. The Duke of Lorraine deftly withdrew from his bargain, leaving James in great straits for money and uncertain what to do. His mother was too angry to assist him, and had forbidden his sister, the Princess of Orange, to receive him in Holland. Forlornly he wandered from place to place in the Low Countries, always dutifully attended by Byron and Bennet, until the Queen, believing him repentant, recalled him to Paris in June, 1651. " The Lord Byron and Mr. Bennet, who had comforted each other in their sufferings, were glad enough to see that there was some end put to their peregrinations, and that by returning to the queen they were like to find some rest again ".'

4 Rennet's presence with his master in Jersey during this time is attested by a letter addressed to him by Abraham Cowley, dated April 3o, 165o, N. S-, the postscript of which reads: " My Lord [Jermyn] desires you to present his humble Duty to the Duke of York." (Brown, *Miscellanea Aulica,* 132.) Cowley was at this time secretary to Lord Jermyn, and wrote regularly to Bennet forwarding the news from Paris as long as the Duke of York remained on the island. Cowley's letters are all in the *Miscellanea Aulica, passim.*

8 Clarendon, *Life,* bk. VI, par. 23.

This was neither the beginning nor the end of dissension in the exiled Court. As we have seen, Bennet had at first associated himself with the Queen's clique, ruled over by her favorite, Lord Jermyn, and this had caused old Secretary Nicholas, who hated the Queen and all she smiled on, to speak of Bennet contemptuously as " a creature of Lord Jermyn's, as all men know that know any thing ".7 But when the young King returned to Paris after the failure of his adventure in Scotland, Bennet fell away from the Queen's party and joined a group of young men in whose society Charles II found much pleasure. Sir Edward Hyde, Charles's Chancellor of the Exchequer, who was jealous of anyinfluence that endangered his own, considered the new " cabal " a pernicious combination of frivolity and ambition.' First among the frivolous was Bennet's cousin, Will Crofts, an easy-going, fun-loving gentleman in the Queen's service, who enjoyed the distinction of being one of the few exiles not in financial straits. Lord Wil- mot and the Irishman, Daniel O'Neill, were men of greater wit, but Hyde had no reason to dread their predominance in the King's affairs. The ablest and also the most ambitious of the fellowship, if we except Ben- net, was William Coventry, son of a former Lord Keeper, a man highly endowed for leadership and not at all the sort of boon companion agreeable to Charles II. Being wholly devoid of a sense of humor and often savagely irritable, Coventry must have tolerated with difficulty the frolicsome Crofts, but he was on terms of the warmest intimacy with Bennet, who may have stood sponsor for him with the less serious members. For Bennet was highly adaptable and could put on frivolity as a garment or sobriety as a cloak, always maintaining a mental detachment and poise that gave him an advantage over men of greater sincerity. Those who knew him but slightly thought him cold and arrogant. On closer acquaintance they would be surprisedlif it seemed worth while to surprise themlby his affability.'Like Coventry he was very ambitious, but unlike Coventry he was careful to show a disarming deference to the older men in the King's confidencelHyde, Ormonde, and Nicholas. Hyde suspected that both Coventry and Bennet were urging Charles to make them privy councillors, an aspiration which he felt obliged to oppose.10 Fortunately for his peace of mind the " cabal" had a short life though a merry one: Coventry and Wilmot were sent off on diplomatic errands, O'Neill was generally in attendance on the Princess of Orange at the Hague, and the departure of the Duke of York in April, 1652, to serve as a volunteer in the French army, forced Bennet to leave Paris and betake himself to the camp. Each summer for the next three years he accompanied his master through the campaign, spending the winters at the capital.

8 *Ibid.,* par. 26.

7 *Nicholas Papers,* I, 294, April 15/25, 1652, Nicholas to Mr. Smith (Lord Hatton).

8 *Clarendon State Papers,* III, 74, June 8, 1652, N. S., Hyde to Nicholas; *ibid.,* 77, June *22,* 1652, N. S., the same to the same.

"As for Mr. Ben [net] ", wrote Lord Hatton, "all I can say is for the better; for doubtless he hath given great satisfaction by the affableness he now shewes to all, and his former estranging made him deemed proud." *(Nicholas Papers,* II, 102, Oct. 16, 1654, N. S., Hatton to Nicholas.) Burnet *(Own Time,* I, 180), the Earl of Ailesbury *(Memoirs, I,* 13), and the Duke of York (Macpherson, *Original Papers,* I, 48) all refer to Bennet's pride in strong terms. Clarendon, however, seems to have been impressed with his social tact: " He was in his nature so very civil, that no man was more easily lived with, except his interest was concerned;

In 1654 Cardinal Mazarin opened negotiations with Cromwell, having in view an alliance between France and England. The King, knowing that Cromwell would be certain to demand the expulsion of the sons of Charles I from France, did not await the outcome, but departed for Cologne in June. The Duke of York was to remain for the present with the French army, and Bennet, to his sorrow, must remain too. But the King did not forget him: " You must be very kind to Harry Bennet", he commanded his brother, " and communicate freely with him; for as you are sure he is full of Duty and Integrity to you, so I must tell you, that I shall trust him more than any other about you, and

. . . He practised such a kind of civility, and had such a mean in making professions that they were oftentimes mistaken for friendship, which he never meant, or was guilty of to any man." *(Clarendon State Papers,* III, Supplement, Ixxxi, Character of Sir Henry Bennet.) *Ibid.,* Ill, 74, June 8, 1652, N. S., Hyde to Nicholas.

cause him to be instructed at large in those Businesses of mine, when I cannot particularly write to you myself.""

The Duke was far from feeling more kindly towards his secretary because of the affection Charles displayed for him. In the conviction that kings should be obeyed, he suffered Bennet's attendance, but he looked upon him as a spy, and disliked him heartily. Sir John Berkeley, the Duke's favorite, a bullying, determined man with whom Bennet had quarreled, seeing that the secretary had now no protector at the Palais Royal, snubbed him freely. " Sir John Berkeley governes in transcendency," writes one observer, " and in that family Mr. Bennet is but a cypher, though truly he carries himself e exceeding well, and to the great satisfaction of lookers on." M So uncomfortable was his situation that in December, 1654, Bennet begged the King's permission to accompany the young Duke of Gloucester, who was about to leave Paris for Cologne. Charles's reply, which has many times been quoted as characteristic of the writer, shows to what degree Bennet enjoyed the royal regard:

Harry, you may easily believe that my approbation for your coming hither would not be very hard to get, and if you had no other business here, than to give me an account how Arras was relieved, or who danc'd best in the Mask at Paris, you should be as welcome as I can make you. I will not say any more to you now, because I hope it will not be many days before you will see how we pass our time at Collen, which tho' it be not so well as I could wish, yet I think it is as well as some of you do at Paris; at least some that are here would

11 *Miscellanea Aulica,* 108. Private Instructions for my Brother the Duke of York, July 13, 1654, N. S. *"Nicholas Papers,* II, 156, Jan. 1, 1655, N. S., Hatton to Nicholas.

not pass their time so well there as they do here, and it may be you will be one of that number. On? of the greatest Alterations you will find here is, that my Lord Taff is become one of the best Dancers in the Country, and is the chief man at all the Balls; and I believe he is as good at it, as one of your Friends at Paris is at making French Verses: I have nothing to add to this, but to tell you you will find me still a true Bablon."

Charij:s Rex."

Bennet soon proved himself one of those who passed their time better at Cologne than at Paris, and willingly prolonged his stay until April, 1655, a delay which the Duke of York and his friends considered undutiful and open to suspicion. We learn that" Mr. Bennet is exceedingly undervalued by Duke Yorke, Lord Jermyn and Sir J. Berkeley in publick discourse ";u that he is " not at all looked on unless with an ill eye ";" and that he " hath noe countenance from top to botome at the Palais Royall"." But the young man showed himself pro- vokingly indifferent to all this condemnation, for, during his sojourn at Cologne, he had cultivated to good purpose the friendship of the King's most trusted advisers, Sir Edward Hyde and the Marquis of Ormonde, and thus fortified could ignore the black looks of Lord Jermyn and Sir John Berkeley, the frigidity of theQueen and the Duke of York." He began to look upon himself as the King's representative rather than as the Duke's servant, and to assume a more authoritative manner towards his nominal master than he had hitherto ventured. Charles continued to correspond with him by every post and in a familiar style very different from the reserve of his letters to the Duke of York. With Bennet he discussed his political hopes as freely as the cut of his clothes or the latest gossip.1" He even sent him money occasionally, with the assurance: " It should have been more if I had it." "

18 A cant phrase in frequent use with the King and his friends. Charles, writing to Bennet of the Duke of York, says: " I assure you, he has behaved himself like a Bablon." *(Misc. Aulica,* 111, May 25, 1655, N. S.) Again, " I think I may say it to a Bablonist, that I hope to see you in your Master's Company before many Months past." *(Ibid., 123,* Nov. 9, 1655, N. S., the same to the same.) And O'Neill remarks cryptically to the King: " Bablon's liberty has noe friend but his fidelity." *(Thurloe State Papers,* I, 682, Dec. 3, N. S., 1655.) I have not been able to find the origin of the expression.

14 Brown, *Miscellanea Aulica,* 109, Dec. 22, 1654, N. S.

18 *Nicholas Papers,* II, 230, March 23, 1655, N. S., Hatton to Nicholas. 11 *Ibid.,* 297, May 21, 1655, N. S., the same to the same.

" *Ibid.,* 343, June 8/18, 1655, N. S., the same to the same.

In October, 1655, the long-imminent treaty between France and England was finally signed. In return for an alliance against Spain, Mazarin agreed to the expulsion from France of the Duke of York and certain of the more prominent Royalists, specified by name. James was not without expectation that the Cardinal would provide for him a command beyond the borders of France, so that he need not quit the French service in which he had been very happy. Hoping for the King's consent in case the offer were made, he sent Bennet once more to Cologne to learn what disposition Charles proposed to make of him when the treaty should go into effect.21

18 " As for Mr. Bennet, he is happy that by Marquis of Ormonde's and Sir Edward Hyde's sudden favor he is soe well with the King, whilst he suffers nothing att Pallais Royall but seeming neglect of Sir John Berkeley." *(Nicholas Papers,* II, 215, March 12, 1655, N. S., the same to the same.) " I doubt not Mr. Bennett is in the height of grace, but I admire not their judgements who soe soone place him in their bosomes for falling out with their adversaries." *(Ibid.,* 247, April 9, 1655, N. S., the same to the same.) See also Clarke's *James 11,* I, 271, 275-

1B The King's letters to Bennet, from May, 1655, to August, 1656, are printed in the *Miscellanea Aulica,* 111-128.

"*Ibid.,* 12o, Oct. 18, 1655, N. S., Charles II to Bennet.

M *Thurloe State Papers,* I, 686, Dec. 1o, 1655, N. S., Bennet to Charles II.

When Bennet arrived, the King was deep in negotiations with Spain, which power, threatened by the agreement of Cromwell with France, now bowed to the necessity of saddling itself with an impecunious ally. Bennet stayed to await the outcome, and made himself as useful as he could to Hyde, who, for working purposes, embodied the complete ministry of Charles II. Nicholas observed jealously that Bennet was now Hyde's " most intimate counsellor, and some say destined to be secretary *[i. e.,* of State] which, whenever it be, he will be such a thorn in Hyde's flesh as will trouble him more than the gout"." Nicholas was a true prophet, but the thorn was to pierce his own flesh first.

The treaty of alliance with Spain was finally signed on April 12, 1656, N. S. As Bennet was to spend four years of his life entreating Spain to carry out her part of the agreement, it is necessary to outline its chief articles: Spain promised to furnish the King with four thousand foot and two thousand horse, and with arms, ammunition, and money for an invasion of England in the course of the present year, whenever the King could give satisfactory assurance of a port secure for the landing of the forces. On his side, Charles engaged to restore all conquests made by England in the West Indies since the year 1630, and that no new English plantations should be made in that quarter. When he should be reestablished on his throne, he must furnish twelve ships of war to the Spanish navy, and maintain them for five years; he must renounce all friendship with Portugal and allow Spain to recruit in both England and Ireland. In a secret article signed the following day,

"*Cal. St. P., Dom., 1655-1656,* p. 170, Feb. 8/18, 1655/6.

Charles promised to suspend all penal laws against Roman Catholics, to grant them full liberty in the exercise of their religion, and to carry out the treaty with the Irish Catholics signed by Ormonde in 1649."

Leaving the King established at Bruges, which had been assigned to him as a residence by the Spanish ministers in Flanders, Bennet returned to Paris with news of the treaty, and with some peremptory instructions for the Duke of York. The prospect of having to serve in the Spanish army against his beloved Turenne was so distasteful to James that he had written his brother urgently for leave to remain in the French service. Charles's refusal was the more emphatic because he suspected that the Duke was secretly engaged in a correspondence with some Royalists in England, to continue which he was anxious to remain in Paris. Ben- net was instructed to prevent the Duke of York from taking any part in the summer's campaign, and to hasten his departure for Flanders as soon as possible; alsolthough the point was not mentioned in his written instructionslto investigate the matter of the Royalists. All of this he communicated to the Duke rather more roughly and freely than becomes a secretary in dealing with a prince." His irritation was increased by a suspicion that the Queen, Lord Jermyn, and Sir John Berkeley were encouraging James to disregard the King's orders. Bennet had long ago ceased to expectanything more satisfying than polite neglect from the

Cardinal in the cause of the exiles; and therefore it tried his patience sorely to find the Duke beguiled by Mazarin's hints of a command in Savoy.

Cal. Clarendon State Papers, III, 1o9-11o, April 12, 1656, N. S., secret treaty between the King and Philip IV of Spain; *ibid.,* 11o, April 13, 1656, N. S., reserved and special article of the preceding treaty.

24 Cla1ke, *James II,* I, 27o-272; *Misc. Aulica,* 125, June 2o, 1656, N. S., Instructions for Harry Bennet; *ibid., 126,* July 7, 1656, N. S., Charles II to Bennet; *Clarendon State Papers,* III, 321, Jan. 28, 1657, N. S., Duke of York's Instructions for Mr. Blague.

All summer James lingered and hesitated at Paris. Seeing him on the verge of mutiny, Bennet thought best to suggest that probably it would not be necessary for him to take the field against France. On this understanding the Duke started for Flanders, feeling all the martyr's melancholy joy. He had been commanded to leave Sir John Berkeley at Paris, but on that point James stood firm: Sir John went with him to Bruges.2"

The rewards of submission are small. James had learned at the French Court to look upon himself as a hero and a general; at Bruges he was made to feel his utter insignificance. He was told that he must serve in the Spanish army; his protests were ignored and he had no part in the King's counsels, though his secretary was petted and consulted. " All the said Sir Henry Bennet's comportments towards me", wrote James afterwards, " were so void of respect, as they made me conclude he had no affection for me, but was rather a spy, and as by the effects I have found a misrep- resenter of my words and actions and inclinations "." Notwithstanding Bennet's reprehensible behavior, James was commanded to show him favor beyond all others in his household, particularly in communicatingwith the Spanish ministers, since Charles had now resolved to send Bennet as his resident to Spain.28

" I am only sorry that after all this tryall wee can yet thinke the Cardinall a fitting person to advise with in things that soe nearly concerne us." *(Nicholas Papers,* III, 126, Nov. 16, 1655, N. S., Bennet to Nicholas.)

Clarendon State Papers, III, 321, Jan. 28, 16S7, N. S., Duke of York's Instructions for Mr. Blague; Clarke, *James 11,* I, 276.

17 *Clarendon State Papers,* III, 322.

It had been the King's first intention, encouraged by Ormonde and Hyde, to make Bennet his Secretary of State,20 and to send Digby, now Earl of Bristol, to Madrid. That nobleman had come out of France a month before James's arrival at Bruges. He had a quarrel of his own with Mazarin, and therefore promoted with enthusiasm the new understanding between the English Court and Spain. Don Juan, who had recently taken command of the armies in Flanders, was charmed with him, and while Charles and his other advisers were kept at a significant distance from Spanish headquarters, the Earl of Bristol was made welcome at Brussels. As he was the only man having the King's confidence who could speak Spanish, his fitness for the mission to Spain was obvious. But an unexpected check arose in the refusal of Mazarin to give him a pass through France, for which reason, and because the Earl was making himself very useful at Brussels, he was restored to the place of Secretary of State, which he had held in the reign of Charles I, and Bennet was consoled with the appointment to

Spain. For the greaterdignity of the young diplomat the King knighted him and made him a gentleman of the privy chamber.50

28 *Clarendon State Papers,* III, *322.*

20 A rumor of this intention had, as we have seen, disquieted Nicholas the preceding winter (see p. 23). Two letters from Ormonde written several years later sustain the idea that the secretaryship was promised to Bennet at this time: " I know Harry Bennett was long since in possession of a promise that when there should be opportunity for it he should be secretary of state." (Carte MSS., 143, f. 18, Oct. 19, 1662, Ormonde to Clarendon. Copy.) " Againe I am still to seeke in what particular I have given the Secretary [Bennet] cause since his coming out of Spaine to conclude my kindnesse was lesse then when I contributed my share towards the Kings sending him thither and towards his being then design'd for the place he now holds." *(Ibid.,* 49, f. 183, May 13, 1663, Ormonde to O'Neill.)

While Bennet was thus exalted, Sir John Berkeley was as ostentatiously slighted. The Duke of York added his favorite's wrongs to his own, felt them intolerable and rebelled. On January 5, 1657, he slipped quietly away, taking with him only the servants he could trust, and retired into Holland, intending to return to France unless he should have assurance of better treatment from the King." When his absence was discovered and his purpose guessed, the Court he had abandoned was dismayed, for the Duke's military reputation made him an important factor in any design upon England, and the Spanish ministers were counting upon his presence to attract English and Irish soldiers from the French army into their own. Don Juan looked grave, and hinted that under the circumstances the invasion of England must be postponed." Bristol, who had hitherto tried to govern the Duke with a high hand, now counselled " even unreasonable compliance"." Charles sent Ormonde in all haste after the indignant prince, with leave to make all the concessions that should be necessary. These proved to be less extensive than all had supposed. The Duke complained bitterly of Bennet's insolence and disloyalty, but was placated by Ormonde's promise that he should reorganize his household as he saw fit. When he returned to Bruges the King received him kindly and raised Sir JohnBerkeley to the peerage to seal the reconciliation. James lost no time in dismissing Bennet from his service, but found him too firmly intrenched in the King's favor to be reached with actual punishment." Under the circumstances, however, the ex-secretary must have felt that his presence in Bruges was embarrassing, and so, a short time after the Duke of York's return, he started on the long journey to Madrid.

80 In his instructions, dated Jan. 2, 1657, N. S., he is styled " Sir Henry Bennet Knight, one of the Gentlemen of Our Privy Chamber." (Clarendon MSS., 53, f. 149.)

a Clarke, *James II,* I, 288-291.

"" *Cat. Clarendon State Papers,* III, 224, Jan. 8, 1657, N. S., Bristol to Hyde; *ibid.,* 226, Jan. 9, 1657, N. S., the same to the same.

" *Ibid.,* 229, Jan. 18, 1657, N. S., the same to the same.

84 James represents the mission to Spain as given to Bennet in compensation for the loss of the post of secretary (Clarke, *James II,* I, 292), but as Bennet's instructions are dated two or three days before the Duke of York left Bruges (see p. 27, footnote 30), that is clearly impossible.

4

SECTION 4

CHAPTER III.
Resident In Spain.

The advisers of Charles II hoped that Bennet's presence at Madrid would enable them to reach with their complaints the fountain-head of Spanish authority. On the other hand, the Spanish ministers in Flanders were not ill satisfied with this opportunity of remitting English affairs to Madrid, which would furnish a pretext to muddle and retard them. The year 1656 had come to an end, and the year 1657 had begun without seeing any preparations under way for the recovery of England in accordance with the treaty between Charles II and the King of Spain. The task of defending the Spanish Netherlands against the armies of France, of protecting the treasure galleons from Cromwell's fleet, and of persisting still in the attempt to reduce the rebellion in Portugal, completely exhausted the resources of the decaying Spanish monarchy, and made idle the promises to Charles II. But the non-fulfilment of the treaty was not entirely due to the failings of Spain. Charles on his side had been unable to give the stipulated assurance that a considerable port would declare for him at his first step from Flanders. Spain, with a show of reason, insisted that a movement in the King's favor must begin in England before assistance could be hazarded from abroad. Charles and his council declared that the King's friends in England must be encouraged by a demonstration from abroad before they could risk an insurrection. Four years were to elapsewhile each implored the other to act, and then the Restoration came about after another fashion.

In view of the helplessness of both parties to the treaty of 1656, it is not surprising that Bennet's sojourn in Spain is neither a brilliant nor an interesting chapter of English diplomacy. The Restoration was not hastened or retarded a single minute by his efforts, nor was it turned by a hair's breadth from the course it would have followed if he had been in China. Nevertheless, because he returned with honor and reputation, whereas he had come obscurely, almost in disgrace, the five years of his stay in Spain form an important period of his life.

Sir Harry's instructions, drawn by Hyde, were of a visionary and extravagant tenor. He was to convey, by such means as should present themselves, promises of pardon and preferment to the officers of Cromwell's fleet which was known to be lying off the coast of Spain. If successful in this, he was to give them new commissions in the King's name. At Madrid he must ingratiate himself with Don Luis de Haro, favorite and minister of the moribund Philip IV, and the most powerful man in Spain. With his assistance, Bennet was instructed to press the Spanish Council for a more open espousal of the King's cause, that the Royalists in England might be emboldened thereby; for despatch of orders and arms for the expedition to England; for the freedom of Spanish ports to ships commissioned by Charles II; and for a sum of twenty thousand crowns in addition to the King's pensionlalready in arrearsl to defray the royal debts. Lastly, he was to represent as convincingly as possible the readiness of Ireland to revolt from Cromwell's government, and to proposethat the Irish troops in the service of Spain and the four regiments newly formed of English and Irish who had left the French service to follow the Duke of York, be constituted an army under the command of a Catholic. This army, transported and maintained at Spanish expense, was to reconquer Ireland.1

About the middle of February, 1657, Bennet had reached Paris. Henrietta Maria, to whom he delivered a letter from the King, gladly vented on him her anger at the alliance with Spain, and her disappointment at the return of the Duke of York to Flanders. She made clear to him that his presence at the Palais Royal was unwelcome. " To which", says Bennet, " I having without any other reply made a low leg, the interview ended."2 Thus encouraged, the resident pursued his journey to Madrid, and near the end of March wrote to Hyde from that city.

In his first interview with Don Luis de Haro he touched upon the reasons for his coming, and found the minister extremely courteous and extremely vague. All that Bennet could elicit was the oracular assertion that Philip IV " would be ready to hearken to anything for the King's advantage ".' A week later the resident was accorded a still more colorless audience of the King of Spain.4 He visited as was customary several members of the Council, but found them preoccupied with the difficulties of equipping an army for Portugal. They displayed a baffling ignorance of affairs in England,and no thirst for information. The hope of a reconciliation with Cromwell still haunted them, preventing an open recognition of the King of England's representative, whose complaints they were unable to heed, and therefore unwilling to hear.

1 *Col. Clarendon State Papers,* III, *222,* Jan. *2,* 1657, N. S., Instructions of Sir Henry Bennet,

Clarendon State Papers, III, 328, Feb. 23, 1657, N. S., Bennet to Hyde (not to Ormonde).

' *Cal. Clarendon State Papers,* III, 264, March 28, 1657, N. S., the same to the same.

Ibid., 267. April 4, 1657, N. S., the same to the same.

Against all the obstacles of his position Bennet tilted with the assurance of inexperience. He presented a memorial embodying all the demands suggested in his instructions, and wrote cheerfully to Hyde that he looked for satisfaction in most of them." Almost a month later he learned to his chagrin that his brave memorial had been lost. More depressing still, his money was exhausted and recognition of him as the King's resident was withheld. Nevertheless he presented his memorial again, and waited.

In this beginning is the epitome of Bennet's experience in Spain, which it would be tedious to chronicle in detail. He found the ministers, to whom he was finally referred by the Council of State, " full of complimental expressions ", but his memorials were never read at the council board." He was unable to carry through a single point of his instructions. The liberty of the ports was never actually granted and never actually denied, the question being referred from Madrid to Brussels and back again, until no man could say where it was pigeonholed at last. Blake's victory off Santa Cruz in April, 1657, Put an end to all hope of tampering with the loyalty of the Protector's fleet. Open recognition of Charles II as King of England was refused on the ground of the expense which his residence in Flanders otherwise than incognito would cause.7 Thegift for the King's debts was a more remote possibility than the regulation of the royal pension, which sank ever further into arrears." The proposal that Spain should give up her Irish troops for an invasion of Ireland, the success of which was problematical, when she was using every means to find men for the armies of Portugal and Flanders, was foredoomed to failure, as a man of less obtuseness in foreign affairs than Hyde would have known. The expedition to England, which required men, money, arms, and ships, was deferred first to the end of the summer's campaign of 1657, then to the following winter, then to March, 1658, then vaguely to the future.

1 Cal. Clarendon State Papers, III, 268, April 7, 1657, N. S., the same to the same.

Clarendon MSS., 55, f. 29, June 13, 1657, N. S., the same to the same. 7 *Ibid.,* 55, f. 78, June 27, 1657, N. S., the same to the same.

Through this dreary series of delays and disappointments Sir Henry Bennet had labored diligently to bring about a better issue. He was a man not ill-suited to his errand, being persistent yet smooth in address, and able to ignore rebuff. But his arguments and reproaches had not the leverage to stir the Council of Spain. He admitted his failure: " I will not flatter my employment soe much as to saye I have obtaind any thing here to my satisfaction in my Masters businesse. If I have merited any thing, it is by telling plainely the truth which I have constantly done."" Having this comfort, he did not blame himself for his ill success; he did not even blame Spain, whose appalling poverty was the root of all that went amiss. He was more inclined to blame the English Royalists, the factor he was least acquainted with, particularly after the death of Cromwell in 1658, which

In July, 1659, the King's pension was twelve months in arrears. *(Ibid., 61, f.* 3o5, July 4, 1659, N. S., Charles II to Mordaunt.

State Papers, Spain, 43, f. 3o, April 24, 1658, N. S., Bennet to Nicholas.

brought about a sudden revival of interest in English affairs at Madrid. But when it was known that England was quiet, there was a swift subsidence of the hopeful symptoms. Bennet was questioned daily by Don Luis or others of the Council regarding the King's plans, and mourned that he could not reply as he would have liked. " I dare not lye for feare of being caught in it, and soe loose the oportunity of doing it to some good purpose hereafter." "

The Protector's death and the consequent weakening of the alliance between England and France enabled Spain to draw the latter into a treaty. A suspension of arms was proclaimed in May, 1659, and in the summer Mazarin and Don Luis de Haro met on the frontier to negotiate the Peace of the Pyrenees. Bennet saw in this meeting a possibility of inducing France to unite with Spainlfrom whom alone nothing was to be expectedlfor the restoration of Charles II. He felt reasonably sure of Don Luis's good will to this end, provided the Cardinal would agree. To gain Mazarin, the resident urged that Charles himself come to the place of treaty to plead his cause in person. By every ordinary he pressed Hyde to consent to this plan, and he was able to fortify his own reasoning with the approbation of Don Luis de Haro." The King had hoped to conduct in person a rising which his friends in England had organized for that summer, but the discovery of the plot, and the failure of an unsupported attempt of the Royalists in Cheshire, decided him to try his fortune at the treaty. Because some of his followers feared arrestif the King were recognized in France, Charles made a long, rough journey by unfrequented routes, and did not arrive at Fuentarabia until late October, when the treaty was far advanced.

10 Clarendon MSS., 59, f. 132, Oct. 3o, 1658, N. S., Bennet to Hyde.

11 *Ibid., 62,* f. 125, San Sebastian, July 26, 1659, N. S., the same to the same.

In the meantime, Bennet had himself reached Fuentarabia in the magnificent train of Don Luis de Haro. This minister had always manifested much sympathy for the hard fate of Charles II. The complaisant and kindly spirit which made him the favorite of Philip IV could not qualify him for coldly intellectual statesmanship. He wished to see all who depended on him satisfied and grateful, even if what they wanted was entirely unreasonable. He was very sensible to obligations of honor, and, partly from circumstance, partly from inclination, now found himself the champion of distressed princes, having the Prince of Conde and the Duke of Lorraine on his conscience as well as Charles II. Bennet's deferential persistence had not failed to make an impression on this soft and generous nature. The friendship of Don Luis was the sole result of his three years' residence at Madrid, and it seemed to be the only hope at this time for the affairs of Charles II.

It was not difficult for a man of Mazarin's penetration to read the character of his opponent, to divine his astounding ignorance of foreign affairs, and the weak will that made it easy to divert him from his opinions."The Cardinal had decided that the question of England must wait until the essential points of the treaty were settled, and it waited accordingly. Neither Sir William Lockhart, ambassador from the English Parliament, who was non-committally harbored by Mazarin on the French side of the Bidassoa, nor Sir Henry Bennet, on the Spanish side, found himself a personage of conspicuous importance when the conferences began in the second week of August. The latter, irritated because Hyde had given him no positive orders what to do or say, and uneasy because the King delayed so long, saw little chance of turning the negotiations to good account. Don Luis, who had treated Bennet with marked friendliness on the journey to the frontier, seating him next to himself at table, and offering the King of England's health after that of Philip had been honored," now, under the influence of Mazarin, began to vacillate, and gave audience to Lockhart at the Cardinal's request. It was not, to be sure, an interview very satisfactory to Lockhart," but it was especially vexing to Bennet because of a humiliation which had befallen him a few days before.

a" Et quoiqu'il importe de parler de Dom Louis commed'un fort grand et habile Ministre, et informe a fond de toutes choses, je suis oblige de faire savoir confidemment a leurs Majestes, lesquelles pourtant pour leur service et par toutes sortes de raisons doivent affecter d'en parler autre- ment, que le jugement que je fais de Dom Louis est qu'il n'est pas inform a fond des affaires etrangeres, ce qui est cause de son irresolution et du doute qu'il a de decider sur les moindres choses, car tout est capable de l'arreter court, et c'est la raison pour laquelle il remet toujours a faire reponse sur cent choses, et sur cent expediens que je lui propose sur le champ." *(Lettres du Cardinal Mazarin,* I, 452, Sept. 1o, 1659, N. S., Maiarin to Le Tellier.)

He had received instructions from Hyde to pay a visit to the Cardinal as if of his own initiative, and had convinced himself that Mazarin, though he might, if forewarned, discourage his coming, would not refuse to receive him when he presented himself at the door. In this he miscalculated Mazarin's determination to preserve appearances with Lockhart. He mounted the steps of the Cardinal's lodgings " as if we were the bestfriends in the world ", wrote Mazarin, " and his master were at Paris in the interests of the King" as he is at Brussels in those of the King of Spain ". At the door he was met by the captain of his Eminence's guards, who said that without an order from the King of France, the Cardinal could not receive him. But Mazarin was too cautious not to salve the wound, reflecting that anything might occur in the present unsettled state of England. An hour later this same captain of the guards sought out Bennet and whispered in his ear that the Cardinal bade him not be troubled at this refusal, which was dictated by due consideration for the King of England, and that this should be manifest within two days. With this crumb of comfort the resident was obliged to retire to the Spanish side of the river and await the promised demonstration which two days, certainly, did not suffice to bring forth.18

18 Clarendon MSS., 62, f. 125, July 26, 1659, N. S., Bennet to Hyde. 14 See Lockhart's report of it to the President of the Council of State, *Clfrendon Stat Papers,* III, 544, A"g- ". 16S9, N. S. (?)

The conferences were drawing to an end when on October 26 Charles arrived at Fuentarabia. Don Luis received him with all the chivalrous courtesy that the occasion demanded, but the Cardinal declined still to depart from the neutrality he had prescribed to himself in English affairs, and refused to see the King. He did consent at last to give audience to Ormonde, and afterwards to Bennet, hinted that assistance would be forthcoming from France, and promised to meet Charles at Bayonne, which, however, he failed to do. Don Luis spoke fluently of the intentions of Spain in the King's behalf, but the sole practical gain that Charles carried back with him to Flanders was the sum of twentythousand crowns, which he had received as the gift of Philip IV.

15 *I. e.,* Louis XIV.

18 This incident is reported by Bennet to Hyde (Clarendon MSS., 63, f. 122, Aug. 15, 1659, N. S.), and by Mazarin to Le Tellier. *(Lettres du Cardinal Masarin,* I, 361, Aug. 3o, 1659, N. S.)

Bennet was not without some consolation for the failure of his plan. His knowledge of Spanish had enabled him to act as interpreter for his master, who showed him all the old kindness and familiarity, and promised that at the next opportunity Sir Harry should be his Secretary of State." Happy in this expectation the resident returned to Madrid and to the old work of coaxing Don Luis to carry out his promises, of which the minister was no more capable than he had been before. But as earnest of his good-will he offered the command of the Spanish fleet to the Duke of York," and it was with reflections upon this subject that Bennet filled his letters, until news of the Restoration|which came rather as a surprise to him|gave new direction to his thoughts.

That event, which changed the destinies of so many men, better and worse, effected a prompt alteration in the position of the English resident in Spain. From being the independent, almost irresponsible agent of a king without a kingdom, he became now an important factor in the foreign policy of England. His attitude towards the crown to which he was accredited, and his relations with the chief advisers of Charles II were to be henceforth of political as well as of personal significance.

Whatever had been the shortcomings of Spain in dealing with Charles II, Bennet had no reason to complain of the treatment he personally had received at Madrid. While the exiles in Flanders experienced all the straits of poverty and all the cruelty of creditors, Sir Harry, by Don Luis's kindness, lived in a house of his own, rode abroad in a coach, possessed a " rich sables coat", and had ten servants to do him reverence." This establishment was theoretically accompanied by a pension, which fell into arrears with the promptness natural to pensions granted by Spain." The contrast between his borrowed state and his empty pockets afforded him both vexation and amusement, but he was not the man to despise the shadow for lack of the substance, and so made the most of the flourishes incident to his station. Don Luis covered the worst deficiencies in his pension by occasional gifts, and so Bennet drifted along comfortably enough until the Restoration. Then he felt that this arrangement no longer accorded with his master's dignity, or with his own. " I hope it will not bee unseasonable," he wrote to Ormonde, " to put your Excellence in minde that since I was at Fuen- tarabia, Don Lewis hath given mee but 120 pistols to bring my guests and mee backe hither, and to paye them wholly many months, as my selfe also to this day, from whence forwarde I doe not thinke it will become mee to aske any more money in this Court, the conclusion herein being easy, I doe not make it."

" When Bennet actually became Secretary of State, the appointment was, according to Clarendon, consequent upon " some promises the king had made to him when he was at Fuentarabia ". *(Continuation of Life,* par. 43o.)

11 Clarendon MSS., 69, f. 45, Feb. 13, 166o, N. S., Bennet to Charles II.

But this recognition of his changed status was difficult to set on foot, owing to the complete disorganization of the finances in England at the Restoration. The first remittance that Bennet received from his government was a privy seal for one thousand pounds, which did not reach him till December, 166o,a and he had no more until after his return to England in the spring of 1661. It seems probable that his allowances from the Spanish crown were continued to him through the last year of his stay, either under the guise of presents from Don Luis, or as arrears of his pre-Restoration pension. This was no longer disinterested charity. The affection with which Charles II regarded Bennet could not have escaped the notice of the Spanish minister at Fuentar- abia. It was the part of political wisdom to oblige a man who might counterbalance the French influence which early showed its strength at the English court. When Bennet left Madrid, the parting gift which was presented to him in the name of Philip IV was so bountiful that it enabled him to journey " in a better equipage and with more grandeur than any foreign Minister had ever returned "."

" Carte MSS., 213, *l.* 643, March 6, 166o, N. S., Bennet to Ormonde; Clarendon MSS., 57, f. 72, Feb. 6, 1658, N. S., the same to Hyde.

"Already in October, 1657, Bennet wrote to Hyde that his allowances were two months in arrears. *(Ibid.,* 56, f. 168, Oct. 24, 1657, N. S.)

a Carte MSS., 46, f. 3, June 9, 166o, N. S.

All this was not without some effect; Bennet retained throughout his life a certain predilection for the countryin which he made his diplomatic debut. He affected the Castilian stateliness of bearing, which the Duke of Buckingham found easy to mimic; he cultivated the Castilian habit of secrecy; he had the Castilian love of magnificence, joined with the Castilian indifference to debt. Politically he inclined to an alliance between England and Spain, but in this he was far from quixotic. Indeed, he held the English terms so high that Spain was never sufficiently hard-pressed to accept them.

22 Nicholas refers to the money as having been sent, in a letter to Bennet of Nov. *2g,* 166o (State Papers, Spain, 44, f. 255, draft), and the warrant is entered in the Treasury Books under the date of Dec. 24, 166o (Co*l. Treasury Books, 166o-1667,* p. 1o9), where by error Bennet is mentioned as " Sir John Bennett, His Majesty's Resident in Spain ".

28 *Clarendon State Papers,* III, Supplement, Ixxxiii. Clarendon adds that Bennet continued to receive money from Spain after his return to England ' under the notion of continuing his Dispense " *(ibid.),* but I believe the statement sprang from malice rather than conviction, and is not consistent with Bennet's natural caution, or with his practice. When the French ambassador offered him a pension after the signature of the Treaty of Dover, he declined it, saying that he had never received presents of the sort from any prince other than his own master, and though the offer was more than once renewed, he persisted in his refusal. (See pp. 168-17o of this biography.)

It is hardly surprising that Bennet did not return from the court of the Most Catholic King unsuspected of a lapse into popery. The doubt sprang partly from his int with Bristol, who had announced his conversion to the Catholic faith in 1658, and had for that reason been deprived of his office of Secretary of State. The friendship between the two men was strengthened after the Restoration, when they made common cause against Hyde's French policy. Rumor easily attributed to them the same agreement in the point of religion.

Among the men who had known Bennet well abroad, suspicion as to the state of his conscience may have arisen from the repeated efforts he had made to bring pressure to bear on Spain by establishing more cordial relations between Charles II and the Holy See. From time to time he besought Hyde to send to Rome some discreet person who should give all possible assurance

Pyrenees; and though he was unsuccessful in his proceedings for his employer, yet he did not altogether lose his time; for he perfectly acquired, in his exterior, the serious air and profound gravity of the Spaniards, and imitated pretty well their tardiness in business." (Grammont, *Memoirs of the Court of Charles 11 by Count Grammont,* 143.)

of favorable treatment of Catholics in the event of the King's reinstatement." Just how far the King was to go in his negotiations with the Pope was to Bennet purely a question of expediency." Delay in making the application would, he thought, force the King " to declare himself to a point that must utterly undoe him at home ". When the King was at Fuentarabia, Ben- net, in despair of joint action by France and Spain for his master's reestablishment, may have proposed that Charles announce his conversion. But, if so, opposition from Ormonde, and perhaps also from other Englishmen who were consulted at the time, gained the day against this last attempt to make of the Restoration a Catholic crusade.28 It is safe to say that if the proposal came from Bennet, it was the decision of a politician and not of a proselyte.

25 See his letters to Hyde in the *Clarendon State Papers,* III, 343, June 13, 1657, N. S.; 371, Oct. 3, 1657, N. S.; also in the Clarendon MSS., 55, f. 322, Aug. 29, 1657, N. S.; 56, f. 273, Dec. 5, 1657, N. S.; 58, f. 51, May 29, 1658, N. S.; 59, f. 225, Dec. 4, 1658, N. S.

2 " . . . you have but one waye left that is by securing yourselves of the friendship of the Pope secretly and upon such terms as may reasonably give him satisfaction without selling the King's conscience or exposing his reputation to the reproaches of those of whose assistance he cannot be secured after such an application." *(Clarendon State Papers,* III, 343, June 13, 1657, N. S., Bennet to Hyde.) "... all wise and good men will be pleased if Rome can be gained and yet England not be lost." *(Ibid.,* 371, Oct. 3, 1657, N. S., the same to the same.)

27 *Ibid.,* 344, June 13, 1657, N. S., the same to the same.

28 There are two very different versions of this story. The first purports to have been related originally by the Duke of Ormonde to Hough, Bishop of Worcester. Its substance is as follows: During the King's stay at Fuentarabia, Bennet came to Ormonde and complained of the King's obstinacy in refusing to declare himself a Roman Catholic, since, when once the admission was made, Spain and France would unite for his Restoration. He begged Ormonde to persuade the King that his interests demanded this step. When Ormonde refused, Bennet argued that the King was really a Catholic, but hesitated to make his conversion public. Shortly afterwards Bristol also

approached Ormonde, to inveigh against the folly and madness of Bennet and others who would persuade the King to confess himself a Roman Catholic, which would certainly ruin his chances of recovering England. (Carte, *Life of Ormonde,* bk. VI, par. 91-93). The other version relates that Bristol and Bennet, being bothconverts to the Church of Rome, were observed by Culpeper, one day at Fuentarabia, accompanying the King from mass. Culpeper afterwards sought Bennet out and said: " I see what you are at: Is this the way to bring our Master home to his three Kingdoms? Well, Sir, if ever you and I live to see England together, I will have your Head, or you shall have mine." And Bennet was so terrified by these words that he did not set foot in England until after Culpeper's death, which occurredlvery abruptly, hints the writerla few months after the Restoration. (Kennet, *Complete History,* III, 220; see also North's comments on the story, *Examen,* 25-27.) This latter tale has an improbable sound, and its insinuations that Bennet remained away from England out of fear of Culpeper, and that he contrived Culpeper's death, are entirely unfounded. The story attributed to Ormonde is more reasonable, and it does not seem possible that Hough should have invented it. On the other hand, it is difficult to imagine Ormonde confiding the incident to any one. Among the many letters preserved among the Carte and Clarendon MSS., written from Fuentarabia by Ormonde, Bristol, Culpeper, O'Neill, Armorer, and Bennet, there is not a word to indicate that the King's conversion was broached at all, or that a dispute on that or any other subject divided the King's followers during his stay. Yetland this seems to confirm the story told by Ormonde to HoughlJames remarks that Ormonde and O'Neill noticed Charles's leaning towards the Catholic religion " in the King's journey to Spain ". (Macpherson, *Original Papers,* I, 40.)

The last year of Bennet's stay in Spain was far from happy in spite of the improvement in material circumstances. He longed to return to England where the rewards of loyalty were being apportioned in his absence; the secretaryship of state which he had coveted went to another man. Moreover he was not in sympathy with the foreign policy of his government, which, under Hyde's leadership, was making advances to France and negotiating an alliance with Portugal, involving the marriage of the King to Catharine of Braganza. The resident would have been the last to advise abandoning the profitable trade with Portugal out of consideration for Spain,2' but he did not sanction a political alliancewith a people he had learned to look upon as rebels, an alliance which must mean the sacrifice of an advantageous treaty with Spain. His opposition was felt and resented by Hyde, and the personal friendship which had hitherto united them began to break down.20 Hyde was now Lord Chancellor and at the coronation became Earl of Clarendon. From such a pinnacle of dignity other men looked very small to him, and even a slight variation on their part from unquestioning obedience was set down as insubordination. Bennet was too prudent to venture on insubordination, but he made no secret of his disapproval, or of his desire to be recalled.In England the good-natured Daniel O'Neill joined his petition to Bennet's, and easily obtained the King's consent.'1 Letters of revocation were despatched at the end of January, 1661," and in April Sir Harry Bennet reappeared in London with that grandeur of equipage so offensive to his old friend the Lord Chancellor Clarendon."

18 See the account of his argument with Don Luis on this point, in a letter to Charles II of Dec. 8, 1660, N. S. (Lister, *Life of Clarendon,* III,

80 There was, however, no open quarrel between the two men previous to Bennet's return, though the Chancellor afterwards wanted to think that Bennet had behaved very badly towards him at this time. As an instance of his insubordination he declares that Bennet ignored precise instructions in regard to the treatment of the Jesuit, Peter Talbot. *(Clarendon Slate Papers,* III, Supplement, Ixxxiii.) But Clarendon's instructions were not precise, and he was himself in doubt whether Talbot were friend or foe. (See his letter to Bennet of Sept. 6, 1659, N. S., *Clarendon State Papers,* III, 552, and one to Ormonde, Carte, *Original Letters,* II, 277, Nov. 22, 1659, N. S.) Neither is it possible to accept unreservedly Clarendon's statement that the King's consent to the renewal of the treaty of 163o between England and Spain was procured privately by O'Neill, at Bennet's suggestion, and was never consulted in England *(Continuation of Life,* par. 399). The renewal does not seem to have been debated in Council (the Order in Council for the publication of the day of cessation of hostilities makes no mention of the renewal of the treaty, Register of the Privy Council, Whitehall, Aug. 3, 166o), but that is far from conclusive evidence that Hyde knew nothing about it. The renewal was published in England by a proclamation, which must have emanated, not from O'Neill, but from the Secretary of State's office, at this time practically under Hyde's direction. Copies of the English and Spanish proclamations are among the State Papers, Spain (44, ff. 318-319). That of Spain is dated Sept. 11, 166o, N. S.; that of England, on the day of cessation, Sept. 1o/2o, 166o. The renewal was almost immediately recognized as a blunder, for the Treaty of 163o prohibited either party from giving assistance to the other's enemies, and from entering into any treaty prejudicial to the other. It was embarrassing to Hyde, in view of the fact that English commissioners were at work with the Portuguese ambassador upon a treaty, to have to explain away this engagement to the choleric Baron de Batteville, ambassador of Philip IV. Therefore he was glad to throw the blamelin retrospect at leastlon Bennet.

" Clarendon, *Continuation of Life,* par. 399.

82 The recall was not carried through without the knowledge of either Secretary of State as Clarendon asserts *(ibid.;* alsO, *Clarendon Slate Papers,* III, Supplement, Ixxxiii), for Nicholas, in a letter to Bennet of Jan. 31, 1660/1, writes: " You will, ere this comes to your handes, have I question not, welcomed my last, wherein I sent you his Majesty's leave to come over, signified in three letters, one to the King of Spain, one to Don Luis, and a third to yourselfe." (State Papers, Spain, 44, f. 309, draft.)

88 I have not been able to find the exact date of Bennet's arrival in England; it is possible that he was in time for the coronation in April. The first mention of his presence in London occurs in a letter from Nicholas to Joseph Kent, of May 2, 1661 *(Cal. St. P., Dom., 1660-1661,* p. 580). The last letter which Nicholas appears to have despatched to him at Madrid bears the date of Feb. 14 (State Papers, Spain, 44, f. 387, draft). Clarendon says it was not known that he had left Madrid until he had reached Paris *(Continuation of Life,* par. 399).

5

SECTION 5

CHAPTER IV.
Secretary Of State.

" The truth is wee have traveled sufficiently, 'tis time wee went home to putt our discretion in practise."' Thus Bennet wrote from Spain on the eve of the Restoration. He was naturally discreet and he had learned finesse in five years of waiting on the pleasure of the Escurial. He arrived in London with the ceremony becoming a personage of importance, and he appeared at Court with the confidence of a man whose fortune is made. In reality he was entering late, and with the disadvantage of having no very presentable claim, the contest for reward and place that had raged unceasingly since Charles had returned to his kingdom. His sole standing at Court was that of gentleman of the bedchamber, the profits of which would certainly not justify the manner of life he had learned in Spain. His family could be neither help nor hinderance to him. Sir John Bennet had died in I658,2 his wife the following year,' and the estate at Harlington was now the inheritance of the eldest son, with whom Harry Bennet was on amicable but not intimate terms. His younger brothers, like himself, were endeavoring to attract the royal favor.

Bennet was now forty-three years old. He had not the distinguished beauty of the Earl of Bristol, nor the grace and sparkle of the Duke of Buckingham, but hewas a man of stately, ministerial presence. The grandee's dignity he had cultivated became his tall figure well, yet it was recognized as exotic and furnished considerable amusement to the wags of the Court. He devoted much thought to his appearance, and was always richly dressed|" an arrant fop, from top to toe ",' jeers Buckingham, who should have been a judge of foppery. His features were regular and not unpleasing, but the eyes were somewhat too pale in color and slightly prominent, the chin heavy.' Across his nose he wore a strip of black courtplaster covering the scar he had received at Andover. " Scars in the face ", remarks the author of Grammont's *Memoirs,* " commonly give a man a certain fierce and martial air, which sets him off to advantage, but it was quite the contrary with him, and this remarkable plaster so well suited his mysterious looks, that it seemed an addition to his gravity and self-sufficiency."11 Sir John Evelyn thought him "the best bred and courtly person his Majesty has about him ",7 and Clarendon, at a time when he hated Bennet most bitterly, admitted: " he may well be reckoned in the number of the finest gentlemen of the time".' Among friends, or with persons he intended to flatter, he would relax the formality of his bearing, and no manat Court could talk more charmingly.' The testimony of an enemy acknowledges his gift for " the best turns of wit in particular conversation that I have known ".10

1 Carte MSS., *221, t.* 1, April 10, 1660, N. S., Bennet to Ormonde. ' Parish Registers of Harlington, Middlesex. *Ibid.*

4 Buckingham's *Works,* II, 163, Advice to a Painter, To Draw My L. A ton, Grand Minister of State.

8 " Two goggle-eyes, so clear, tho' very dead,

That one may see thro' them, quite thro" his head." *(Ibid.)* Portraits of Arlington are reproduced in Birch's *Heads of Illustrious Persons,* in Lodge's *Portraits,* and in the *Memoirs of Grammont* (Harding, ed., London, 1793). A portrait by Lely in very poor preservation hangs just outside the door of the dining-hall of Christ Church. It represents Arlington in his robes of the Garter, holding the white staff of Lord Chamberlain.

Memoirs of the Court of Charles II by Count Grammont, 143.

1 *Diary,* Sept. 10, 1677.

8 *Clarendon State Papers,* III, Supplement, Ixxxi.

" The King ", says Clarendon, " received him with great kindness, as a man whose company he always liked." " Charles was delighted with the foreign mien of his resident, and in jesting allusion to the proposed Portuguese marriage, which he knew was hateful to Bennet, threatened to cut his Spanish beard with a pair of Portuguese scissors.12 The gay party that assembled nightly under the leadership of Barbara Palmer, the King's mistress, welcomed Sir Harry to its revels. He was welcomed also by the Spanish ambassador, the Baron de Batteville, whose acquaintance he had made long ago at San Sebastian. But the Count d'Estrades, ambassador of Louis XIV, in whose instructions Ben- net was bracketed with the obnoxious Earl of Bristol as a partisan of Spain, u watched him suspiciously, finding him more difficult to circumvent than the Earl, whose courses were open to the day.

At the King's command, Clarendon used his influence to obtain a seat for Bennet in the Cavalier Parliament which met for ifs first session a few weeks after his return to England. He was accordingly chosen as member for Callington in Cornwall early in June, 1661, although, as the Chancellor afterwards declared, " heknew no more of the constitution and laws of England than he did of China "."

'Clarendon says: "... he would speak well and reasonably to any purpose." *(Clarendon State Papers,* III, Supplement, Ixxxi.) Pepys confirms this: "He speaks well, and hath pretty slight superficial parts, I believe." *(Diary,* Feb. 24, 1666/7.)

10 Temple, *Works,* II, 492.

11 *Clarendon Slate Papers,* III, Supplement, Ixxxiii.

" Hist. MSS. Comm., *$th Report,* 151, MSS. of the Duke of Sutherland, May 7, 1661, Francis Newport to Richard Leveson.

"Arch. Aff. iftr., Angleterre, 76, f. 175, Instruction baillee a Monsieur le Comte d'Estrades . . . du 23 May, 1661.

Bennet had at once to decide whether he would ally himself with the party of the government, or with its opponents. The first included the men under whose auspices he had gone as resident to Spain; it was organized, and in occupation of the highest places in the gift of the crown. The Lord Chancellor commanded it. His lieutenants were the Earl of Southampton, Lord Treasurer, and the Duke of Ormonde, to whom the government of Ireland had been restored. The senior Secretary of State, Sir Edward Nicholas, did Clarendon's bidding in the transaction of foreign affairs. The Chancellor's opinion prevailed in the working committee of the Council. In the House of Commons he had formed a clique of men of fortune and position, who used their influence in the way that he deemed advisable. His orthodoxy won to his support the strength of the restored Anglican Church. The Duke of York, heir-presumptive to the throne, was his son-in-law.

But behind this front of power lurked the weakness that was to destroy it. Clarendon could dictate; he could not lead. He governed according to his own lights, conceding as little to the wisdom of his colleagues as to public opinion. He knew that the King did not enjoy his society, but he reckoned on the royal gratitude and his own usefulness to preserve him. Afuture in which he should be no longer useful was beyond his imagination.

14 *Continuation of Life,* par. 400-404. From Clarendon's account one would infer that Bennet was not a member of Parliament until 1663, but his name appears for the first time in a committee list of June 21, 1661 *(Commons' Journal).* At the general election Callington had returned Sir Allen Broderick. But Sir Allen had been returned by Orford als0, and chose to sit for the latter. Callington, then, at Clarendon's suggestion, elected Bennet.

The opposition to his regime was hardly sufficiently fused to be a party at all. It comprehended all who for any cause were enemies of the Chancellor: the clowns of the Court, whose silliness he rebuked; " the Lady " whom he refused to honor; greedy courtiers to whose grants he refused the seal; political dilettantes, such as the Duke of Buckingham and the Earl of Bristol, whom he thwarted. These were seemingly contemptible rivals, but they were the companions most diverting, and therefore most dear to the King. There were, however, weightier elements: men who disliked the religious settlement promoted by Clarendon; men who disliked his foreign policy; and men of capacity and ambition in the Council or in Parliament who were ill content with the humble parts they must play under the autocratic Chancellor.

The self-appointed leader of this faction was the Earl of Bristol, who now regarded himself as the champion of the English Catholics, though somewhat against the will of the more thoughtful among them. The King had always an indulgent affection for him, and this was cemented by the assiduity with which Bristol courted the imperious mistress. By reason of his faith he could not hold office or sit in Council, but Charles, in spite of the Chancellor's admonitions, kept no secrets from him, and he meddled as he pleased. His determination to secure toleration for the Catholics, his opposition to the Portuguese marriage, and his daring speeches in the House of Lords, irritated the Chancellor to the last degree, though he knew himself to be still the stronger.

It is possible that Bennet was already committed to the Opposition before his return from Spain, but it is more probable that a man of his discretion would not be in haste to array himself against the party in power. The Chancellor, though suspicious of his Spanish sympathies, was willing to play him off against Sir Charles Berkeley, a favorite with both the King and the Duke of York, whom Clarendon detested for his encouragement of Charles in his pleasures, as well as for more personal reasons." But Bennet, seeing that he was expected to draw the Chancellor's chestnuts from the fire without advantage to himself, retired from the contest and made friends with Berkeley, though the two had been on very bad terms when Bennet went off to Spain.1" From Ormonde, whom he always sincerely admired, Bennet had hoped some activity in his behalf," but the Lord Lieutenant shunned other men's quarrels whenever possible, and was careful not to cross his friend the Chancellor. Feeling himself slighted, Bennet reverted naturally to his earliest patron, the Earl of Bristol, and with him made a last attempt to break off the treaty with Portugal. Although he held no office justifying interference in politics, his knowledge of Spanish, a tongue little heard in England, madehim useful in communicating with Batteville.18 But the diplomacy of Louis XIV, who, for his own reasons, desired to have the flickering rebellion in Portugal sustained by the English alliance, and the determination of Clarendon, who overbore a considerable opposition in Council, gained the day. The marriage treaty was signed in June, and in September, in consequence of a street brawl for precedence between the servants of the French and Spanish embassies, Batteville was ordered by the King to keep his house. When Bennet at the ambassador's request asked permission to visit him, Charles replied shortly that if he had business with Batteville he could apply to the Secretary of State."

"" The chancellor brought Sir Henry Bennet, afterwards Earl of Arlington, into the King's favour, who, soon after, turned against him. He meant to oppose by him, Falmouth." (Macpherson, *Original Papers,* I, 23.) " Arlington came back from Spain, and tried to get into favour, supported at first by the chancellor and Bristol against Falmouth." *(Ibid.,* 24-25.)

1 Clarke, *James II,* I, 275.

" Bennet told O'Neill that before his return from Spain he had believed that Ormonde would contribute more to his advancement than was actually the case. (Carte MSS., 32, f. 346, April 4, 1663, O'Neill to Ormonde.)

In this first trial of strength with the greatest man in England Bennet had won nothing more profitable than a snubbing, but in the next encounter he was more successful. The one important charge at Court yet unfilled was that of Privy Purse which the King had promised to Clarendon for one of his relatives.2' But Charles was offended at the opposition which the Chancellor had recently offered in Parliament to certain proposals for the relief of Catholics, though he had previously promised not to contest them.21 As a rebuke to this breach offaith, the King on August 16 gave the privy purse to Sir Henry Bennet. To Clarendon's protest, as well against the public slight to himself in the elevation of his enemy," as against the disappointment of his relative, Charles replied by referring to the matter of the Catholics, and added that Bennet was better suited to the place." But though the King was resolved to prove himself the master of Clarendon, he was no less resolved to be the master of Bristol and Bennet, and, when these two ventured to criticize the Chancellor in his presence, gave them to understand that he knew the Earl of Clarendon's virtues and defects better than they, and that he wished them to live at peace with him. The next day he brought Bristol and Clarendon together and forced them to a reconciliation in which Bennet was doubtless included."

18 " L'Ambassadeur d'Espagne a eu depuis huict Jours trois audiences secretes ou il a este tousjours conduit par le Chevalier Benet." (Arch. Aff. E"tr., Angleterrc, 75, f. 134, Aug. 29, 1661, N. S., D'Estrades to Louis XIV.) D'Estrades's instructions state that Batteville " est appuye dans ses Negociations asses ouvertement par le Comte de Bristol et le Chevalier Benet". *(Ibid.,* 76, f. 175, May 23, 1661, N. S.)

"Ibid., 75, f. 260, Dec. 1, 1661, N. S., Batailler to [Lionne ?].

20 Clarendon, in telling the story *(Continuation of Life,* par. 400; *Clarendon State Papers,* III, Supplement, Ixxxiii), does not mention that the claimant was his kinsman, but D'Estrades was informed that the Chancellor intended the place for " a Lord, one of his friends and relatives ". (Arch. Aff. Etr., Angleterre, 75, f. 133, Aug. 29, 1661, N. S., D'Estrades to Louis XIV.) . 132.

If Bennet had been content with the privy purse, Clarendon might in the lapse of time have forgotten his grudge, but to a man avid of wealth and power this office was only an insignificant beginning. In January, 1662, Sir Harry begged his master to appoint him ambassador to France, and was strongly seconded by the Earl of Bristol and Barbara Palmer, now Lady Castle- maine. Charles was on the point of consenting when rumor brought the matter to the astonished ears of the Count d'Estrades, who hastened to inform the King ofFrance. Louis commanded his ambassador to obstruct by all possible means the appointment of a man so ardent in the interests of Spain. It was not very difficult. D'Estrades represented to Clarendon the danger of entrusting what was certain to be an important negotiation to a person in whom the Chancellor himself had no confidence. Clarendon was easily convinced, and in turn pointed out to Charles the resentment that the King of France might conceive if a man suspected of being a pensioner of Philip IV were sent to the Court of St. Germain. Unable to combat this argument, the King gave way and named as his ambassador Lord Holles, who belonged to Clarendon's party."

a According to D'Estrades, Bennet was already in August, 1661, the *ennemy declare* of the Chancellor. *(Ibid.)*

" *Ibid.* I have followed D'Estrades's account throughout. He is always fair to Clarendon, who was his political ally. Clarendon's narrative of the affair of the Catholics *(Continuation of Life,* par. 287-290) makes no mention of his own attitude, nor does he connect this matter with his disappointment about the privy purse.

"Arch. Aff. Etr., Angleterre, 75, f. 133, Aug. 29, 1661, N. S., D'Estrades to Louis XIV.

If Bennet recognized the Chancellor's hand in this disappointment, he made no sign, but continued on terms of outward friendliness with him through the summer of *1662.™* They worked together to effect a compromise between Charles and his wretched foreign queen in regard to the admission of the Countess of Castlemaine to be lady of the queen's bedchamber." Bennet began to believe that Clarendon had put aside his resentment, and would no longer oppose his advancement, but in this he was speedily undeceived.

At about the time when Bennet was obliged to forego the embassy to France, he had received, by Lady Cas- tlemaine's persuasion with the King, promise of theextremely lucrative place of Postmaster General." The Post Office had been farmed out in 1660 to one Colonel Henry Bishop for a term of seven years,2' but many complaints of dishonesty and inefficiencylinstigated, perhaps, by persons who hoped to succeed to his placel had been made against him, and Bennet hoped to force the surrender of his lease.'0 He had approached Clarendon in the matter, and believed he had won his support. But when the question was discussed in Council, the Chancellor changed his mind, and with his legal expertness effectively quashed Bennet's case. " Our f rind Harry Bennet iss in disorder ", reported O'Neill to Ormonde. " My Lord chancelor uppon whome hee depended in the bissines of the post office, att a hearing the other day att counsell, hee soe justifyed Bishop that the matter iss wher it was, and will bee soe until his terme is out for ought I see, though the King iss strangly troubled att it, and sayes hee will have it tryed att law. The passione I find the King in for this afront ass hee tearms itt, makes mee feare My lord chancelor has done that that heele not find his account in, for this puts the King uppon an other designe that Henry Bennet will find more his advantage in and that will less please the chancelor."8i

25 D'Estrades, *Lettres,* I, *232,* Feb. 6, 1662, N. S., the same to the same; *ibid., 237,* Feb. 12, 1662, N. S., Louis XIV to D'Estrades; *ibid.,* 263, Feb., 1662, D'Estrades to Louis XIV.

Among the Clarendon MSS. (77, f. 71) there is a cordial letter from Bennet to Clarendon, written from Deal, whither he had gone with the King to meet the Queen Mother on her arrival from France. The letter is dated July 22, 1662.

2 7 Carte MSS., 32, f. 23, Sept. 9, 1662, O'Neill to Ormonde.

2' D'Estrades, *Lettres, I, 233,* Feb. 6, 1662, N. S., D'Estrades to Louis XIV.

" *Cal. St. P., Dom., 16601661,* p. 209.

80 For the complaints against Bishop, see *ibid., 1661-1662,* pp. 55-57. To this latter date, approximately, should be assigned a petition of Sir Henry Bennet and Charles Cornwallis (miscalendarcd under Dec. ? 1660, p. 445) for a grant of the office of Postmaster General (that to Henry Bishop being void in law) with reference thereon to the Attorney General, ordering that the petition be granted if Bishop's patent be found

void. The Attorney General, however, decided in Bishop's favor *(ibid., 1661-1662,* p. 92, Attorney General Palmer to Secretary Nicholas).

Carte MSS., 32, f. 26, Sept. 13, 1662.

With a promptness seldom granted to prophecy, O'Neill's premonition was fulfilled within a month. On October 15, 1662, Bennet was sworn Secretary of State and took his seat at the Council board. This change had necessitated the removal of one of the secretaries then incumbent. The elder of these, Sir Edward Nicholas, had been a loyal servant of Charles I, and of his son, though not a man of brilliant initiative. The other, Sir William Morice, had been appointed on the eve of the Restoration at the suggestion of his kinsman, the all-powerful General Monck. Morice seems to have been an honorable, sober, industrious gentleman, but he was completely at sea in foreign affairs. Monck's notable recommendation of himlthat he could speak French and write shorthandlwas an exaggeration of his fitness. He could not speak French. Only the minor affairs of his office were entrusted to him; he had not even lodgings at Whitehall, and seldom appeared at Court, having no admiration for the amusements that prevailed there.

But for the still-feared power of Monck, it would have been Sir William Morice who had made way for the favorite of the King. As his removal was not practicable, it had to be Sir Edward Nicholas. A sense of shame, to which Charles was not always impervious, made him provide an honorable retirement for his old servant. Using Jack Ashburnham, a gentleman of the bedchamber, as intermediary, he offered to relieve Nicholas of his duties which must be onerous to one of his years, and promised a handsome recompense for his place." Nicholas, though disappointed that his son

" Lister, *Life of Clarendon,* III, 223, Oct. 7, 1662, Nicholas to Ormonde.

was not to succeed him, did not at first think ill of his bargain." Soon, however, the whisperings of the Court over the causes and consequences of the change made him suspicious." Charles had wanted Clarendon to facilitate the arrangement, but from this the Chancellor excused himself and held entirely aloof, thereby pleasing neither the King, Nicholas, nor Bennet.5

But the King's mind was made up: Nicholas retired and Bennet succeeded him. Clarendon accepted the change as cheerfully as he could, attributing the appointment rather to the King's personal affection for Bennetlhowever unfortunatelthan to an intention to alter the ministry. He scouted the suggestion that Nicholas was removed against his will, or that he himself was likely to suffer the same fate."1 At the King's desire he acquiesced in another reconciliation with Ben- net, the previous one having been impaired by the quarrel over the Post Office.27

The secretaryship of state was at this time an office whose powers and importance were limited only by thewill of the sovereign. Thus, though Morice and Ben- net were nominally equal in dignity, the former, lacking the confidence of the Court, was but a clerk, while the latter, who " had the art of observing the King's temper and managing it beyond all the men of that time "," was a minister whose eminence encroached on the premiership so jealously guarded by Clarendon.

88 " I confesse ", he wrote to Ormonde, " if I may have such a recom- pence as is proposed, I shall for my owne particular blesse God and the King for it." *(Ibid.)*

84 *Ibid.,* 225, Oct. 11, 1662, the same to the same.

" I can assure you the King iss very much unsatisfyed with the Chancellor, first for the oppositione and then for the litle assistance hee gave him in the removing of Mr. Secretary Nicholas to his satisfaction which mought easily have beene done for the good man was not unwilling to retyre uppon good tearmes; I doubt hee is not soe now, which is attributed to the other more then to himself. His slowness in interposing made the King make use of Jack Ashburnham ..." (Carte MSS., 32, f. 67, Oct. 11, 1662, O'Neill to Ormonde.)

" Lister, *Life of Clarendon,* III, 228, Nov. 1, 1662, Clarendon to Ormonde.

87" Le Chevalier Benet fut declare hier Secretaire d'Etat; le Roi d'Angleterre lui ordonna d'aller voir le Chancelier et de bien vivre avec lui; je crois que l'Amitie sera mediocre entre ces deux Personnes." (D'Es- trades, *Lettres,* I, 395, Oct. 27, 1662, N. S., D'Estrades to Louis XIV.)

For the transaction of business and the control of correspondence relating to foreign affairs, the countries with which England had diplomatic relations were in theory equally apportioned between the two secretaries, while Ireland and the colonies were included in the province of the one elder in office." Practically, Ben- net's superiority was plainly admitted in the partition: He had Spain, France, Portugal, the Dutch, Flanders, Italy, Savoy, Turkey, Barbary, and the Indies, leaving to Morice the relatively unimportant cognizance of the affairs of Denmark, Sweden, the Empire and the German princes, the Hansa Towns, Russia, Poland, Switzerland, and of all promiscuous, unlocalized concerns. But when any delicate negotiation fell within Morice's province, its handling was sooner or later taken over by Bennet. At Ormonde's request, Irish affairs passed through the hands of the new secretary.40 Colonial business also gradually drifted into his office, to the exclusion of Morice.

These responsibilities were by no means all that fell to the secretaries of state: they were not only the Foreign Office and the Colonial Office, but the Home Office as well. They supervised the Post Office, and managed the intelligence or secret service which supplied the government with information of all that occurred at home or abroad. They exercised the censorship of the press. All communications between sovereign and subjects, of what nature soever, passed through their hands. Persons suspected of conspiring against the peace of the kingdom or against the King's person or authority, were examined by one or both of the secretaries. Both were, by virtue of their office, members of the Privy Council and of the Committee of Foreign Affairs, and one or the other was a member of every other committee formed from the Council. It was an unwritten law that one secretary must be a member of the House of Commons."

88 Burnet, *Own Time,* I, 18o.

" Beatson, *Index,* I, 397.

""Carte MSS., 143, f. 15, Oct. 15, 1662, Ormonde to the King. It is clear from a letter from Ormonde's secretary, Sir George Lane, to Morice (Clarendon MSS., 8o, f. 227, Oct. 14, 1663), that the latter had claimed the Irish correspondence as his right.

Bennet entered office just after the government had passed through a grave crisis, and while it was still uncertain of safety. When Parliament rose on May 19, 1662, the King's assent was registered to two extremely unpopular measures of taxation, the chimney tax and the excise, and also to a still more dangerous measure, the Act of Uniformity, which, designed to enforce the strictest conformity to the Church of

England, struck down the hopes of Presbyterians and Independents alike. So menacing was the dissatisfaction throughout the country that Bennet had advised the King to prepare for insurrection in the interval ofthree months before the act should go into effect, by raising new troops to hold the North and West and withdrawing a regiment from Dunkirk to keep the peace in London." But he opposed the demand of the Presbyterians to be exempted by the King from the operation of the act, believing that such exemption would publish the panic of the government and irritate the House of Commons without being broad enough to appease the discontent." Nor did he think the situation would be bettered by calling a new parliamentlanother suggestion of the Presbyterians. The present parliament, Bennet told the King, was " the onely bulwarque now betwixt the disaffected people and the government ", and its dissolution would be " one of the greatest misfortunes that could befall you ". With the wariness of parliaments that always distinguished him, he advised the King to await the next session, and then to use his influence for a mitigation of the act."

tt The actual scope of Sennet's duties, exclusive of foreign affairs, can be best determined by an examination of the papers which came in and went out of his office during the years of his secretaryship, 1662-1674, as abstracted in the *Calendar of State Papers, Domestic.* See also Beatson's *Index,* I, 397; Nicholas Faunt's ' Discourse touching the Office of Principal Secretary of Estate ", etc., 1592 (ed. Charles Hughes, *English Historical Review,* XX, 499).

Charles resolved to follow this advice. The standing forces were slightly increased, and the act went into effect without exemption or mitigation on the twentyfourth of August, 1662. On that day eighteen hundred non-conformist clergymen were deprived of their benefices.1 They submitted quietly, nor was concerted resistance to the law encountered anywhere. But as the autumn drew on, meekness gave way to unrest and defiance, not without slight symptoms of conspiracy, and this furnished arguments to the men who were urging conciliation on the King."

a Lister, *Life of Clarendon,* III, 198-201, Bennet to the King, without date, but from internal evidence, written in June or July, 1662.

a Ibid. Also a letter from Bennet to Ormonde of Sept. 9, 1662: " The not concluding any mitigation fitt upon the Act of Uniformity will, wee be- leeve, fasten our owne party and the Parlement better to us, whereas the indulgence that was proposed would certainly have disobliged them and not gaind the other party, which had been an unhappy midle to have affected." (Carte MSS., 221, f. 9.)

Lister, *Life of Clarendon,* III, 199, Bennet to the King.

48" after the authority bee thus strengthened, should your

Majesty bee pleased to declare you will effectively employ yourselfe, at the next meeting of the Parliament to obtaine a mitigation of those things that are now complained of as grievous; and then, I say, it will bee reasonable (and not a moment sooner) to use that easinesse and complyance which in the beginning, will bee looked upon only as a marque of extraordinary feare, and hasten the discontented partys to attempt something upon your Majesty and your government." *(Ibid.,* 201.)

Foremost among these was Lord Ashley, Chancellor of the Exchequer, who belonged to the Anti-Claren- donians though his wife was a niece of the Lord Treasurer Southampton. In person he was slightlalmost emaciated. A long nose, a pointed chin, an ironic mouth, humorous, eager eyes, gave warning of the boldest mind and the quickest wit discoverable at the Court of Charles II. He was the most effective orator in the House of Lords and criticized the government quite fearlessly, even under the presiding eye of the Lord Chancellor, who had learned to dread the peculiar magnetic cadence of his voice. Too restless and too selfish to be a statesman, he was an exceptionally able politician, unhampered by prejudices, conventions, or scruples. Like his friend Bennet, Ashley was latitudina- rian in religious matters, and ready to extend as much liberty to non-conformists, whose political patron hedesired to be, as the times would admit. Joined with him was Lord Robartes, the Privy Seal, a Presbyterian who wanted toleration for his co-religionists, and the Earl of Bristol, who demanded relief for the Catholics.

Bate, *The Declaration of Indulgence, 1672, 29,* and Appendix II. The number is usually given as twenty-four hundred.

41 Many arrests were made at this time on suspicion of plots against the government, and a few executions were ordered, as Bennet wrote Ormonde, " to justify that there was a plott which few will beleeve ". (Carte MSS., 46, f. 19, Nov. *22,* 1662.) Bate (p. 29) says that disturbances were few and far between, but the French ambassador, Comenge, reported that the ill-feeling gradually increased, that some plots had been discovered, and that the royal family was constantly threatened by the fanatics. (Arch. Aff. $tr., Angleterre, 79, f. 34, Jan. 22, 1663, N. S., Comenge to Louis XIV.)

These men united in reminding Charles of that care for tender consciences which he had promised in the Declaration issued from Breda prior to the Restoration. Their arguments made the greater impression on Charles because he was relieved of the daily monitor- ship of Clarendon, who, attacked by his old enemy, the gout, kept his bed at Worcester House. Spurred on by Ashley and encouraged by Bennet's more cautious counsel, the King determined to issue a general Declaration which should allay the discontent without impinging upon the authority of Parliament. This document, which is called, rather misleadingly, the First Declaration of Indulgence, was drafted by Bennet, and made public on the twenty-sixth of December, 1662."

The purpose of the Declaration, as one finds it stated therein, was to reassure His Majesty's loving and dutiful subjects on four points: first, his determination to uphold the Act of Indemnity ;' secondly, his abhorrenceof a rule by military force; thirdly, his intention, now that the uniformity of the Church had been established by his care, to carry out the Declaration of Breda in the point of relief to tender consciences. " We shall make it Our special Care so far forth as in Us lies, without invading the Freedom of Parliament, to incline their Wisdom at this next approaching Sessions, to concur with Us in the making some such Act for that purpose, as may enable Us to exercise with a more universal satisfaction, that Power of Dispensing which We conceive to be inherent in Us. Nor can We doubt of their chearful cooperating with Us in a thing wherein We do conceive Our selves so far engaged, both in Honour, and in what We owe to the Peace of Our Dominions

" James II speaks of the Declaration as having been solicited by " Roberts, Ashley and others ". (Macpherson, *Original Papers,* I, 36-37.) Burnet lays responsibility for the suggestion on Bristol and the Catholics. " Bennet ", he says, " did not meet with them, but was known to be in the secret; as the Lord Stafford told me in the Tower a little before his death." *(Own Time,* I, 345.) Comenge wrote that Bennet drafted the Declaration, and this is to be inferred also from Clarendon's account (Lister, *Life of Clarendon,* III, 233, Jan. 31, 1663, Clarendon to Ormonde). Bennet, in writing to Ormonde, assumes the attitude of authorship: " I herewith sende your Grace his Majesty's Declaration which is what I promisd you in my last. It is finishd but this evening and I with the same dispatch desird to sende it you, that it might not bee subject to any ill relations from others." (Carte MSS., 221, f. 15, Dec. 30, 1662.)

48 The Act of Indemnity, passed by the Convention Parliament in 1660, offered pardon and indemnity to all political offenderslthe Regicides exceptedlfor acts committed between June 1, 1637, and June 24, 1660.

Lastly, while repelling all insinuations of a yearning for popery in the royal breast, and professing approval of laws intended to hinder the spread of that doctrine, the King admitted his dislike of the sanguinary laws against Catholics, and avowed: " We shall with as much freedom profess unto the world, that it is not in Our Intention to exclude Our Roman Catholick Subjects ... from all share in the benefit of such an Act, as in pursuance of Our Promises, the wisdom of Our Parliament shall think fit to offer unto Us for the ease of tender Consciences." 51

Both Dissenters and Catholics might reasonably wonder how their status was affected by this announcement. Clearly Bennet had not departed from the opinion he had previously expressed to the King, that mitigation of the act was not safely within the scope of the

KHis Majesties Declaration to All His loving Subjects, Dec. 26, 1661. London: printed by John Bill and Christopher Barker. *Ibid.*

prerogative. The King asserted that the power of dispensing lay inherent in him, but to exercise it he must be enabled by act of Parliament. Until Parliament should meet, therefore, the Act of Uniformity remained intact. Why, then, was the Declaration put forth at all ? Why did not the King wait until he could address both Houses in a speech from the throne ? Ostensibly, of course, to soothe the present unrest by promising a remedy, but really to make that promise so overt that Parliament must feel engaged to fulfil it, unless the Houses were prepared to hazard a quarrel with the King. The art of this proceeding savors of Ashley rather than of Bennet, who, unprompted, would have preferred to wait until the meeting of Parliament. The matter and the form of the Declaration are almost certainly Bennet's.

In taking this step it had not been Charles's intention to ignore or to slight the Lord Chancellor. Twice he sent Bennet over to Worcester House with the draft of the Declaration. Clarendon heard it, suggested certain changes which Bennet made accordingly, and seemed to approve in so far as a man with the gout could bring himself to approve of anything. " I told him ", wrote the Chancellor afterwards, " by that time he had writ as many declarations as I had done, he would find they are a very ticklish commodity." '

" Ticklish " proved to be a gentler adjective than the sensation made by the Declaration merited. Nonconformist opinion that had condemned the Act of Uniformity, was now diverted to fall upon the Declaration instead, in which the Anglicans for once joined them in all cordiality. Protestant Dissent refused to

M Lister, *Life of Clarendon,* III, 233, Jan. 31, 1662/3, Clarendon to Ormonde.

have anything to do with a toleration which included the Catholics.™

The fate of the Declaration lay, by its own admission, in the hands of Parliament, which reconvened on February 18, 1663. The Court had made great effort to secure a favorable majority in the Commons, calling on all members upon whom it could rely, to attend, and flattering the men to whom the House was most willing to listen." The speech from the throne referred confidently to the Declaration, and explained that its purpose was not to grant a toleration to Catholics, nor to enable them to hold office.55 All in vain. The Commons believed that the Court would not have used so much ingenuity in any but a very bad cause. If the King wished to relieve the Catholics as a reward for their fidelity, why did he not say so openly to his faithful Commons ? What dark purpose of betraying England to popery might not underlie the subtlety of this proceeding? In their vote of thanks the Commons excepted that portion of the King's speech which dealtwith the Declaration; then they drew up an address wherein it was pointed out that the sovereign had not the right to invalidate a law to which he had signified his assent, and that the indulgence which he wished to exercise would establish schism by law, and destroy the public peace. Further, they demanded a proclamation banishing priests and Jesuits from the kingdom, and, pending the King's reply, introduced a bill against the growth of popery. Supply was delayed, and, it was clear, would continue to be delayed as long as the Declaration had lease of life. Charles saw that he must yield, and so, on the sixteenth of March, made answer to the address, that though he found what he had said not well understood, he would not continue the argument." In the Upper House a bill was introduced by Lord Robartes, and strongly upheld by Ashley, granting to the King the power of dispensing for which he had asked. Hitherto the Chancellor had absented himself from the House of Lords on the score of illness, anxious to avoid the dangers which either defense or condemnation of the Declaration presented. Now that it was safely out of the way, he took his place on the woolsack and, applauded by the Bishops, encouraged opposition to the bill brought in by Robartes until it failed of commitment."

58" That which here ch0ques most people in it ", wrote Bennet to Ormonde, " is the favorable mention of Roman Catholiques." (Carte MSS., 221, f. 15, Dec. 3o, 1662.) In January a Puritan minister was arrested for preaching against the Declaration. (Arch. Aff. Etr., Angle- terre, 79, f. 37, Jan. *22,* 1663, N. S., Comenge to Louis XIV.) The King attempted to conciliate the Presbyterians by g1ving audience to some of their leading ministers, but won no satisfaction from them. (Bate, 38.) Gilbert Sheldon, archbishop of Canterbury, did not hesitate to inform Charles that by the Declaration " you labour to set up that most damnable and heretical Doctrine of the Church of Rome, whore of Babylon". *(Ibid.)*

84 Thus Bennet wrote Ormonde to send over from Ireland Henry Coventry and Sir Winston Churchill in time for the meeting of Parliament. (Lister, *Life of Clarendon,* III, 232, Jan. 13, 1662/3.) Bristol introduced Sir Richard Temple to the King as a man who could induce the Commons to refrain from contesting the Declaration. (Carte MSS., 32, f. 597. June 2o, 1663, O'Neill to Ormonde.)

B Cobbett, *Parliamentary History,* IV, col. 259-26o.

A sense of personal injury greatly intensified Ben- net's chagrin over the failure of his policy. As in the affair of the Post Office, he had depended on Clarendon's support, but the Chancellor had sacrificed him, and, as it seemed to Bennet, had wrecked the King's business for that session out of sheer official jealousy.

M Cobbett, *Parliamentary History,* IV, col. 26o-263.

OT Clarendon, *Continuation of Life,* par. 583-592.

Clarendon, on his part, asserted that the folly of Ben- net in putting forward the Declaration had ruined the session: " he doth every day so weake and unskilf ull things as he will never have the reputation of a good minister, nor is in any degree able for that province." " The hostility of the two ministers was the talk of the Court.50 The King, smarting from the humiliation of seeing his wishes disregarded in both Houses of Parliament, found it hard to forgive Clarendon, and for a while showed his displeasure so frankly that many believed he would demand the seals.50 But Charles, angry as he was, knew better than any man his need of Clarendon, and was unwilling to deprive himself of his services at a time when Parliament was refractory. Late in May he brought together the Chancellor and the Secretary and, half by persuasion, half by authority, won them to a trucelthe third since Bennet's return to England.51

It proved to be the most enduring of the three, for both men were really alarmed over the unmanageableness of Parliament, and neither felt that he had come off wholly unscathed. Bennet set aside his policy of toleration, and never again actively pursued it, though twice thereafter, once in the House of Commons and once in the Committee of Foreign Affairs, he voted in favor of measures for the relief of Dissenters."2 As earnest of his good faith towards Clarendon, Bennet forsook the party of the Earl of Bristol, who complained loudly of this abandonment in which he was too vain to read a warning."8 He swore that if the King did not admit Ashley and Robartes to the committee of the Council formed for the deliberation of affairs requiring secrecy, he would force the committee to disband.54 Charles was worn out by his effrontery, and, as it happened, Bristol's friend and patroness, Lady Castlemaine, was also in disfavor for having quarreled with Mistress Stewart. A plot authorized by the King but originating, perhaps, with Clarendon, was devised to retire the Earl from politics by drawing upon him the anger of the House of Commons. Bristol showed unexpected dexterity in avoiding this snare, but promptly fell into one of his own making by an ill-considered and unsupported attempt to impeach Clarendon. In the House of Commons he might have succeeded, but in the Lords he was certain to fail. When the session came to an end theEarl prudently disappeared; a proclamation of banishment was hurled after him, and for four years the stage of English politics knew him not.

M Lister, *Life of Clarendon,* III, 244, April 11, 1663, Clarendon to Ormonde.

58 O'Neill wrote to Ormonde: " These two neither in their owne defence nor odium surlye can not agree. How much this disunion hurts the King I need not tell you." (Carte MSS., 214, f. 471, April 18, 1663.)

w " It seems the present favourites now are my Lord Bristoll, Duke of Buckingham, Sir H. Bennet, my Lord Ashley, and Sir Charles Berkeley; who, among them, have cast my Lord Chancellor upon his back past ever getting up again; there being now little for him to do, and he waits at Court attending to speak to the King as others do." (Pepys, *Diary,* May 15, 1663.)

81 Both Clarendon and Bennet expressed the hope to Ormonde that the reconciliation would endure. (Carte MSS-, 47, f. 56; *ibid.,* 221, f. 48.) The French ambassador wrote to his master on June 11/21: "Monsieur le Chancelier et le Chevalier Benest sont apparemment dans la meilleure Intelligence du monde par le soin qu'en a pris le Roy qui demeure depositaire des paroles qu'ils se sont donnes l'un a l'autre." (Arch. Aff. $tr., Angleterre, 79, f. 226.)

H When Arlington's impeachment was being debated in the Commons, Sir Gilbert Gerrard asserted that at the time of the Conventicle Act, 1664, the Secretary voted for a proviso allowing the dispensing power to the King. (Grey, *Debates,* II, 271.) For his attitude in regard to the second Declaration of Indulgence, see pp. 184-185 of this biography.)

" Le Chancelier et le Chevalier Benet sont unis sans que le comte de Bristol y soit compris, qui se plaint du procede du Chevalier Benet qui l'a abandonne de la plus mauvaise grace du monde." (Arch. Aff. Etr., Angleterre, 79, f. *231,* June 25, 1663, N. S., Comenge to Louis XIV.)

84 *Ibid.,* 79, ff. 234-237, June 25, 1663, N. S., Ruvigny to Louis XIV.

Bennet had stigmatized the rash attack on Clarendon as " madness ", and expressed a public-spirited regret that such things could be.55 So inscrutable was his behavior that not even his friend O'Neill was certain whether it covered loyalty to the Chancellor or to Bristol." Probably he considered the situation too delicate for a discreet man to jump at conclusions, and so awaited the event before committing himself to either party.

Carte MSS., 32, f. 7o8, July 11, 1663, O'Neill to Ormonde.

M " Ungratfull Mountague, Master of the Horse, is deep in this Caball against the Chancellor of England. How far Sir Henry Bennet is in their designe I can not learne, but I doubt more then hee should, for hee and Mountague are very great frinds." *(Ibid.,* 33, f. 12o, Sept. 6, 1663, the same to the same.)

6

SECTION 6

CHAPTER V.
The Dutch War.

Notwithstanding his reconciliation with the Lord Chancellor, and the care with which both ministers preserved the appearances of it, Bennet advanced but slowly to the mastery of his own department of foreign affairs. Nicholas and Morice had done little more in their office than record Clarendon's decisions. The Committee of Foreign Affairs, which included, besides the Chancellor and the two secretaries, the Duke of York, Southampton, and Albemarle, had been organized by Clarendon and had hitherto reflected his opinions in default of any of its own. From this supremacy he did not propose to abdicate in favor of a secretary whose sole experience was that vagrant mission to Spain. When Richard Bellings, whom the Chancellor had sent to Rome to solicit a Cardinal's hat for Lord Aubigny, wrote to Bennet in reference to that affair, Clarendon declared angrily that Bellings did not deserve to be trusted, forgetting that Italy was in Bennet's province, and that he had every right to know what the King's envoy did there.1 The Count de Comenge did not venture to transact business with the Secretary for fear of exciting Clarendon's jealousy, until he had express direction from Charles to do so; and he suspected thatthe reason the negotiation of a commercial treaty, begun in England, was suddenly transferred to France for completion, and Sir Richard Fanshaw was sent to Spain as ambassador, was because the Chancellor saw that in any negotiation carried on in England the Secretary claimed too prominent a part.8

1Arch. Aff. $tr., Angleterre, 77, f. 32o, Dec. 14, 1662, N. S., Batailler to [Lionne ?]. *'Ibid.,* 79, f. 31, Jan. 15, 1663, N. S., Comenge to Louis XIV.

Courtiers, no less than foreign ministers, felt the delicacy of the situation when they tried to conciliate the King's favorite without provoking the displeasure of the King's most powerful minister. The Earl of Sandwich, finding it difficult to keep his footing in the clash of faction at Court, approached the Secretary, says Pepys, with the gift of " a gold cup of 1001. which he refuses, with a compliment; but my Lord would have been glad he had taken it, that he might have had some obligations upon him, which he thinks possible the other may refuse to prevent it; not that he hath any reason to doubt his kindness ".4 But Sandwich, in pursuit of the Secretary's kindness, and flattering himself that he had won it, soon discovered, " That my Lord Chancellor do from hence begin to be cold to him ", seeing him " so great " with Bennet."

It could have been no pleasure to Clarendon to note that Bennet's facility with languages brought him into more frequent and informal intercourse with the representatives of other courts than the Chancellor couldenjoy who spoke no tongue but his own. Bennet was a good Latinist; he could speak French and Spanish with ease; he could, on emergency, draw upon a small stock of Italian. He was far more accessible than Clarendon both to business and pleasure, for the Chancellor was constantly housed in the miserable company of the gout.'

8 " Je vous ay mande plusieurs fois, que le Milord Holis est tout a fait devoue a Monsieur le Chancelier Heyden [c] qui se servira de toute sorte de voyes et de moyens pour luy faire tomber les affaires entre les mains afin d'en estre absolument le maistre, et d'en ravir la cognoissance et le merite au reste du conseil. II prend les mesmes mesurcs avec le Sieur Fanchos nom1ne pour Ambassadeur d'Espagne, au crevecoeur du Chevalier Benet qui voudroit bien y avoir part." *(Ibid.,* 8o, f. 13o, Nov. 19, 1663, N. S., the same to Lionne.)

4 Pepys, *Diary,* April 29, 1663.

'Ibid., July 15, 1664; Oct. 25, 1665.

The King's plan, devised for the sake of a quiet life, was to leave the transaction of foreign affairs to Ben- net under the supervision of the Chancellor. It resulted in each man showing a certain hollow deference for the opinion of the other in public, while exerting to the utmost his influence over the King in private. In Council and in the Committee of Foreign Affairs, Clarendon was wont to talk a great deal in his stately, wordy fashion. Bennet sometimes dared an almost imperceptible sneer at the Chancellor's " eloquence ".7 He himself spoke very seldom on such official occasions, rather from caution than from inability to express himself. " His talent", observes Clarendon, " was in private, where he frequently procured, very inconveniently, changes and alterations from public determinations." 8 It was one of Clarendon's grievances that hecould not know how often or how familiarly Bennet talked with the King. When the new Secretary had taken over Nicholas's lodgings at Whitehall, a door had been opened from his office onto a little staircase which ascended to the royal apartments above," and this, no doubt, facilitated the vexing " changes and alterations ". In recompense, Clarendon, out of his larger experience, was able to find many flaws in the papers drawn-by the younger man. " I use all freedom and opennesse ", wrote the Chancellor to Ormonde, " and when any thinge is shewed to me of dispatch as frequently it is, I do excepte and advize as I see cause, and I thinke it is well taken, for without all doubte all directions and orders of importance should be carefully worded and with greate cleerenesse; busynesse is a new language that men are not suddaynely acquainted with." M

Comenge, who was three months in England before he saw the Chancellor on his feet, observed that, " par l'Indisposition dudit Chan- celier, qui ne luypermet pas un accez assez facile a tous ceux qui ont des affaires a luy, elles pourroient bien d'elles mesmes tomber entre les mains du Chevalier Benet qui est accostable et qui sans doute ne les refuseroit pas." (Arch. Aff. Etr., Angleterre, 79, f. 31, Jan. 15, 1663, N. S., Comenge to Louis XIV.)

1 " . . . nous connumes bien par ce qu'il nous avoit dit au commencement de son discours, et par la maniere dont il nous avoit parle de l'elo- quence de Monsieur le Chancelier, qu'il n'est pas en trop bonne intelligence avec lui." (Egerton MSS., 812, f. 136, May 24, 1665, N. S., French ambassadors to Louis XIV.)

8 Clarendon, *Continuation of Life,* par. 740.

Aside from the personal jealousy, a wide divergence in views upon foreign affairs further estranged the ministers. Clarendon's ambition had been to form a close alliance with France, and to this endlalthough other considerations contributedlhe had advised the alliance with Portugal, which had antagonized Spain; and the sale of Dunkirk, which neither Spaniards nor Dutch desired to see in the hands of Louis XIV. Then he had the mortification of seeing France conclude a defensive league with England's great commercial rival, the Dutch. Charles, who might at the Restoration have had a good treaty with the Dutch, was obliged to accept one that gave him no advantage and left the points in dispute open to further wrangling.

"Carte MSS., 32, f. 67, Oct. 11, 1662, O'Neill to Ormonde.

M *Ibid.,* 47, f. 56, June 19, 1663, Clarendon to Ormonde.

Bennet had no sympathy with the Chancellor's inclination for France. French despatches, which ever since his return to England had referred to him as a " Spaniard ", were thus far right, that he could see greater advantages accruing from a well-paid protection of the weak, than from building up the power of the strong. He was willing to extend the protection of England to Spain against the future aggressions of France, but he set the price high. Fanshaw was instructed to demand freedom of trade in the West Indies for English ships, and an assiento which would insure to the Royal African Company a monopoly of the profitable slave trade to the Spanish colonies." The promotion of commerce was, indeed, the keynote of the new Secretary's foreign policy. Though his interest in the national development along this line received some impetus from the fact that he was a shareholder in the Royal African Company, and, like many of the great men at Court, thought it a fair way to fortune, it would be unjust to attribute his concern for the expansion of trade to self-seeking purely. Commerce was not merely the occupation of a large and influential number of Englishmen ; it was the national greatness and the national jealousy; it symbolized in some fashion that mighty boast of the dominion of the seas. To be outstripped commercially was intolerable to English pride as well as to English pockets, and in this point if in few others the Secretary shared the feeling of his countrymen.

It was impossible, however, to expect Spain to throw open her closely-guarded empire while England was giving military assistance to the Portuguese rebels; andit was equally impossible for Charles to renounce the treaty by which he had promised that assistance. Bennet saw that to clear the way for his policy, a peace or truce must be established between Spain and Portugal. Even before he became Secretary of State he was making inquiry of his friends in the Spanish Court as to how the mediation of England would be received.12 But Spain, fearful of arousing the anger of France, shut her eyes to the future and rebuffed the English advances by insisting on the abandonment of Portugal and the restitution of Tangier and Jamaica before an alliance could be considered."

11 *Arlington's Letters,* II, 1-12, Jan. 14, 1663/4, Instructions to Sir Richard Fanshaw.

Bennet had also to contend with the inclination of his master in favor of France. Although Charles felt himself much injured by the treaty which Louis had made with the Dutch, he could not easily bring himself to repay his good brother in kind. When D'Estrades was recalled in the autumn of 1662, he carried back to France such glowing accounts of Charles's ardor for an alliance that Louis hastily sent over the Count de Comenge in December, with instructions to conclude a treaty."

But Comenge found a new hand at the helm. His importunities were evaded on various pretexts: that negotiation could not begin until he had made hisformal entry;" that a commercial treaty must precede a political alliance ;18 that the King of England's dignity demanded that the French ambassador be the first to open proposals." Clarendon finally sent the scarcely begun commercial treaty to France with Lord Holles, who went thither as ambassador in November, 1663. Holles was a stiff-necked Presbyterian, and he involved himself in a contest for precedence in the French Court, from which he was with difficulty extricated. Then he took up the commercial treaty. But there was no possibility of agreement between Bennet's insistence that France should allow English traders the privileges granted by treaty to the Dutch, and Colbert's contention that in such case England should make the same or equivalent concessions to French merchants.18 The commercial treaty was still being languidly argued when war broke out between England and the Dutch.

18 " Since my last I received from my old friende Don Christoval in answer to one of mine which with leave I wrote to him asking whither they weare in that court in a temper of entring into a Peace or truce with Portugal and by the mediation of Englande which he verry discreetely saies is a matter to delicat for him to propose. What his meaning is by it time only can tell us." (Carte MSS., 221, f. 9, Sept. 9, 1662, Bennet to Ormonde.)

" Project of a league between Spain and England, given to Sir Richard Kanshaw by the Duke of Medina de las Torres, March 1o/2o, 1664/5. (Clarendon MSS., 83, f. 74.)

14 Jusserand, *A French Ambassador at the Court of Charles the Second,*

This quarrel was a result of the commercial rivalry which had long marked the relations of the two great sea-powers. The boggled treaty signed the month before Bennet became Secretary had done nothing to relieve the situation, and popular prejudice in Englandhad done much to embitter it. Bennet's natural preference was always for the security of peace, but he was ambitious to establish England's commercial supremacy, and believed, in common with most Englishmen, that the Dutch resistancelif they resisted at alllwould be short and spiritless." What influenced him most, perhaps, was the fact that the party with which he had allied himself in the House of Commons was enthusiastic for the war.

15 D'Estrades, *Lettres,* II, 183, April 13, 1663, N. S., Louis XIV to D'Estrades.

18 Commissioners were appointed to negotiate a treaty of commerce with Comenge late in May, but Louis XIV had no faith in their sincerity towards France. (Arch. Aft. Etr., Angleterre, 78, f. 194, July 19, 1663, N. S., Louis XIV to Comenge.)

1T *Ibid.,* 79, f. 2oo, May 24, 1663, N. S., Comenge to Louis XIV.

18 "... they say ", wrote Holles on this point, " when I urged they had granted it to Cromwell, that it never was before in any Treaty, they might doe it then, but since having made a stricter union with the Dutch, and receiving greater priviledges from them then from any other, they had granted them the like, therfore others could not expect the same that would not grant them, which wee would not, instancing that in Holland the French were used as Natives ..." (State Papers, France, 119, f. 192, Dec. 3/13, 1664, Holles to Bennet.)

Bennet had never aspired to leadership in the House. As in Council, he never spokelexcept, as Clarendon suggests, " in his ear who sat next him to the disadvantage of some who had spoken ".M He was resigned to the existence of Parliament, but in spirit he was never a part of it. When the Commons showed a reluctance to grant supply, " It is a hard case ", said the Secretary of State philosophically, " but Parlaments hardly give money soe wee must have patience and shuffle againe." " And after a prorogation he once confessed: " Altho there be safety (as Solomon says) in a multitude of Counsellors, yet we cannot but think our selves at ease when we are fairly rid of them.""How to humor the House of Commons was a problem over which Bennet spent a lifetime of study. Clarendon, as we have seen, had organized a committee of members on whom he could rely to influence the House in the direction recommended by him. The result was not wholly satisfactory to the King, who was disappointed in the modest income allowed him, and in the several attempts he had made to fulfil the Declaration of Breda by a relaxation of the laws against nonconformity. This, Bennet explained to his master, was because the House was not properly acquainted with the royal wishes. Ignoring the Chancellor's whips, he undertook to form a party in the Hous% which should serve the Kinglmen who, as Clarendon said, " spake confidently and often ", and were " busy and pragmatical ".a In this Bennet was abetted by his old friend William Coventry, one of the leaders of the House, and, as secretary to the Lord High Admiral, the duke of York, virtual administrator of the navy. Though he served the Duke, he was one of the most inveterate anti- Clarendonians in the Commons.

18 " As for their hopes of wearing us out without fighting wee doubt not also to bee hard for them that way." (Additional MSS., 22920, f. 78, Feb. 6, 1664/5, Bennet to Downing.) The English ministers were probably much influenced by Sir George

Downing, Charles's ambassador at the Hague, who insisted that the Dutch would yield rather than come to a war. (See Downing's letters to Bennet, State Papers, Holland, 171, f. 25, July 25, 1664; *ibid., f.* 125, Aug. 26, 1664.) The French King and his ministers thought that neither Dutch nor English expected the other to hazard a war. (Egerton MSS., 812, f. 2 *ct seq.,* April 4, 1665, N. S., Memoire du Roi, Pour servir d'instruction a Monsieur le Due de Ver- neuil et aux Sieurs Comte de Comenge et De Courtin, Ambassadeurs extraordinaires de sa Majeste en Angleterre. See als0, Japikse, *Ver- wikkelingen,* pp. 340-342.)

20 Clarendon, *Continuation of Life,* par. 413.

21 Carte MSS., 221, f. 52, June 6, 1663, Bennet to Ormonde.

a Miscellanea Auiica, 357, May 14, 1664, Bennet to Ormonde.

Bennet's particular confidant was not Coventry but the member for Totnes, Thomas Clifford, little known when Parliament assembled in 1661, but soon attracting a considerable following by the strength of his convictions and the eloquence with which he pressed them on the attention of the House. Bishop Burnet tells that at his first coming to London, Clifford sought the patronage of Clarendon, but was repulsed, and then struck in with the Chancellor's opponents.24 However that may be, certainly no love was lost between the first minister and the hot-tempered gentleman from Devon.

K Clarendon, *Continuation of Life,* par. 404-405.

M Burnet, *Own Time,* I, 402.

It was therefore with much displeasure that Clarendon heard and obeyed the King's command to call Bennet, Coventry, and Clifford henceforth to the committee for parliamentary management. Their advent was anything but welcome to the Chancellor's junto.28

It was the party led by Coventry and Clifford that embraced the Dutch War most ardently. They were for the most part young inexperienced men, eager for great doings and jealous of the maritime power of the Dutch. Clarendon considered the matter more seriously. He and Southampton alone realized the heavy expense that a war, even if successful, would entail on the already necessitous Crown, and they had reason to believe that if the war were undertaken and failed, the blame would be visited upon them as the most responsible members of the government. They were of a very small minority. In the House of Lords Ashley made stirring speeches in favor of the war. At Lady Castle- maine's suppers, where politics as well as pleasure found place in the evening's diversions, the war spirit reigned unchallenged. Ashley and Bennet were always fraternally present; so were the Duke of Buckingham and Charles Berkeley, now Lord Fitzharding, both of whom aspired to military renown; so was another advocate of the war, the Earl of Lauderdale, a man who in appearance was stupid and uncouth, but under his repulsive exterior concealed great ability and greater cunning. He was Secretary of State for Scotland, and had recently obtained the dismissal of the royal Commissioner, the Earl of Middleton, in favor of a creature of his own. Quite openly he boasted that he had ruined one

"Clarendon, *Continuation of Life,* par. 4o6-413.

of the mainstays of the Chancellor.2' The fastidious Sir Henry Bennet, who had looked somewhat coldly on the coarse Scotsman at the outset of their acquaintance, had been dazzled by Lauderdale's brilliant assertion of the royal authority in Scotland, and hastened to make friends with him."

The King had at first no great liking for the war, but the enthusiasm of the Court, particularly of that part of it whose society he most affected, gradually prevailed with him in spite of opposition from Clarendon and Southampton. But the decision lay not with the King, nor with the Chancellor, but with Parliament. When in November, 1664, the Commons voted the supplylenormous for that timelof two and a half million pounds for the equipment of the fleet, the government stood committed to the war.28

The handsome gift of Parliament seemed so ample for the expenses of the fleet, that the King determined to apply prize money, of which it was expected there would be a great deal, to other needs of the Crownwhich he felt more poignantly. Therefore in December, 1664, he appointed a large Commission of Prizeslall the great nobles pleading for a place on itlwith Ashley as treasurer and Bennet as comptroller.20 By the terms of their patent, the moneys due the Crown from the sale of prizes were not to be turned into the Exchequer, but should remain a fund apart from which sums should be disbursed only on the King's order.80 Lord Ashley's services were to be requited with a salary of $1500 a year; Bennet was to receive $1ooo, and the other members *$500* apiece.21 Naturally this arrangement contributed to the warmth with which Bennet and his fellow-commissioners espoused the war.

" Arch. Aff. $tr., Angleterre, 80, f. 74, Aug. 20, 1663, N. S., Comenge to Louis XIV.

27 " My lord Lauderdaile came last night hither. The great things that are done in Scotland in the vindication of his Majesties Authority in all points have made him very wellcome to those that cared not much for him before. I confesse ingeniously for my owne part hee hath cozened me and I am glad to bee soe to his Majesties advantage." (Carte MSS., 46, f. 108, Nov. 3, 1663, Bennet to Ormonde.)

28 This sum had been proposed by Clarendon in the conclave for the preparation of business for Parliament. The Chancellor hoped, perhaps, that the Houses could be frightened out of their fondness for the war by large figures. Bennet and Coventry, confident that the war would be brief and successful, favored asking only a small supply, enough to set out the fleet and maintain it through the summer; then when some advantage gained should afford opportunity, a larger sum might easily be obtainedlsay at Michaelmas. The Chancellor and the Treasurer wisely rejected this hand-to-mouth policy, and it was finally decided to propose the amount first suggested. (Clarendon, *Continuation of Life,* par. 534-549.)

The course that France would take became now a question of the highest importance to both prospective belligerents. Louis was bound by treaty to aid the Dutch in a defensive war, but as each party claimed that the other was the aggressor, it was an engagement not impossible to evade. Bennet set aside the Spanish policy with which he had made no headway, and turned to court the power he had hitherto repulsed. He persuaded the King to send Lord Fitzharding, as if on a private errand, to Paris, to sound the intentions of Louis XIV.52 Fitzharding was instructed to ask first the completion of the commercial treaty on the terms demanded by England; this settled,

Charles would be prepared to enter at once into " straiter articles of defense ".ss Diplomatically vague as this suggestion was,

" *Cal. St. P., Dom., 1664-1665,* p. *122.*

80 Clarendon, *Continuation of Life,* par. 581.

81 So according to the Dutch ambassador's report to the States General. (State Papers, Holland, 174, f. 192, Feb. 13, 1665, N. S.)

82 Clarendon's hatred of Fitzharding precludes the idea that he had any share in sending him.

88 State Papers, France, 119, f. 151, Nov. 1664. Draft of Fitzharding's instructions, in Bennet's hand.

t

it could be expanded into an offer to abandon Spain in any contest between that crown and France for the Spanish Netherlands, in return for the renunciation of the Dutch league by Louis. But much as Louis desired the alliance of England, his intentions in regard to Flanders demanded still more imperatively that he keep the Dutch bound to him by a sufficient observance of his treaty. Though he was not sorry to see the two great commercial powers on ill terms, he wished to avert a war in which he must be involved to the postponement of his own designs. So, without giving Fitzharding more than a complimentary answer," he sent after him into England his *Celebre Ambassade,* by which he joined to his ordinary ambassador, the Count de Co- menge, two others, the Duke de Verneuil, whose function was to add lustre to the embassy, and Pierre Courtin, master of requests and an able diplomat. The purpose of the *Celebre Ambassade* wasto offer the mediation of France to Charles II.

Almost from the moment of their landing the ambassadors realized that the war could not be averted. " Never ", Comenge had written, " has such joy reigned in England, forlaside from the celebration of Christmas, which is to them our carnival-timelthey talk of nothing but triumphs and victories, with so much confidence that it is a crime to be dubious about it and to fear reverses of fortune."

84 ' I hoope ", wrote Fitzharding to Bennet, " you will have the satisfaction to see at my returne that my journey will not alltogather have bin unprofitable to his Majestys service and that if all be not as you desire, at least you will know how it is." (State Papers, France, f. 17o, Nov. 2o, 1664.) On Nov. 28 Bennet wrote to Holles as if he thought that there was at least a possibility of winning France: "... we cannot but think, that with the Ships we have at Sea, and the Money we shall quickly have in our Purses, our friendship ought to be as acceptable to them as our Enemies'.' *(Arlington's Letters,* II, 61-62.) Lord Holles was even more certain that an open breach with France was not to be feared: " I am confident they will not openly engage for the Dutch, and any other assistance a Treaty will not prevent, no more then that with Spaine keepes them from assisting Portugall, and the more wee appeare apprehensive of it, to make it a busines, the worse it will be I thinck." (State Papers, France, 119, f. 192, Dec. 3, 1664.)

Nevertheless, to gain time for their master, the Frenchmen began their talk of peace. They met with angry opposition from the Commissioners of Prizes, and Bennet, to whom as Secretary of State the ambassadors were referred, took the same high tone. He defended warmly the drastic rules in regard to neutral commerce which had been adopted by the commission in order to prevent French ships from carrying for the Dutch during the war.'6 He declared that it was useless to think of peace until the Dutch had lost a battle and were thereby made more tractable.87 When Comengedesired to know on what conditions the King would lay down his arms, the Secretary took away the ambassador's breath by the statementlthough advancing it as his personal opinionlthat his master could not be secure in any peace with the States General which did not deliver into his hands certain Dutch towns in guarantee for the fulfilment of the treaty, as England had held Brill in the time of Elizabeth.TM Bennet at first opposed even the acceptance of Louis's mediation, lest the prospect of peace divert possible allies, but on this point he was overruled by the King." Then, changing front, he encouraged the ambassadors to linger in England throughout the year 1665 and to hope that some agreement might be reached. But this was mere sparring for time. England had found but one ally on the Continent, the Bishop of Miinster, who in this summer attacked the United Provinces by land. He was able to hold his own well against the paltry land forces of the States General, but if Louis should recall his ambassadors from England and send French troops to the assistance of the Dutch, the Bishop would most certainly be crushed. " We do what we can ", Bennet wrote to William Temple, then agent of Charles II with the Bishop of Miinster, " to divert France from molesting the Bishop: and accordingly have lately humour'd them in offering something towards a Treaty withHolland; which wee hear takes reasonably well with them; notwithstanding which we cannot be confident of them in the end, such is their Partiality to Holland: But if at the worst, it will gain the Bishop some time, we have a great part of our end." '"

"Arch. Aff. $tr., Angleterre, 84, f. 86, Dec. 29, 1664, N. S., Comenge to Lionne.

Egerton MSS., 812, f. *127,* May 21, 1665, N. S., the French ambassadors to Louis XIV. The treatment which neutrals might expect from belligerents depended in this day not upon any generally accepted ruling, but on the treaties in force at the moment between the parties concerned. The rule that free ships make free goods had been accepted mutually by the French and Dutch in 1650, but no such agreement existed between France and England. Thus the Commissioners of Prizes were free to adopt such rules as seemed prudent to them in dealing with French commerce, and they chose to be very severe in the spring of 1665. Later, however, the King's compliance for France, and, perhaps, the realization of the ministers that a little provocation would draw Louis XIV into the war, made them more lenient in practice though the theory of *robe d'ennemy confisque celle d'amy* was not abandoned. For a brief account of the development of neutral rights in this respect, see Woolsey, *Introduction to the Study of International Law,* 316-320. In the Record Office are two protesting memorials from the French ambassadors (State Papers, France, 120, f. 98, Nov. 24, 1664, N. S., and f. 131, April 22, 1665, N. S.); also an answer from the Commissioners of Prizes *(ibid.,* 118, f. 130). Clarendon, who disliked the Commissioners personally, and the Commission officially, says that the rules were very unjust. *(Continuation of Life,* par. 572-574.) Writing on May 21, 1665, N. S., the French ambassadors say: "... la pluspart des marchandises saisies aiant este reclamees par les marchans francois il les a fallu rendre." (Egerton MSS., 812, f. 124.)

"Arch. Aff. Etr., Angleterre, 83, f. 192, Jan. 29, 1665, N. S., Comenge to Louis XIV.

"Arch. Aff. $tr., Angleterre, 83, f. 192, Jan. 29, 1665, N. S., Comengc to Louis XIV.

80 To the French ambassadors the Secretary said that the acceptance of the mediation would anger the Londoners, who were bent on war, and would incite them to refuse a loan of money to the King. (Egerton MSS., 812, f. 54, April 27, 1665, N. S., the French ambassadors to Louis XIV.) But to Fanshaw Bennet expressed the fear that the delays of Spain in allying with England were " improved by a jealousie, that we would make an end of the Dutch War at the recommendation of France, and that the conclusion of it would be consequently a stricter union with that Crown ". *(Arlington's Letters,* II, 96, Nov. 4, 1665.)

The indifference which the Secretary displayed to the tentatives of peace offered by the *Celcbre Ambassade,* sprang from a double conviction: first, that Spain was now in good faith ready to embrace the English alliance; second, that however much bluster the French ambassadors might expend for the edification of the Dutch, Louis XIV would either keep clear of the war altogether, or, under color of assisting his ally, would carry out the long-planned occupation of Flanders.41

40 *Ibid.,* I, 18, Aug. 24, 1665. With the same purpose in view, the Secretary agreed to a proposal from Downing, who still lingered on at the Hague, that he should begin secret negotiations with the States General for a peace which France should have no hand in: " If you can helpe to distract them by making a fair advance on our side, with whom they certainly had much rather treate, *[i. e.,* than through France] and, effectively, wee would not be sorry to doe it, so wee saw them fairly disposed to aggree with us." (State Papers, Holland, 177, f. 54, July 14, 1665, copy in Williamson's hand.) It is evident from the careless way in which the Secretary stated the English conditions, that he had no intention of negotiating seriously at this time: " It is not possible to set down the precise termes upon which the King would be willing to have a peace, because they must never have the advantage to say any offer hath bin made by the King, but if from thence a reasonable overture be made to pay in some convenient time the charges we have been of, to give good conditions in the East Indys by which we may equali share that trade; reparation for what is taken at Guiny, and if such propositions were ushered in by somt friendli actions towards the Prince of Orange, it is very probable that a treaty might be entred into which in a short time might produce a peace.'; (Additional MSS., 22920, f. 152, July 21, 1665, Arlington to Downing.) Downing was not able to accomplish anything on the basis of these instructions during the two months following that he remained at the

In the meantime, the King of France is making vast preparations
a st the spring for forces superior to any he ever had, which he
i rs only with the appearance of a breach with us, who are not like to
him occasion of making use of them ... in conclusion, it is plain
are designed against the house of Austria and yet not to omit any
.sion of giving us trouble here at home if they can do it." *(Memoirsof the Family of Taafc,* 73, Dec. 21, 1665, Arlington to the Earl of Car- lingford, English envoy at Vienna.) Even after France declared war, the Secretary was still half-inclined to believe that it was a feint to cover an attack upon Flanders: " Those who come out of France say confidently the design is not upon us, but Flanders; and from Madrid we

hear that the French Ambassador, in his Masters name, hath laid claim to the Provinces of Brabant and Renault; a few days will unriddle this matter." *(Miscellanea Aulica,* 374, Jan. 3o, 1665/6, Arlington to Ormonde.)

The same breeze that had wafted the *Celebre Am- bassade* across the Channel, had brought also the Count de Molina, ambassador from Spain. Neither was delighted to note the presence of the other, nor, as the Secretary remarked, " do the compliments run very currantly betwixt them ". While Bennet blandly turned aside the French proposals for peace, he used all his address to draw Spain into alliance with England. The death of Philip IV in September, 1665, which gave the King of France opportunity to claim the Spanish Low Countries whenever it should suit his convenience, hastened the pace of the Count de Molina. After many conferences with Clarendon and the Secretary, he agreed to certain conditions as the basis of an offensive and defensive league: Charles II was to mediate a peace between Spain and Portugal, and if the Portuguese should persist in refusing reasonable terms, he would give them no further assistance against Spain. When this peace was made, Spain and England would conclude a close alliance, " making our selves Friends to Friends and Enemies to Enemies of each other ",48 It was probably understood on both sides that Spain was not to declare against the Dutch (on whom even more than on England she must eventually rely if Flanders were to be saved), unless France should carry out the threat which her ambassadors had made familiar to theears of the English ministers, of entering the war to assist the Dutch.4 The prospective success of this negotiation with Molina, and the cheerful support which Parliament, meeting at Oxford in October, offered for the continuance of the war, decided the ministers to refuse the last pacific proposals of the *Cel&bre Ambassade,* which then, with many warnings, took its departure for France."

" *Arlington's Letters,* II, 78, May 4, 1665. To Sir Richard Fanshaw.

44 The terms of this agreement are reported by Arlington to Fanshaw. *(Ibid.,* II, 95-1o1, Nov. 4, 1665.)

In the absorption of foreign affairs we must not omit to notice that at Oxford the Secretary took his seat for the first time in the House of Lords, an event of much personal satisfaction to him, for he was a great respecter of titles. He hesitated long over the choice of a name. *Lord Bennet* was not acceptable; perhaps it was not sufficiently sonorous, or, more probably, it had an unpleasing association with Bennet's erring grandfather. He revolved Colnbrook, Lymington, and Paddington uncertainly in his mind," then fixed upon Baron Cheney, a title which had been honorably borne by a family of that name in the reign of Elizabeth, to which the Crofts were remotely related." But thepatent in this form was never sealed, there being Cheneys still extant, who, though not of the direct line, protested against the assumption by the Secretary of a title to which they themselves aspired." Bennet obligingly withdrew from his pretension and at last adopted the name of the village where he had spent his childhood, though the manor at Harlington was not his but his brother's. From the Secretary's personal indifference to the H., or because the Heralds' Office fell into a cockney error, Bennet was created Baron Arlington. If he did not prefer this form, he accepted it, at least, without demur, and ever afterwards so subscribed himself.

44 The Count de Molina assured the Dutch ambassador in London that Spain was very well disposed towards the States General and would be very willing to undertake the work of mediation, if they so desired. (State Papers, Holland, 176, f. 160, June 15, 1665, N. S., English translation of a letter from Van Gogh, Dutch ambassador, to the States General; *ibid.,* f. 166, June 26, 1665, N. S., the same to the same.) A member of the Spanish Council, Don Blasco de Loyola, told the Archbishop of Embrun: "Messieurs les Hollandais sont nos amis, nous ne voulons pas rompre avec eux: nous ne voulons que garder ce qui nous appartient." (Mignet, *Negotiations,* I, 433.)

48 The refusal of the last offers towards peace made by the French ambassadors was communicated to them by Arlington on the seventh or eighth of November. (Jusserand, *A French Ambassador at the Court of Charles the Second,* 176.) This answer had been decided in the Committee of Foreign Affairs, all the ministers apparently concurring. (Clarendon, *Continuation of Life,* par. 707-713.)

"i *Cal. St. P., Dom., 1664-1665* p. 246.

41 In the *Miscellanea Genealogica et Heraldica* (new series, III, 384) it is stated that Henry, Lord Cheney (d. 1587) married Jane, daughter ofThomas, Lord Wentworth of Nettlested, and that Margaret, daughter of the same Lord Wentworth, married Sir John Crofts, Bennet's grandfather. This is corrected by the editor of the *Little Saxham Parish Registers,* (p. 169 *et seq.),* who says that Lady Cheney belonged to the Wentworths of Berkshire. Yet there was certainly some connection between the Crofts and the Cheneys, for in Bennet's patent for the title of Cheney it is clearly stated: " insignire nobili et antiquo nomine ac titulo Baronis de Cheney unde genus materno sanguine deducit ". (Egerton MSS. 2543, *f.* 142.)

The winter of 1665 proved the turning-point of the war. Until then the balance of success had been in favor of England, and an advantageous conclusion seemed always within the grasp of the King whenever he should care to avail himself of it. The ministers, though not free from anxiety on the side of France, hoped for assistance from Spain, from Sweden, and from the Emperor and some of the German princes in case Louis XIV should make good his guaranty to the Dutch. Englishmen generally welcomed the prospect of a war with France, being jealous of her commercial aspirations as well as of her political arrogance. Many prominent men at Court shared this feeling: Albemarlewas eager to crush the growing French navy out of existence; Ashley and Lauderdale thought longingly of the prizes that could be made at the expense of French trade.4"

48 Clarendon, *Continuation of Life,* par. 604.

Arlington, on the contrary, began to feel uneasy. His affection for the war had always been somewhat artificially stimulated, and his post enabled him to forecast possibilities better than the other ministers. He was experiencing the difficulty of finding allies; he had noted that Spain made no sign when French troops crossed her territory without permission, to punish the Bishop of Miinster; the States General as yet showed no disposition to sue for peace. His state of mind was shrewdly guessed by Courtin. " Almost all the English ", he reported, " would be as ardent for a war with France as they were for that with Holland. My Lord Arlington knows this disposition well and, according to our judgment, he who sees farther than the English who have not traveled, believes that the declaration of France in favor of the Dutch would be very injurious to his master, but ... at the same time that, as we believe, he fears France will declare against England, we cannot avoid the suspicion that at the bottom of his heart he plans to assist Spain, and that if any one induces the King of England to come to an agreement with the States, either directly or by the interposition of the Count de Molina, in order to make a league against France in case the latter attempts something on the side of the Netherlands, it is he who will bring it to pass." M

40 The French ambassadors refer to Albemarle, Ashley, and Lauder- dale as particularly desirous of a war with France. Egerton MSS., 812, f. 173, June 1, 1665, N. S., to Lionne.

80 *Ibid.*

Courtin was right in believing that the Secretary would be glad to bring the Dutch War to an end before coming to blows with France.51 When the *Celebre Ambassade* was preparing to return to France, he wrote to Ormonde in evident dejection: " Wee are upon the point of breaking with France before wee are secure of Spaine or indeede of any other friende abroade whatever face wee put upon it, which joind with the smale meanes wee have to drive on the warre makes us secretly wish for peace but wee see noe overtures made for attaining it and the professd seeking it would too much expose us both at home and abroade which is our present condition." M This view of the situation led him to send an agent, Gabriel Silvius, secretly to Holland in November, 1665, to encourage the Dutch in the direction of peace.88

The events of the year 1666 more than justified the Secretary's misgivings. Louis XIV declared war on England on January 6, and the effect on other powers was immediate. Denmark also declared against England. Brandenburg and the Dukes of Brunswick and Liineburg joined the Dutch against the Bishop of Miinster, who, encompassed by enemies and seeing no assistance forthcoming from any quarter, was obliged to make peace in April, leaving England without a single ally. The Emperor waited to see what action Spain would take, and Spain, relieved that the French arms were not to be directed against her as she had feared, was enticed by the wiles of Louis's ambassador away from the treaty begun by the Count de Molina." Sweden, without the subsidies that England could not give, was unable to do more than offer her mediation. The intrigue that Silvius set on foot with the Orange party in Holland, to force the States into a peace apart from France, promised well for a time, but in August it was discovered and crushed by the Grand Pensionary of Holland, Jan de Witt, whose influence kept the States inflexible in the French alliance.55

51 " The best News we have out of Holland ", wrote Arlington to Ormonde at the end of the campaign of 1665, "is, that their vast expences and losses this year make the Generality call for Peace, and the Province of Overyssel has made a formal Proposition to the States General, which is likewise Printed, to send the Prince of Orange, as ambassadour, to the King to make Peace; but it is likely when De Wit returns these things will be supprest." *(Miscellanea Aulica,* 366, Nov. 1, 1665.)

02 Carte MSS., 221, f. 98, Nov. 3o, 1665.

M Silvius was sent to Holland with a view to encouraging the partisans of the House of Orange in the desire they had already manifested for a peace with England. He had the enthusiastic support of Henri Fleury de Coulant, Lord of Buat, who endeavored to organize an opposition in the States General which should force De Witt to make peace. Buat's correspondence with Arlington was discovered by the Pensionary in August, and the conspirator was arrested and tried for treason. See Clarendon's account of this affair *(Continuation of Life,* par. 835-855), also Wicquefort's *Histoire des Provinces-Unies,* III, 255-265, and J. Hora Siccama's biography, " Sir Gabriel de Sylvius ", in the *Revue d'Histoire Diplomatique,* XIV, 598.

Arlington's diplomacy had failed in every quarter of Europe: he had been over-sanguine in his rel1ance on the House of Austria; he had not realized the potency of the better-financed negotiations of France; he had underestimated the determination of the ruling faction in Holland, which, for fear of reaction in favor of the Prince of Orange, must fight the war through to success. But the main cause of his failure to find allies without buying them was the fact that the war no longer represented the paramount anxiety of Europe, and its continuance distorted the true alignment of European relations. Menaced by the greatness of

M An ample account of the French negotiations which drew Spain away from England is in Mignet's *Negotiations, I,* partie II, section III.

M Buat was condemned for treason and beheaded at the Hague in October.

France, English and Dutch alike had lost spirit in their quarrel. Arlington expressed this change in public sentiment when he wrote plaintively to Ormonde, "... and now, contrary to what it was last yeare, everybody now cries let us have peace with the Dutch and warre with France, *fiat voluntas dei."* M Arlington, as we have seen, had tried to change the focus of the war by bringing Spain into it and thus forcing the hand of France. For he knew that with the accession of Spain, the *casus belli* would no longer be commercial rights and the empire of the sea, but the preservation of Flandersla cause which must sooner or later detach the Dutch from France. But he had been defeated by the ostrich-like policy of the Council of Spain. The plan in itself was good.

An account of the naval battles by which the war was fought out has properly no place in a biography of Arlington. It happened, however, that a serious mistake for which he was partly responsible occurred in the campaign of 1666 and materially lessened England's chance of a speedy and successful end to the war. The Committee of Foreign Affairs, which was virtually the government of England, relied upon the Secretaries of State to furnish that intelligence of the movements of the enemy necessary for the direction of the English fleet. The secret service of the reign of Charles II was never as efficient as that organized by Thurloe for the Protector. One slip had already occurred in the spring of 1665, when a Dutch merchant fleet, very rich, passed through the Channel to Flushing without any advertisement of its nearness being given to the Englishl

TM Carte MSS., 46, f. 255, Feb. 17, 1665/6.

fleet." In the campaign of 1666 it was of great importance that the French squadron, under the Duke de Beaufort, should not join the Dutch. Popular sentiment, enraged at the idea of France daring to have a fleet at all, demanded that Beaufort's ships should be blown out of the water forthwith. This year it happened that the English fleet was ready first. The government, relying upon Arlington's assurance that the Dutch could not soon come out, and that Beaufort was about to leave La Rochelle, decided to send Prince Rupert with thirty ships in search of the French." Secretary Morice, having letters of his own from Holland which convinced him that the Dutch fleet was almost ready to sail, opposed this plan, but Arlington's confidence carried the day.80 That the Dutch knew of the proposed division is doubtful, but they suspected it, and completed the equipment of their fleet in such haste that it was able to leave the Texel May 22, Old Style.TM The ministers heard a rumor of its departureon the twenty-fourth, but, on Arlington's assurance still, did not credit it. Nevertheless, the Secretary wrote to the Duke of Albemarle, who commanded the main body of the fleet, reporting the intelligence but not revoking the orders to Rupert." This letter, by the negligence of the posts, was three days in transmission. Even so, it was in time to prevent the division had the admirals believed that the Dutch were out, but they were as doubting as the government.TM Rupert sailed away on May 29 to find Beaufort, who in reality had not yet left the Mediterranean, and Albemarle proceeded with his squadron towards the Gunfleet, whither he had been ordered. On the evening of May 30, the government was at last convinced that the Dutch were at sea; the Duke of York signed orders for Rupert's recall, and Coventry hurried with them to Arlington's lodgings, for it was the Secretary's function to see to their despatch.'8 Unfortunately the hour was late and Arlington had retired; his servants, ignorant of the importance of the orders, did not wake him. The next day the Secretary sent the orders off by an express, and theyreached Rupert June 1 at Portsmouth, whither he had been forced to return by stress of weather.'4 That very day the Dutch fleet met Albemarle's division in the Downs, and the General, eager to have the entire glory of a victory, at once engaged. His squadron had already been roughly handled when Rupert came to the rescue; even then, after four days' fighting, the advantage remained with the Dutch, although there was an approximate equality of loss.

81 The French ambassadors, commenting upon this negligence and upon the fact that the government did not know the whereabouts of the Dutch Smyrna fleet, wrote: " Il nous paroist que le Roy d'Angleterre n'est pas trop bien averti la dessus, quoique ce soit une des choses des plus impor- tantes dont il ait interet d'estre bien informe." (Egerton MSS., 812, f. 103, May 16, 1665, N. S., to Lionne.)

88 On May 15, Arlington wrote to Ormonde that the Dutch fleet was in such want of men that it would not soon be abroad, and therefore, the English fleet " being likely to want employment, his Majesty hath resolved of sending Prince Rupert with about 30 good shipps to goe find out Monsieur de Beaufort upon the coast of Rochelle ... If wee have the good luck to meete and beate them, it will bee a great and comfortable successe ". (Carte MSS., 46, f. 300.)

w Clarendon, *Continuation of Life,* par. 869.

80 Arlington's secretary, Williamson, after a careful review of all the intelligence letters of this time from Holland, concluded that the Dutch did not know of the division, but, he says: " They suspected it 16/26 May (vid. F. J. from Anvers 16/26 May) when the Counsell was not so much as taken here, or but the very day it was so." (State Papers, Holland, 180, f. 207, memorandum in Williamson's hand concerning the division of the fleet.) But, since Carteret and Coventry discussed the division withAlbemarle on May 14 (Hist. MSS. Comm., *l$th Report,* part II, p. *56,* MSS. of J. Eliot Hodgkinlthe Duke of Albemarle's explanation to the House of Commons of

circumstances connected with the division of the fleet), it is not impossible that the Dutch got wind of the resolution, which must have been taken in Committee a day or two before.

n Albemarle's explanation to the House of Commons, as in the preceding note. A letter from Arlington to Ormonde, written on May 29, shows that he was still ignorant of the whereabouts of the Dutch. Referring to Rupert's departure, he wrote: "... we suppose he will bee informed by straggling shipps by that time hee comes to the mouth of the Channel that hee may the quicklyer returne to joine the body of the fleete for feare the Dutch who are stronger this yeare then the last, and perhaps upon that confidence and seeing our fleete seperated, may presently resolve to fall upon us." (Carte MSS., 46, f. 310.)

K Albemarle's explanation to the House of Commons.

3 Clarendon, *Continuation of Life,* par. 872-873; Pepys, *Diary,* June 24, 1666, and Feb. 17, 1667/8.

All over England arose a clamor of indignation at the carelessness and incapacity of the government. " The seperation of your fleet", declared a correspondent from Holland, " is cause you have not gaignd a great Victory. All the World admires you have been so ill informed." ra It seemed more than likely that Parliament would likewise admire when it should assemble in the autumn. Pepys heard on August *26* that " both my Lord Arlington and Sir W. Coventry . . . have reason to fear, and are afeard of this Parliament coming on." M The success of the fleet in two engagements which occurred later in the summer could not atone in public estimation for the loss of the Four Days' Battle. In September the Great Fire laid waste two-thirds of London, and added much to the general feeling of depression.

The Houses came together in no amiable mood, and a stormy and difficult session ensued, lasting all winter, for the Commons, having lost their confidence in the ministers and their affection for the war, were slow togrant further supply. The ministers were quarreling among themselves. Arlington and Coventry disagreed over the responsibility for the delay of the orders to Rupert.'7 The Lord Chancellor blamed Arlington for advising the King to yield to a bill prohibiting the importation of Irish cattle on which the Commons were aggressively determined.08 As between Clarendon and Coventry, there had never been harmony, and now open hostility reigned." Ashley, who was always apt to bolt to the popular party, joined the Duke of Buckingham in promoting the Cattle Bill in the House of Lords, regardless of the King's displeasure. " There are scarce any two that dare trust one the other ", wrote a Privy Councillor, " but every man is jealous of his neighbour and those in power practising to supplant one another, and wants and debts increasing." TM In this gloom and discord the winter of 1666-1667 was passed. The submissions of the Court at last induced the Commons to grant supply once more, and on February 8 the King thankfully prorogued his Parliament. It remained for the shattered government to pull itself together as best it might to continue or to end the Dutch War.

" Hist. MSS. Comm., *l$th Report,* part II, p. 54, MSS. of J. Eliot Hodgkin. Prince Rupert's explanation to the House of Commons of circumstances connected with the division of the fleet.

c5 State Papers, Holland, 180, f. 204. Intelligence letter undated.

"*Diary,* Aug. 26, 1666.

"*Diary,* Sept. 15, 1666; *ibid.,* Feti. 17, 1667/8. Clarendon, *Continuation of Life,* par. 873.

" Clarendon told Lord Conway that Arlington had persuaded the King to pass the Cattle Bill, assuring him that this concession would induce the Commons to grant supply. (Carte MSS., 35, f. 259, Jan. 19, 1666/7, Con- way to Ormonde.) Arlington, lamenting the delay of supply, says: "... if wee had thought fit to gratify them in the beginning in some things they weare sett upon, the session had been at an ende by this time." *(Ibid.,* 46, f. 434, Jan. 5, 1666/7, to Ormonde.)

60 Pepys, *Diary,* Aug. 26, 1666.

7'Carte MSS., 217, f. 433, Jan. 4, 1666/7, the Earl of Anglesey to Ormonde.

7

SECTION 7

CHAPTER VI.
The Fall Of Clarendon.

In the spring of 1666, the Secretary of State surprised his friends and amused his enemies by getting married. Hitherto he had shown himself almost insultingly oblivious to feminine charm except to note its influence on his impressionable master. His regular attendance at Lady Castlemaine's suppers was a tribute to her power over the King: he came because he was afraid to stay away. When he observed Charles's fancy veering in the direction of Frances Stewart, Arlington hastened to pay his court to the new favorite. Gammont has told how he called upon her to offer his most humble services and best advices. Now Mistress Stewart, who had a mirthful and childlike disposition, had been often amused by the Duke of Buckingham's mimicry of the Secretary's pompous carriage; Arlington's grave discourse brought the recollection vividly before her, and she began to laugh so uncontrollably that he quitted her in vast annoyance.1 Nevertheless, he was careful to invite her to sup at Goring House, whither her presence brought the King also,2 and it is not surprising to find him a member of that shameful committee that Pepys has named, " to get Mrs. Stewart for the King ".2 In thus seeking the favor of the ladies, he was too coldblooded to succeed as had Bristol and Buckingham.The *turns* of wit and classic quotations which delighted such scholarly gentlemen as Evelyn, Sheffield, and Temple, provoked no tribute more flattering than a yawn from the beauties whose faces, as they smile from the walls of Hampton Court, do not suggest a taste for the classics. Now that his youth was past, Arlington would have been glad had his master found the society of women less alluring, but he was too wise to press the point. He once talked to Clarendon very soberly and regretfully of the King's manner of life, and of its effect upon his service and government. But it was charactistic of Arlington that when Charles himself, coming upon them by chance in the midst of this conversation, inquired what they were talking about, he should turn the matter into a jest, and join the King in mocking the solemnity of the Chancellor.4 He adapted himself with perfect grace and tact to the royal pleasures, but was not moved to imitate them. At the time of his marriage his name had never been coupled in sentimental connection with that of any woman," and the only friends he ever made among the ladies, Ralph Montagu's sister, Lady Harvey, and Lady Scroope, were renowned for sharp tongues and ready wit, rather than for beauty.

1 *Memoirs of the Court of Charles II by Count Grammont,* 143.

2 Jusserand, *A French Ambassador at the Court of Charles II,* 151. *"Diary,* Nov. 6, 166j.

The bride was a Dutchwoman, Isabella, daughter of Louis of Nassau, Lord of Beverwaert. This gentleman, a natural son of Prince Maurice, had been chief of the embassy sent to England by the States General after the Restoration, and was a man whose justice andpatriotism made him respected by all parties in the United Provinces. Arlington may have met him in London after his return from Spain, and, if he was not too busy establishing himself at Court, may have remarked the beauty of the Dutch ambassador's daughters la beauty which they inherited from their mother, a daughter of the Count of Horn. If so, the vision of loveliness was in remote prospect, for his bride was a stranger to him when she came to England for the second time in 1666. Before the Restoration her sister Emilia had married the Earl of Ossory, eldest son of Arlington's old friend, the Duke of Ormonde. Certainly a lady whom the Prince of Orange addressed as *ma cousine,* who was descended from the noble family of Horn, and sister-in-law to the Duke of Ormonde's heir, who, moreover, brought with her a portion of a hundred thousand guilders, was a *partie* capable of shedding lustre on the newness of the title and fortune of the first Baron Arlington. Beverwaert had died in 1664, and the formalities of the match were good- naturedly undertaken by Ossory, always the Secretary's devoted friend. It was at his country house, Moor Park, that the wedding took place very quietly on the sixteenth of April, 1666. The King manifested a friendly approval of the marriage, and Lady Arlington was at once appointed a lady of the bedchamber to the Queen.

Clarendon, *Continuation of Life,* par. 919-921.

8 Comenge refers once to Mistress Scrope, first Lady of the Bedchamber to the Queen, as Bennet's mistress, but since the fact escaped Pepys and all the other newsmongers of the time, I believe he was mistaken. (Jus- serand, *op. cit.,* 151.)

When the betrothal was rumored abroad, it produced a flurry of interest that is evidence of the Secretary's importance in European politics. The governor- general of the Spanish Netherlands, hearing that Mademoiselle de Beverwaert would sail from Antwerp, received her handsomely and offered a Spanish frigatefor her transportation.' D'Estrades, the French ambassador at the Hague, considered gravely the diplomatic possibilities of the match, and only his master's prohibition prevented him from tampering with the lady's politics/ The Elector of Brandenburg sent one of his gentlemen to the Hague expressly to convey his congratulations.' The Dowager Princess of Orange was no less complimentary in her attentions, to counteract which the leaders of the Louvestein party made a point of calling on Mademoiselle de Beverwaert.0

As to the lady herself, we have the bridegroom's testimony that she fulfilled all the good he had heard of her, " and that was not a little ".10 From a Dutch correspondent we learn that " Mademoiselle Beverwert is a fine discreet lady, personable and well shap'd, and will certainly prove an excellent wife. She is not given to coqueterie ".u Sir John Evelyn found her good- natured and obliging, but hints at ambition and extravagance.12 Such faults as these, however, were merits in the eyes of her husband, who longed to make a figure in society, and had now no need to count the cost.

In the marriage contract we note the Secretary's expectation that in five years he will be in receipt of a " full and clear yearly value of foure thousand poundsover and above charges and incumbrances whatsoever, publick Taxes onely excepted " from his estates alone." This, for a man who five years ago owned nothing but the equipage with which he made his appearance at Court, testifies to skill and energy in acquisition. But four thousand pounds a year, even at the date of Arlington's marriage, represents but a fraction of his income. From his place he received the modest sum of eighteen hundred pounds a yearlnot enough, he declared, to give him wherewithal to dine the next week after he left it." But there were fees in addition, and if some of these swelled to the proportions of bribes, it is not likely that Arlington turned from them, or that any man of his time would have been more scrupulous. In 1665, upon the death of Daniel O'Neill who had succeeded Bishop as Postmaster, Arlington and Lord Berkeley took over the lease, and at its expiration in December, 1666, Arlington became sole Postmaster, and entitled to a large share of the profits of that office.15 Out of the confiscations in Ireland he had received the estate of Lord Clanmalira, worth about a thousand pounds a year." By a proviso inserted in the Explanatory Act, he was allowed the sum of ten thousand pounds fromthe Irish revenue." His estate was still in the making." The King had leased to him for a long term of years Marylebone Park and St. John's Wood, which merited their names then, though now they are well within the vast circumference of London.1" Holmby House, once the prison of Charles I, had been restored by his son and presented to Arlington, who afterwards sold it to the Duke of York.20 In its stead he purchased a country seat called Euston Hall, in Suffolk not far from Saxham where he was born, and but fifteen miles from Newmarket whither the Court went every year for the races. The house he transformed into " a very noble pile . . . with a vast expense made not only capable and roomsome but very magnificent and commodious, as well within as without, nor less splendidly furnished ". The grounds were given baronial extent in 1671 by the King's license to impark two thousand acres in the surrounding parishes."

State Papers, Spain, 50, f. 196, April, 1666, the Marquis de Castel Rodrigo to Mademoiselle de Beverwaert.

7Arch. Aff. $tr., Hollande, 79, Jan. *21, 1666,* N. S., D'Estrades to Lionne. Quoted in the *Bijdragen en Mededeelingen van het Historisch Genootschap,* XXVII, 552, footnote.

'Ibid.

Ibid.

10 Carte MSS., 46, f. 286, April 21, 1666, Arlington to Ormonde. *i Ibid.,* 222, f. 81, Jan. 15, 1666, N. S., intelligence letter to Sir Philip Frowde. a Evelyn, *Diary,* Sept. 10, 1677.

18 Carte MSS., 69, f. 6o8, April 16, 1666.

"*Ibid.,* 46, f. 37, April 11, 1663, Bennet to Ormonde.

18 *Cal. St. P., Dom., 1665-1666, p.* 5. Arlington paid $5382 1o s. a year to the Duke of York, on whom the King had conferred the rent of the Post Office. Part of the profits paid for the secret service, and there may have been other charges, as well as current expenses to be deducted from the profits, but it is probable that Arlington cleared a large amount. D'Estrades, writing in 1662, said the place was worth two hundred thousand francs a year, but that is probably an exaggeration. (D'Estrades, *Lettres, I, 232.)*

"Carte MSS., 42, f. 744; *ibid.,* 43, f. 569.

11 Carte, *Life of Ormonde,* bk. VI, par. 173-174. The royal warrant is in the Carte MSS., 43, f. 326, Jan. 3o, 1663/4. When Arlington was defending himself before the House of Commons, he explained that the ten thousand pounds from Ireland had been allowed him for secret service (p. 232), but the truth of his statement is open to question. He was entirely safe in saying that the money had been expended for intelligence, since he had never to render an account of money so spent.

18 An indication of the value of Arlington's estate at the time of his death is furnished by his will (Probate Office, Somerset House), from which it is apparent that the large grants he had received were but for his life, and that the remainder was not to his daughter, but to his daughter's husband the Duke of Grafton and his heirs. As payment for Arlington's acceptance of this condition, the King had promised him the sum of eighty thousand pounds, only part of which had been received in 1685. This amount represents the value of the renunciation, not of the estate itself which may have been much greater.

" *Cal. St. P., Dom., 1663-1664,* p. 585.

20 Magalotti, *Travels of Cosmo the Third,* 248.

21 Evelyn, *Diary,* Oct. 16, 1671.

22 *Cal. St. P., Dom., 1671,* p. 592.

For his London residence the Secretary had bought Goring House from the last Lord Goring. It stood on the site where James I had attempted the cultivation of mulberry trees for his silk-worms, and where Buckingham Palace now stands." A country quiet still reigned in the neighborhood; open fields stretched away on either side, and in front lay the royal pleasure ground, St. James's Park. Evelyn, whose taste suggested many improvements here and at Euston, says the house was " ill-built but the place capable of being made a pretty villa ". Arlington lavished immense sums in its improvement until it was a treasure-house of beautiful things. Here he practised the fine art of entertaining which he understood and loved better than any man in

England, and in which Lady Arlington, happily, proved no less gifted than himself. Anyone who by any title could claim the notice of polite society was made welcome at Goring House. Foreigners found the Secretary's hospitality particularly pleasant by reason of his easy command of tongues. The old French exile Saint- Evremond was a frequent guest, and when he went to Holland in 1668, did not neglect to make graceful acknowledgment of the pleasures he had enjoyed under that roof. So intense was his yearning, he wrote plaintively, for the gay company that gathered at Arlington's table, that he had been impelled to read Livy more than six times to reconcile himself to the spirit of republics."

As we have seen, the session of Parliament that ended on February 8, 1667, left the ministers in much dissatisfaction with one another. Clarendon, Arlington, and Coventry agreed in but one thing, that the Duke ofBuckingham was the instigator of all the troubles of the session. He had posed as the people's champion and encouraged the hue and cry in the Commons over the mismanagement of the war and the extravagance of the government. In the House of Lords he had quarreled with Arlington and the Earl of Ossory over the Irish Cattle Bill,2' which he cared nothing about but promoted because it was popular. As soon as the Houses were prorogued, his punishment was determined. A charge of treasonable correspondence with a vagabond astrologer whom he was known to frequent was trumped up against him by the ministers with the King's approval." The Duke was arrested and spent two weeks in the Tower, but the demonstration of his popularity among Parliament men and in the City made it unwise to proceed further against him, particularly as Lady Castlemaine had interested herself in obtaining his release. He was examined before the Privy Council by Arlington, to whom he showed himself as impertinent and resentful as he dared in the presence of the King. " And it is said ", wrote Pepys, " that when he was charged with making himself popular|as indeed he is, for many of the discontented Parliament . . . did attend at the Council-chamber when he was examined|he should answer that whoever was committed to prison by my Lord Chancellor or my Lord Arlington could not want being popular." x The King,whose anger was never lasting, showed no desire to press the charge, which on examination appeared flimsy enough, if not absolutely untenable, so the Duke was released, more popular than ever and fully disposed to repay with interest the offices of Clarendon and Arlington. Pepys moralized over the episode: " It is worth considering the ill state a Minister of State is in, under such a Prince as our's is; for, undoubtedly, neither of those two great men would have been so fierce against the Duke of Buckingham at the Council-table the other day, had they not been assured of the King's good liking, and supporting them therein: whereas, perhaps at the desire of my Lady Castlemaine . . . the Duke of Buckingham is well received again, and now these men delivered up to the interest he can make for his revenge." M Pepys was a little premature: it is true that Lady Castlemaine had obtained for the Duke the privilege of kissing the King's hand, but he was still in disfavor, and temporarily abandoned the role of leader of the people for that of the devoted and unquestioning subject.

28 Thornbury, *Old and New London,* IV, 62.

" *Diary,* March 29, 1665.

25 State Papers, Holland, 184, f. 266, July 5, 1668.

M Carte MSS., 217, f. 348, Oct. 27, 1666, the Earl of Anglesey to Ormonde.

"For this episode, see Gardner's *George Villiers,* 170-182, and Clarendon, *Continuation of Life,* par. 1118-1132. Arlington certainly played the most conspicuous part in the prosecution, but from the fact that Clarendon upholds his action, it may be inferred that the Chancellor also was a party to the plot.

88 *Diary,* July 17, 1667.

The extinguishing of Buckingham had not simplified the problems by which the government was beset. Supply had been granted so late that it seemed almost impossible to set out the fleet that spring. That the Committee of Foreign Affairs yielded so easily to the seeming impossibility was due to a conviction that peace was at hand. To discover the best terms obtainable for England, the government was busy, in the spring of 1667, with two secret negotiations, the one with France, conducted by the Earl of St. Albans at Paris and managed by Clarendon; the other carried on at theHague by the Imperial envoy, the Baron von Lisola, acting on an understanding with Arlington. The purpose of the first was to discover whether Louis XIV could be bribed into an underhand betrayal of his ally: England would temporarily abstain from interference in any contest for Flanders if Louis would force the Dutch into a treaty of peace favorable to England.20 The purpose of Lisola's journey was to attempt once more a peace with the Dutch apart from France. Lisola was the most astute and determined diplomat with whom Louis XIV had to contend. He had long ago discerned the march of the French King's ambition and was not in the least blinded by Louis's altruism in assisting the Dutch. Though much hampered by the paltering Courts at Vienna and Madrid, he devoted his life to building up a coalition against France, sometimes in accordance with his instructions, sometimes in defiance of them. In this year 1667, he published his answer to Louis's claim on Flanders, an eloquent appeal to the attention of Europe entitled *Le Boucher d'Etat et de Justice,* which ranks among the great political pamphlets of all time, and evoked at the French Court a flattering tribute of hate. Lisola realized that the first step towards the preservation of Flanders was to facilitate peace between England and the Dutch. He believed that De Witt was no longer as firmly attached to France as he had been, the benefits of the French alliance having proved in some respects rather illusory. Arlington's weaker spirit was carried away by the envoy's confidence and energy, and he sent Lisola off to Holland in March with a letter of credence, to see what could be done with DeWitt." In the meanwhile all parties to the war were engaged in a preliminary wrangle over the choice of a place for the treaty.

M *Ibid.*

80 Clarendon, *Continuation of Life,* par. 1o38-1o4o.

Among all these possibilities it seemed certain to the English ministers that peace could not be long delayed, so they did not bestir themselves to make ready the fleet. On the contrary, they advised the King unanimously to forego that expense, and allow such merchant ships as would to go abroad, as if the peace were already made." Arlington, who had noted with pain the languishing of commerce during the war, watched the exodus of merchantmen that availed themselves of this permission, with rare enthusiasm. " It is certain that England never saw such a Trade go out; and if they have the good luck to come home again as safely, we shall have no cause to repent the Councel we have followed herein, whatever the success of the Dutch Fleet." "

Rash remark! Two days after the Secretary spoke thus slightingly of the Dutch fleet, its sails were seen off Harwich. The negotiations of St. Albans and Lisola not only failed of their end, but did actual harm by convincing both French and Dutch of the English bad faith." Moreover, Louis XIV had no intentionof allowing Dutch and English to come too amicably to a peace. Therefore, although the plenipotentiaries of all the belligerents met at Breda in May, the Dutch fleet went to sea as usual. Arlington's information was complete on this point: he knew the Dutch were at sea, but he believed that their coming was " but to make a bravado upon our Coast, to compleate which they are saide to have many land men aborde which wee suppose they will not venture to lande if it weare but for feare of protracting the warre "." This extraordinary blindness would be entirely incomprehensible but for one fact. Louis XIV, without awaiting the issue of negotiations at Breda, had begun his conquest of the Spanish Netherlands. His progress, as the Secretary knew, must inspire the Dutch with fear lest when the barrier between them and France was gone, their independence would be of short duration. The longer the war with England lasted, reasoned Arlington, the more hopeless would become the saving of Flanders, to which the Dutch could certainly not apply themselves until peace were signed. So he believed that the coming of their fleet was only to taunt the English with their unreadiness, which done, they would cruise along the coast of Flanders to have an eye on the proceedings of the French.88 The lords lieutenant of the eastern countieswere ordered to their posts, but there was little excitement or alarm.

" His errand, as the Secretary wrote to the Earl of Sandwich, was, " to try whither hee can prevaile with the leading persons there to accommodate with his Majesty upon faire and honourable grounds". (State Papers, Spain, 52, f. 88, March 11, 1666/7. Draft in Arlington's hand.) Clarendon's account of this trial would lead one to suppose that the envoy went of his own initiative. *(Continuation of Life,* par. 1o34.)

"Ibid., par. 1o18-1o27. According to the Duke of York, the plan was approved by Clarendon, Southampton, and Albemarle. (Clarke, *James II,* I, 425.) -,

"Arlington's Letters, I, 171, June 5, 1667. To Sir Robert Southwell.

84 De Witt confided Lisola's errand to the French ambassador, and himself refused to see the imperial envoy, though he sent him word assuring him of his desire for peace. (D'Estrades, *Lettrei,* V, 98, March 17, 1667,N. S., D'Estrades to Lionne; *ibid.,* 163, April 21, 1667, N. S., the same to Louis XIV; Longin, *Un Diplomats Franc-Comtois,* 94; Pribram, *Franz Paul, Freiherr von Lisola,* 309.) Louis XIV was enraged that Charles should employ against him the man whose diplomatic ability he most feared. By his orders D'Estrades informed De Witt of St. Albans's negotiation at Paris. (D'Estrades, *Lettres,* V, 98, 163.)

88 Carte MSS., 46, f. 481, May 25, 1667, Arlington to Ormonde.

ao " what course they steere is not knowne," wrote Arlington's secretary, " most likely towards our coasts, and thence to cruise before that of Flanders." (State Papers, Domestic, Charles II, 231, f. 25. Williamson's Journal, June 3, 1667.) Arlington seems to have labored under theimpression that Lisola had really convinced De Witt that it was to his interest to hurry through the peace. In the instructions for the ambassadors going to Breda, the Secretary concludes: " And you will then be able to discover how far the Baron Isola (though he be not like to be present) hath proceeded in those professions he made of advanceing the peace, and whether he had done any of those offices with De Witt, which he pretended to have power and inclination to performe. And if Monsieur Friquet the Emperor's Envoye be at Breda, you will live with all kindnes towards him, and by him you will be able to discerne whether Dewitt hath been wrought upon or noe." (State Papers, Holland, 182, f. 245, April 18, 1667. Instructions to Lord Holles and Henry Coventry.)

The event proved that De Witt had his own ideas of the way to hasten the peace. On June n, the Dutch fleet sailed up the Medway to Chatham, broke the chain which had been hurriedly stretched across the river to guard the English great-ships, and burned six men-of- war, carrying off the *Royal Charles.* London was panic-strickenlthen furious. So violent was the demand for protection that, with his Treasury empty, the King was obliged to levy forces, though half-fearful lest they mutiny against him. The terrified ministers fell upon the scapegoat that came most obviously to hand: Sir Peter Pett, Commissioner of the Navy, to whose care the security of Chatham had been entrusted, was sent to the Tower. " If he deserve hanging ", wrote Arlington wistfully, " as most thinke hee does, and have it, much of the staine will be wip'd off of the Gouverment which lyes heavily upon it."87 When Pett came before the Council for examination, the Secretary and Coventry showed him small mercy, declaring that " if he was not guilty, the world would think them all guilty ",88 Arlington was unhappily conscious thatalthough the immediate failure might be fathered upon the Commissioners of the Navy, the basic fault lay in the interpretation of the situation abroad, for which he was justly responsible. His discouragement was extreme: " We are fallen into a more troublesome world than ever I thought I should live to see ", he wrote to Ormonde. " God deliver us well out of it! " " The Privy Council was hurriedly summoned to advise in this crisis, as it was always summoned when the ministers were afraid of responsibility. In accordance with its decision, orders were hastened to the ambassadors at Breda to yield the points they had hitherto contested. Parliament, which stood prorogued to October, was summoned for July 25. But when that day camc, thc " snarling Peacc ", as Templc called it, had been signed. Relieved on that score, the King was glad to prorogue the assembly to its old date in October, and the government began feverishly to put its house in order against the moment when the redoubtable Commons should call for an account. Orders voluminously signed were sent by the Council to justices of the peace throughout England, insisting upon the apprehension of priests and Jesuits, and the full execution of the laws against Popery. The Treasury, upon Southampton's death in May, had been handed over to a commission of five: Albemarle, Ashley, Sir William Coventry, Sir Thomas Clifford, and Sir John Dun- combe.40 The Commissioners now toiled over an inspection of all branches of the revenue and of all recurrent expenses, with the intention of drawing up a program of retrenchment which should enable the King to live within his income.

81 Carte MSS., 46, f. 492, June 18, 1667, Arlington to Ormonde.

88 Pepys, *Diary,* June 19, 1667.

88 Carte MSS., 46, f. 492, June 18, 1667, Arlington to Ormonde.

40 Pepys mentions three times a rumor that Arlington was to become Treasurer in succession to Southampton. *(Diary,* March 18 and 19, 1666/7, and May I, 1667.) From the King's subsequent firmness in refusing this office to Arlington, it does not seem probable that he considered appointing him on this occasion.

The climax of reform was reached in the dismissal of Clarendon. His great office and the authority he claimed for it made him responsible, in the public mind, for all the failures of the government, so that he sheltered the very men he hated: the ill-success of the war, the mismanagement of the fleet, the failure of the foreign policy, and the shame of the peacelall that had gone amiss since the Restoration was attributed to his counsel regardless of consistency. Everywhere he was savagely denounced. He could no longer be useful to the King, and Charles, wearied of his lectures and fault-finding, no longer protected him. His domineering, uncompromising spirit had left him no friend in all the Court, except his son-in-law, the Duke of York.

The motion for the Chancellor's dismissal came from Arlington and Coventry. Realizing the danger in which they themselves would stand when the Commons should meet, they attempted to forestall investigation by concentrating the blame for all ministerial shortcomings and offering up the Chancellor as an exculpatory sacrifice. Coventry made no secret of his determination to have Clarendon removed.41 He advocated it openly and freely, surrendering his place of Secretary to the Duke of York that he might not be hampered by that connection. Such frankness was impossible to Arlington. In faultless phrasing he represented the decision as originating with the King, but it was he and not Coventry who steadied the royal resolution, waver-

"*Ibid.,* Sept. 2, 1667.

ing under the reproaches of the Chancellor and the Duke of York.42 In so far as he was able, Arlington suppressed all symptoms of any personal grudge, justifying the step broadly on the ground of expediency. " I cannot but still bee of the opinion ", he explained to Ormonde, " that not only the publique affaires will bee bettered by this change, but that my Lord Chancellor will find greater ease by it then hee seemes yet to believe hee shall."48 But Clarendon, leaving Whitehall one day after a sad interview with the King, saw Lord Arlington looking down at him " with great gaiety and triumph " from a window of Lady Castlemaine's lodgings, in evident enjoyment of the scene.44

But if he laughed with Lady Castlemaine and so far forgot his pose of personal detachment as to taunt the old man's friends with his impotence4jlthough the incident is unlike Arlington, and may have been an attempt at conciliation that bitterness distortedl-the surrender of the seals by Clarendon was by no means the end of his anxiety. He had yet the Duke of Buckingham to deal with. Buckingham was the man of the hour. His enemies were delivered into his hand, and he could crush them at will. As the day for the meeting of Parliament drew nearer, respect for his popularity with the House of Commons increased. He had nodifficulty in getting himself recognized as a martyr for love of Parliaments and as arbiter of the next session." His first intention was to destroy Arlington, who had played the most conspicuous part in contriving his brief disgrace. To this end he sent a friend to the Chancellor, shortly before the latter's dismissal, desiring him " to deal freely with him concerning the Lord Arlington, whom he knew to be an enemy to both of them; and that he must have him examined upon that conspiracy, which he hoped he would not take ill ". But the Chancellor, who had himself been a party to the astrological episode, felt obliged to assure him that there had been no conspiracy, and that Lord Arlington had done no more than his duty, " which testimony ", he allowed himself to add, " could proceed only from justice, since he well knew that lord did not wish him well "."

42 When he believed that the King might, after all, change his mind, Arlington wrote in his disinterested fashion: " If he does soe, I feare the next sessions of Parliament will be a very troublesome one; and that those things which the Government standes essentially in neede off, will very hardly bee attaind, and my Lorde Chancellor himselfe suffer more then hee would have done if hee had retired. I heartily pray it may be otherwise; but I feare I shall bee a true prophet, and then not bee exposed to soe much censure as I am for my opinion now." (Lister, *Life of Clarendon,* III, 468, Aug. 27, 1667, Arlington to Ormonde.)

"*Ibid.,* 47o, Aug. 31, 1667.

Clarendon, *Continuation of Life,* par. 1143.

45 *Ibid.,* par. 115o.

Thus rebuffed, the Duke looked on indifferently enough when Clarendon was discharged from his office. Arlington and Coventry saw in him the dictator of the House of Commons and exerted themselves to recover his good graces. By their instrumentality Buckingham was graciously received by the King in a "much nearer reconciliation" than the Countess of Castlemaine had been able to effect.48 At the same timethe Duke was restored to the places he had held before his disgrace. This propitiation paved the way for a reconciliation with Arlington, which was, accordingly, formally arranged by mutual friends." In this shallow soil the Secretary labored to cultivate a sudden friendship with all the courtier's arts he knew. Coventry, though less adept at flattery, and less timid, was anxious to attract the Duke into the Court party, though not to make him the head of it. But Buckingham, seeing all the world running to do him honor, enjoyed prolonging the suspense. " He assumes here ", reported the French Ambassador, " a role important enough to surprise strangers, who do not know the extent of his self- sufficiency. He is, indeed, very much considered, and in a way to be sought after by every one."'"

49 " II gouvernoit le Parlement lors qu'il fut separ$ il y a huit mois, Jepuis cela il a perdu toutes ses charges, il a este exile et mis dans la Tour, et aujourdhuy il est considere comme le Martir de cette assemblee. II est vray qu'il est recherche de toute l'Angleterre et mesme des etrangers." (Arch. Aff. Etr., Angleterre, 89, f. 124, Oct. 10, 1667, N. S., Ruvigny to Louis XIV.)

47 Clarendon, *Continuation of Life,* par. 1152.

48 " La Cabale du due de Bouquinquan qui est la plus accreditee du parlement a donne assez de crainte a Milord Arlinton et a Couventri de se joindre aux amis du Chancelier Heiden pour les obliger de reconcilier ce due avec leur maistre lequel l'a restabli dans toutes ses charges." (Arch. Aff. Etr., Angleterre, 89, f. 103, Sept. 29, 1667, N. S., Ruvigny to Louis XIV.)

Second in importance only to the glorification of Buckingham was the reappearance of the Earl of Bristol. In 1664 he had petitioned the King with great pathos to allow him to seek medical treatment in London, he being a prey to several diseases the least of which he affirmed would certainly prove mortal.'1 Now, at the news of the Chancellor's disgrace, he was miraculously whole, and returned in triumph to Court, where he prepared himself to deliver his blow at the fallen man when Parliament should assemble.

The Houses met on October 10, and the Commons displayed at once the consciousness of mastery that the events of the summer allowed them. Arlington and Coventry had hoped they would be content with the dismissal of Clarendon and not take it upon themselves to question or punish the other ministers. Far from accepting so tame a program, the House began at once a rigid inquiry into the miscarriages of the war, in the course of which the Secretary was summoned to account for the faulty intelligence which had caused the division of the fleet in 1666, and Coventry, to explain why no fleet had been sent out in *1667.'* Therefore neither was able to oppose the impeachment of Clarendon which was being prepared in the Commons at the same time that their own conduct was under investigation. " It has been hinted to my Lord Arlington and to Coventry that there must be matter for Parliament, and that they might very well serve, if the Chancellor were taken away." M The most ominous feature of the situation was that the Secretary could no longer be certain of the King, for Charles had been won by Buckingham's promise that the House, when it should be satisfied in regard to the ministers, would give him money." According to Pepys, Buckingham and Bristol were now " the only counsel the King follows, so as Arlington and Coventry are come to signify little ".K The French Ambassador noted a rumor that Arlington was to be dismissed."

Carte MSS., 35, f. 737, Sept. 28, 1667, Carlingford to Ormonde; *ibid.,* 220, f. 301, Oct. 22, 1667, Ossory to Ormonde.

"Arch. Aff. $tr., Angleterre, 89, f. 119, Oct. 6, 1667, N. S., Ruvigny to Louis XIV.

81 *Ibid.,* 84, f. 39, Nov. 24, 1664, N. S., Comenge to Lionne.

82 " Le Chancelier auroit este accuse ce matin si Couventri ct le Milord Arlincton qui sont sur le tapis ne 1'eussent empesche. Le premier qui a este Secretaire de Monsieur le due d'York desirant estre Justine sur sa con- duite dans la Marine. Et 1'autre le souhaitant aussi sur des Avis qu'il a donnez, et dont il estoit mal informe que la flotte Holandoise ne pouvoit pas d'un mois sortir de leurs ports, ny se mettre en Mer, peu de Jours avant le grand combat qui dura quatre Jours." *(Ibid.,* 89, f. 195, Nov. 3, 1667, N. S., Ruvigny to Louis XIV.)

K *Ibid.,* 89, f. 181, Oct. 3o, 1667, N. S., the same to the same.

M Carte MSS., 35, f. 778, Oct. *22,* 1667, Conway to Ormonde.

M *Diary,* Nov. 15, 1667.

BArch. Aft. Etr., Angleterre, 89, f. 192, Oct. 31, 1667, N. S., Ruvigny to Louis XIV.

In this critical situation, the two discredited ministers deserted each other. To Coventry, who was a man of violent dislikes, even the reinstatement of Clarendon was preferable to Buckingham's supremacy. Therefore he showed no enthusiasm for the impeachment and even absented himself from the House one day when the debate raged hottest, thus drawing upon himself the King's disapproval." He made an effort, also to recover the confidence of the Duke of York.08 Arlington was too frightened to revolt. At the King's command, he revised the articles of impeachment to be brought against Clarendon.0' Sir Robert Carr, who had married Arlington's sister Elizabeth, and Sir Thomas Lyttel- ton, the Secretary's most reliable henchman in the Commons, were among those members who volunteered to bring proof of certain of the accusations.'0 In the middle of November, the Commons sent the impeachment to the House of Lords, with a demand that the ex-Chancellor be committed to the Tower. But here Clarendon's adherents developed unexpected strength, and carried a vote against commitment, on the ground that such proceeding was not warranted by a general impeachment in which no specific accusations had been made. From this decision twenty- six of the Lords under Buckingham's leadership registered their dissent, Arlington being one of the number.01

The Commons were not prepared to yield their point; the Lords maintained theirs. Thus matters stood atthe end of November, when, to the general surprise, Clarendon fled to France. He had acted unwisely on a suggestion purporting to come from the King, which may, however, have originated with Arlington, who had much to fear from either the success or the failure of the impeachment. Certainly he knew that Clarendon would go, several days before the flight.'1

87 Carte MSS., 220, f. 326, Jan. 4, 1667/8, Ossory to Ormonde.

KIbid.; also Arch. Aff. $tr., Angleterre, 91, f. 35, Jan. 12, 1668, N. S., Ruvigny to Louis XIV.

"Arch. Aff. $tr., Angleterre, 89, f. 178, Oct. 30, 1667, N. S., the same to the same.

M Clarendon MSS., 85, f. 428. Articles of the impeachment, with names of those undertaking to prove them.

m *Lords' Journal,* Nov. 20, 1667.

This put an end to the defense, but it also checked the Buckingham faction in mid-career. Parliament was uncertain what to do next, and so the Christmas holidays found and dispersed it. It had come to no conclusions regarding the miscarriages of the war, nor had it voted supply. It had not accomplished anything at all, except to minister to the greatness of the Duke of Buckingham.

68 See his letters to Ormonde, Lister, *Life of Clarendon,* III, 472, 473.

8

SECTION 8

CHAPTER VII.
The Triple Alliance.

Who was to succeed the Earl of Clarendon as first minister? To the Duke of Buckingham that question was already answered, and the circumstances of the past few months lent weight to his pretension. But to Buckingham the leading place in the ministry meant not so much an opportunity to govern as the satisfaction of preening himself in the public eye. If he had been capable of a settled policy, he had not the industry necessary to sustain it. Arlington, who knew the instability of the Duke, was content to bide his time and in the meanwhile reestablish his influence over the King. His estrangement from Coventry was now complete, for each regarded the other as a renegade and resented angrily any imputation of fault in himself.1 Mutual detestation reigned frankly between Coventry and Buckingham. Pepys heard with regret, " That this new faction do not endure, nor the King, Sir W. Coventry ; but yet that he is so useful that they cannot be without him; but that he is not now called to the Cabal. That my Lord of Buckingham, Bristoll and Arlington, do seem to agree in these things; but that they do not in their hearts trust one another, but do drive several ways, all of them." *2*

1" I do hear of all bandes that there is a great difference at this day between my Lord Arlington and Sir William Coventry, which I am sorry for." (Pepys, *Diary,* Feb. 13, 1667/8.)

" I am advertised that the difference betweene the Lord Arlington and Sir Will Coventry is growne to that height that it is not likely to be composed." (Carte MSS., 36, t. 218, D'iblin, March 3, 1667/8, Michael Boyle, archbishop of Dublin, to Ormonde.)

a Diary, Dec. 30, 1667.

To the Secretary's intense irritation, Buckingham trespassed on the field which, now that Clarendon was gone, he had hoped to make peculiarly his own, that of foreign affairs. Not only was the Duke a member of the committee for such matters, but he attached himself to the Secretary in all official intercourse with foreign ambassadors and ministers.8 Since Clarendon's dismissal, the Foreign Committee included, besides the two Secretaries and the Duke of Buckingham, the new Lord Keeper, Sir Orlando Bridgman, a man of legal rather than political turn of mind, the Duke of Albe- marle, Lord Robartes, and, of course, the Duke of York when he cared to attend.

The foreign situation was at this time particularly critical. Louis XIV had prospered well in his conquest of Flanders during the summer of 1667lso well that unless Spain were able to find powerful allies, her provinces were lost. But, of the powers most interested in preserving Flanders to Spain, the Emperor was too irresolute and too fearful of France to act; the Dutch were still under the obligations of their alliance withLouis XIV; and England was practically pledged to temporary neutrality by engagements contracted with each of the belligerent powers. When angling for a peace in April, 1667, Charles had been lured into a promise not to enter into any alliance or treaty prejudicial to the interests of France for the space of one year.4 In May of that year the Earl of Sandwich, Charles's ambassador at Madrid, had signed two treaties with Spain: the one a treaty of commerce very advantageous to England; the other, an arrangement for a truce with Portugal, to be accomplished by the mediation of England with that Crown. The latter concluded with a secret article by which the Kings of England and Spain agreed not to assist each other's enemies.' But neither France nor Spain was aware of Charles's engagement to the other, and each hoped to win him to an active alliance.

1 The French ambassador, Ruvigny, tells that when the Committee of Foreign Affairs was reorganized after Clarendon's dismissal, he, fearing Arlington's affection for Spain, impressed upon Buckingham the importance of his obtaining a place on it, in order to redress the balance in favor of France. Buckingham thereupon sent his confidant, Leighton, to the Secretary, to demand that the Duke be included, but Arlington tried to excuse himself on the plea that he lacked the credit. Leighton told him flatly that if the thing were not done in three days, he need expect nothing from the friendship of the Duke of Buckingham. This so alarmed Arlington that he procured the appointment at once. (Arch. Aff. Etr., Angleterre, 91, f. 15, Jan. 5, 1668, N. S., Ruvigny to Louis XIV.) But Buckingham had been appointed to the Committee in October (Carte MSS., 46, f. 567, Oct. 29, 1667, Arlington to Ormonde), whereas Ruvigny, writing on Dec. 26/Jan. 5, relates this incident as of recent occurrence. It is possible that Arlington may have attempted to reorganize the Committee after the

adjournment of Parliament in order to be rid of Buckingham, but I am inclined to believe that Ruvigny was misled by a fabrication of Leighton's whose vocation it was to exalt the Duke of Buckin- ham.

To this end Louis XIV had sent the Huguenot Marquis de Ruvigny to London as his ambassador in the autumn of 1667.' Ruvigny knew England well, and had many friends at Court, among whom he could count the King himself. No ambassador was ever more fully or more accurately informed of what went on in the government to which he was accredited, but he lacked imagination to supplement his knowledge, and was over-apt to despise the intelligence of men that opposed him. He had to reckon with three ambassadors whomthe States General had sent over after the Peace of Breda to sound Charles II on the problem of Flanders. There was also the Count de Molina, the Spanish ambassador, a man, as Clarendon has said, " rather sincere than subtle ", but he was managed and, as it were, edited, by the representative of the other branch of the House of Austria, the Baron von Lisola. This gentleman had returned after his fruitless errand to Holland, bearing instructions to negotiate a defensive league between England, Spain, and the Empire.7

4 This engagement, which was reciprocal in form, had been agreed to by England in return for Louis's promise to restore the West Indian islands which the French had taken from the English during the war. (Mignet, *Negotiations,* II, 43-45.) In the case of English St. Christopher's, the fulfilment of this promise was long delayed.

8 The treaty regarding Portugal, with the secret article, is in volume II of *Arlington's Letters,* 240-254.

6 Mignet, *Negotiations,* II, 505-512, instructions of the Marquis de Ruvigny, Aug. 11, 1667, N. S.

Ruvigny's proposal of an offensive and defensive league was received with enthusiasm by Charles II, who, however, assured him that both Parliament and the Committee of Foreign Affairs were hostile to France, and hinted that only very solid material advantages would win public consent to a French alliance." When the ambassador broached his errand to Arlington, the Secretary remained entirely unmoved, and after a perfunctory compliment, spoke of finishing the commercial treaty, left incomplete by Holles when France declared war upon England. Ruvigny easily penetrated this subterfuge. " The King of England ", he wrote to his master, " desires a union with your Majesty, but he is turned aside by my Lord Arlington, who wishes it no more than the Count de Molina."10

It was true that the Secretary was not considering a league with France at all, but he was revolving certain other possibilities and weighing their relative advantages to England. France, he believed, would be willing to pay Charles II to remain neutral: " It is truethe popular Opinion here is opposite to this, but, when the Necessities of the Kingdom after such a War, and so faulty a Government as we are suppos'd to have liv'd under, shall go into the other Ballance, it is not likely to be long so, nor cannot be maintain'd but by the Parliaments giving his Majesty yet more money than they are either able or willing to do. The present game of France is to take off us *[sic]* from the help of Spain, by showing the likelihood of their making the Peace, by assuring Holland, that they shall have the Profit, and honour of making it: And yet, in the meantime, to prepare so vigorously for the next Years War, as if they never meant indeed to make the Peace. The Game of Holland is to effect it indeed, and in the meantime, Spain doth nothing to invite their neighbours to concurr in their Assistance, but by telling them, that they must oppose this growing greatness of France, because at last it will be prejudicial to them." u

7 Longin, *Un Diplomate Franc-Comtois,* 1o1.

8 Arch. Aff. fetr., Angleterre, 89, f. 93, Sept. 22, 1667, N. S., Ruvigny to Lionne. *Ibid.* "/bid., 89, f. 222, Nov. 14, 1667, N. S., the same to Louis XIV.

One may draw three inferences from this letter: first, that the Secretary was as distrustful of France as in the days of the *Celebre Ambassade;* second, that England would not fight the battles of Spain unless that Crown paid the costs; third, that failing this, a bargain might be struck with France for neutrality. Arlington was at this time trying to discover, through the English ambassador at Madrid, the highest terms at which Spain would buy the English alliance."

11 *Arlington's Letters,* II, 264, Oct. 31, 1667. To the Earl of Sandwich.

12 " At the Receipt of this, I suppose your Excellency will think it fit, to acquaint the Queen, or the Ministers there at least, of his Majesty's Intentions to recall you speedily; and accordingly dispose them to put into your hands, their last offers of the Terms they will give and take from his Majesty, in a stricter Union betwixt the two Crownes ... In my last Letter to your Excellency by Mr Sheers, I took notice of the obscure Overtures, the Duke of Medina de las Torres had made to Mr. Godolphin, of the giving us free Ports in the Indies. Your Excellency knows, betterthan I, how tempting such Propositions will be to this Nation, which is so fond of inlarging the Bounds of their Trade, and, accordingly, endeavour to bring with you, the utmost they will grant of that kind, with any other Particulars, you suppose may be inviting to his Majesty.' *(Arlington's Letters,* II, 264-265, Oct. 17, 1667. To the Earl of Sandwich.)

While the impeachment of Clarendon hung fire, the Secretary's indifference to the French advances did not seem an insuperable obstacle to Ruvigny, who witnessed his fear of Parliament and his forced capitulation to Buckingham. " He is on a slippery path ", thought the ambassador " and turned, rather contemptuously, to woo the bolder spirits.

First, there was the King, who, under Buckingham's influence, himself proposed terms of alliance: money, a share in Louis's future conquests in Flanders, and commercial privileges in France." But later he declared to Ruvigny that the best he could do would be to prevent England from assisting Spain, and even for this neutrality " advantages " must be shown wla state of mind evidently promoted by the Secretary of State. Then, there was the Duke of Buckingham, who burned to distinguish himself in a Continental war, and so preferred an offensive alliance on either side rather than neutrality. But he esteemed the French alliance above that of Spain, and for this reason Ruvigny encouraged his application to foreign affairs. The Duke expected, however, that Louis would make England's participation in his quarrel profitable to her, and hinted as broadly as Charles at a division of conquests." ButLouis had no intention of inviting interference in Flanders, nor of buying neutrality, and so the matter rested for a space. England was accepted by both belligerent powers as mediator, the Dutch and the Swedes having already taken upon themselves the same pacific office.

"Arch. Aff. Err., Angleterre, 89, f. *222,* Nov. 14, 1667, N. S., Ruvigny to Louis XIV.

14 Mignet, *Negotiations,* II, 521-522, Oct. 17, 1667, N. S., the same to the same.

18 Arch. Aff. Etr., Angleterre, 89, f. 217, Nov. 14, 1667, N. S., the same to the same.

M " Le due de Bouquinquan est aussi contraire a cette neutralite et il m'a dit qu'il aimeroit mieux qu'on se joignit a l'Espagne que de laisser Votre Majeste dans le pouvoir de tout prendre, et d'imposer en suite a

On the evening of November 25, while the contest over the commitment of Clarendon still raged between the two Houses, Ruvigny was surprised by a joint visit of the rivals, Buckingham and Arlington. They came by the King's order, explained the Secretary, for two purposes: first, to discuss the basis of a league between France and England; second, to learn exactly the terms which Louis XIV had suggested to the Dutch mediators as the foundation of a peace agreeable to him. Arlington begged courteously that the ambassador satisfy them first in this minor matter, after which they could freely proceed to the more important. Ruvigny, eager to hear what they had to say about an alliance, quickly rehearsed the conditions which Louis had offered to Spain in September: He would keep the conquests he had made in the course of the summer, or Spain should cede to him a line of frontier towns in the Netherlands with the Duchy of Luxembourg or Franche-Comte. For the consideration of these terms Louis offered a suspension of arms lasting until the end of March, 1668. Hitherto Spain had made no move to avail herself of either the truce or the alternative conditions.

When Ruvigny had ended his explanation, Buckingham rushed into the problem of the union, seeking to

I'Angleterre telle loy quelle trouveroit bon de luy donner." (Arch. Aff. Etr., Angleterre, 89, f. 209, Nov. 9, 1667, N. S., Ruvigny to Louis XIV.) See also Mignet, *Negotiations,* II, 525, Oct. *23,* 1667, N. S., the same to the same.

discover what France would give for the alliance, and declaring that Louis must agree to abandon his efforts to strengthen the French marine, which could not fail to arouse jealousy in England. Arlington, who had listened to the Duke's harangue in silence, now interrupted him to say that the present state of England counseled peace rather than war. But Buckingham would not be checked: he was sure, he said, of public consent to a union with France and to participation in the war against Spainlprovided England should find her account therein. Ruvigny assured him that the King of France would consider England's interest as his own, and, neither party being willing to proceed further than this overture just then, the Englishmen took their leave."

Arlington was going about on crutches at this time, owing to injuries he had received by the overturning of his coach. Punctiliously intent on relieving the Duke of the tedium of waiting, he limped slightly in advance of Buckingham and the ambassador to the coach. Ruvigny seized the moment to urge the Duke to hasten at once with his report of the interview to the King, lest Arlington's account prove prejudicial.18

All this Ruvigny wrote to his master that night. Whether Buckingham or Arlington first reached the King with a version of the interview, it is interesting to note the minutes of it jotted down by Arlington the following day.18 The major part is devoted to Ruvigny's statement of the terms of a possible peace with Spain. There follows briefly the substance of theremainder of the conference, emphasis being placed on Buckingham's suggestion that France abandon her efforts to " affect a strength at sea ", and Ruvigny's reply, that he was sure his master would gratify the King of England on that score. Arlington's memorandum closes with an entry made five days later (for it is dated December 1) in expectation of another interview with the French Ambassador: " Propositions for Monsieur de Ruvigny, will his master enter into a league offensive and defensive against Holland and content himselfe with the King our Masters nutrality as to Flanders? This later [latter?] to bee urged upon his demande of the Contrary."2'

"Arch. Aff. $tr., Angleterre, 89, f. 263, Dec. 5, 1667, N. S., "a XI heures du soir ", the same to the same.

18 *Ibid.,* 89, f. 270, Dec. 6, 1667, N. S., the same to the same.

10 Foreign Entry Book, 176. " Teuesday 26" [Nov., 1667]. Minute in Arlington's hand (misplaced in volume).

Such a proposal was startling in its irrelevancy, and Ruvigny was puzzled when he heard it the following day, December 2, from Buckingham and Arlington. He set it down far too easily as the caprice of a government that did not know its own mind, and though he did not admit the practicability of a league against the Dutch, he humored the English ministers by playing with the idea. The upshot of the conference was a paper which, all three men agreed, represented the substance of what had been said. Arlington drafted it, and Ruvigny made a copy to send to his master: " A league has been proposed, offensive and defensive, towards all and against all, and, it is explained, particularly against Holland, and as Monsieur de Ruvigny has represented that the King his master, having a treaty which binds him to the Dutch, could not break with them suddenly, the reply was made, that it would be as difficult to break suddenly with Spain, because of a treaty of commerce with the Spanish, which is very useful to England. Upon this, it was said that one must agree upon the time, the

"Foreign Entry Book, 176. " Decemb. 1. Sunday." Minute in Arlington's hand.

means, and the measures which could be taken to arrive at the execution of this proposition, and to accomplish it with safety." a The noncommittal tone of this statement, which would leave the reader in uncertainty as to whether the league had been proposed by France or England, and the conclusion which intimated that the two kings would unite against the Dutch as soon as a decent lapse of time had allowed them to forget their present treaty obligations, made the paper a more dangerous weapon in Arlington's hands than Ruvigny appreciated.

During the next three weeks the situation remained unchanged. It was out of the question for Louis to provoke a war with the Dutch while his hands were full with Spain, yet Arlington seemed immovably attached to that condition as the price of his master's abstinence from all part in the war for Flanders. Buckingham flitted from one idea to another, even suggesting that Ostend and Nieuport be conquered by Louis XIV and delivered to England in return for the latter's neutrality.28

Now that Clarendon had fled and Parliament was adjourned, Arlington began to regain his power over the King, and, in consequence, his control of foreign affairs. His Spanish colors showed more boldly. In order to increase the popular antipathy to France, he took advantage of Clarendon's choice of that country as a refuge by adroitly insinuating that Louis would intrigue for the banished man's reinstatement,2 a suggestion which obliged the King to treat Clarendon with great severity. The French Secretary of State, Lionne, proposed that Ruvigny complain of Arlington to Charles II, but the Ambassador rejected this as imprudent, " because this King has hitherto concealed nothing from him.... I believe ", he added, " that there is no way of getting rid of this minister other than by decrying him na1vely to the King his master, and by requesting that he be never present at Council when French affairs are under consideration." M A strange proposal, this, to exclude the chief Secretary of State from the discussion of the most important problem arising in his province! " I ought to tell you ", continued Ruvigny, " that he is for neutrality, and that he would sustain that proposal more boldly than he does, were it not for the Duke of Buckingham, who is a sort of pedagogue to him." M

n Arlington's draft of the paper (in French) is in the Record Office, State Papers, France, 123, f. 29o, Dec. 2, 1667; Ruvigny's copy, with his explanation of the circumstances, is in his letter of Dec. 12, N. S., to his master. (Arch. Aff. $tr., Angleterre, 89, f. 277.)

Mignet, *Negociations,* II, 535-539, Dec. 23, 1667, N. S., Ruvigny to Louis XIV.

So confident was Louis of the neutrality of England, that he did nothing to enhance the attractiveness of that role. On the twenty-first of December, Ruvigny communicated to Arlington the project of a treaty drafted by Lionne, which with excessive ingenuity gave the whole profit of the alliance to France: Charles II was to enter into no new engagement with the Dutch while France was at war with Spain, but Louis XIV was not bound by a reciprocal obligation. If the Dutch should break with France, Charles was to assist the Most Christian King with forces to be agreed upon later. When the Dutch were subdued, their commercial empire was to be divided between the allies. As regardsthe war in Flanders, England was to remain neutral, or, with an annual subsidy of 200,000 crowns from France, was to undertake the conquest of the Spanish West Indies. If Charles II would break with Spain on the European side of the Line and aid the King of France with men and ships, his Most Christian Majesty would " consider " attacking a port town in Flanders, which, when taken, should be handed over to England, as Dunkirk had been delivered to Cromwell.28

MArch. Aff. fetr., Anglcterre, 89, f. 288, Dec. 16, 1667, N. S., the same to the same.

24 *Ibid.,* 89, f. 284, Dec. 15, 1667, N. S., the same to Lionne. *Ibid.*

Arlington saw at once that by this project Louis had defeated himself, and with great joy he laid it before the Committee of Foreign Affairs. Not even Buckinghamlnot even the Duke of Yorklnot even the Kinglupheld it. Of the other members, Rupert and Albemarle were scarcely of the intellectual fibre requisite to a grasp of foreign affairs, but for personal reasons they were inclined to follow Buckingham rather than Arlington. Robartes was one of the best-known of Buckingham's adherents. Morice was always jealous of his brother Secretary and, that aside, would be apt to nod as Albemarle nodded. The Lord Keeper alone shared frankly Arlington's distrust of France. Yet not a man of the Committee raised his voice in favor of the French project, or saw in it anything but a slight to England.27

Ruvigny was slow to realize the impression he hadmade. He noticed that the Duke of Buckingham no longer sought him out to talk about an Anglo-French alliance. He observed that the first two weeks of January passed without a meeting of the Committee of Foreign Affairs, and though he scouted Arlington's explanation that the intermission was due to the illness of the Duke of Albemarle and the gout of the Lord Keeper, the true solution escaped him. " The real cause of the rarity of this assembly ", he wrote, " is the natural aversion which they have for business, and because they care very little about the course of events." He knew that Sir William Temple, envoy of Charles II at Brussels, had made a flying trip to England, returning as he came, via Holland, but it was not until ten days after his departure that he mentioned the fact to Lionne. He even added that Temple had been hurried away at the solicitation of Arlington, but the fact had no significance for him.TM He had seen Charles II and his ministers in frequent conference with the Dutch ambassadors, with Lisola, and with Molina, but he was neither alarmed nor suspicious. He found the Dutchmen deliciously funny. " Surely ", he wrote, " they are bravely dressed, and their cocked hats, their cravats, their wide baldrics, their long swords, and, above all, the proud mien of Monsieur Meerman, provoke the raillery of this Court."80

" Mignet, *Negotiations,* II, 539-546, Jan. 4, 1668, N. S., Louis XIV to Ruvigny. A copy of the project in Arlington's hand (State Papers, France, 123, f. 319) is headed, " Monsieur de Ruvigny's project deliverd the *21* deccmb. 67. Project de Ligue entre la France et 1'Angleterre du 4me Jan. 68 ns." The confusion of dates is probably due to the fact that Ruvigny presented the project a few days in advance of the date which Lionne had set for its communication.

27 Arch. Aff. fetr., Angleterre, 91, f. 32, Jan. *12,* 1668, N. S., Ruvigny to Louis XIV.

In his enjoyment of the raillery, Ruvigny penetrated no further into the situation, and so was astounded to learn on January 16 that a treaty of alliance between England and thc Dutch had bccn signed at the Hague three days before.

28 Arch. Aff. $tr., Anglctcrre 91, f. 48, Jan. 19, 1668, N. S., Ruvigny to Louis XIV.

"Ibid., 91, f. 59, Jan. 23, 1668, N. S., the same to Lionne.

Ibid., 89, f. 271, Dec. 6, 1667, N. S., the same to Louis XIV.

The negotiation which came to this climax had been going on in England by the side of that with Ruvigny. While Arlington was haggling over the value of neutrality with the French ambassador, he was trying to plumb the depths of Meerman's instructions. " The Dutch Ambassadors here ", he wrote to Sandwich on November 28, " presse us very hard to make the Peace, wee object that wee know not enough the Mindes of the Parties to goe about it, they reply, if wee will joyne with them effectually in this work, wee must together threaten that Crowne that opposes it notoriously. Wee are now enquiring of the Ministers they have here what sentiments the kings their Masters have towards the Peace. Monsieur de Ruvigny hath told us his, and tomorrow wee goe to see the Spanish Ambassador and the Baron d'Isola to know theirs."

This explains Arlington's interest in the terms France would admit as acceptable when with Buckingham he called on Ruvigny the evening of November 25. On November 29 the Secretary saw Lisola and Molina, but could not extract the information he desired from them." Lisola did not want peace; he wanted a coalition that should force France back to the limits accorded her by the Peace of the Pyrenees. Molina could promise neither the exclusive privileges of trade demanded by Arlington, nor money to equip the sixty men-of-war and arm the 12,000 men which he asked of Charles II for the defense of Flanders.'8

al Carte MSS., 65, f. 587, Nov. 28, 1667, Arlington to Sandwich. (Copy.)

82 See the memorandum by Arlington of the substance of a conference with Lisola and Molina, in which he tried in vain to discover on what terms Spain would make peace at this time, Foreign Entry Book, 176, Nov. 29, 1667.

a8 State Papers, France, 123, f. 297, Dec. *g*, 1667. Account of a conference between the English ministers and the Count de Molina and the Baron de Lisola (French).

The following day Arlington again met the Dutch ambassadors and reported the result of his interviews with Ruvigny, Lisola, and Molina: " They seemed not much surpris'd at it", runs the Secretary's memorandum, " but proceeded to make the proposition of his Majesty's joining his armes to theirs to oblige the Partys to a Peace, and, it being askd them what they meant by it: whether forcing France to surrender what they had taken, or making Spaigne content themselves with moderate conditions, they answered the first would bee a worke too longe and too costly, but the latter would bee easy in the state the affaires of Spaigne weare. To which it being answerd it would bee a hard thing for his Majesty to force his ally to sitt down with soe much losse unlesse hee shewd some disposition toward it, they only replyd it was not to force but oblige him fairly to it, that a Periode might bee put to a warre which was inconvenient to its neighbors . . . In conclusion, wee pressd them to answer how they understood his Majesty's armes should bee joind to theirs, or where, what the allyes would doe. To which they answerd wee weare too particular and pressing in our questions, and that his Majesty ought to answer upon the fundamentall one before they could reply to these wee made them." "

Arlington had already realized that the Dutchmen were at the end of their instructions. On November 25, the day of that interview with Ruvigny on the subject of a union with France, when Buckingham had talked so loudly of war, instructions were drawn up in the Secretary of State's office summoning Sir William

M Foreign Entry Book, 176. Nov. 30, 1667. Minute in Arlington's hand of a conference with the Dutch ambassadors.

Temple to England. On his way he was to talk with De Witt at the Hague. " You shall plainly tell Monsieur de Witte the scope of our sending you to him is to be informed whether the States will really and effectively enter into a league offensive and defensive with us for the protection of the Spanish Netherlands. And if the interests of both Nations shall require it, even against France itselfe." "

In such an intricate maze of diplomacy, it is difficult to trace with certainty the real intentions of the Secretary of State. He was feeling his way with the greatest caution, knowing that a misstep in such a crisis would bring upon him the fate of the

Earl of Clarendon. The possibility of an alliance with France was certainly in the King's mind, and was more or less seriously considered by several members of the Committee of Foreign Affairs, as is shown by the fact that Temple's instructions were allowed to lie on Arlington's desk for two weeks after they were drafted. Ruvigny had his opportunity, but he came to shipwreck in trying to steer around the proposal of a league against the Dutch with which Arlington had complicated the negotiation. Nothing was more remote from the Secretary's plans than another war with the Dutch. On the other hand, the suggestion in the orders to Temple of a coalition against France may have been designed ratherto draw out De Witt than because the Secretary deemed that the best policy. To Ormonde, with whom he was generally sincere, Arlington used a less warlike tone: " Wee are now in an idle time as to our domestique affaires which gives us more to intende our forraine ones. I pray God wee take such good measures in them as to bee quiet the next yeare at least, without which our domestique ones will bee much disordered." M

85 Courtenay, *Memoirs of Sir William Temple,* II, 381-382. The original draft of these instructions, in Williamson's hand, corrected by Arlington, is in the State Papers, Flanders, 37, f. 213. The transmission of these instructions was delayed two weeks after their drafting, while the Committee of Foreign Affairs was awaiting the final offers from Ruvigny and from Lisola and Molina. They reached Temple on Dec. 15/25, and he arrived in London on the twenty-first or twenty-second of that month. (Courtenay, *Memoirs of Sir William Temple,* I, 142; Temple, *Works,* I, 321, Jan. 28, 1668, N. S., Temple to Sir William Godolphin.)

Temple finally received his instructions on December 15, and acted upon them with joyful promptness, for the mission was one that he liked. He found De Witt still of opinion that the preservation of Flanders should be attempted first by the joint mediation of England and the Dutch with the belligerents; if they should meet with failure in this, the allies must then declare war on the obstinate party until he should accept equitable terms of peace. As a basis for the peace, De Witt suggested the alternative terms proposed by Louis himself which Ruvigny had explained to Buckingham and Arlington at the latter's request. Though Spain had made no response to this offer, and the French King's sincerity in making it was open to suspicion, the Pensionary's plan was to force Spain to accept one or the other alternative, and to oblige Louis to abide by his offer."

Temple was convinced, and in the ardor of conviction hastened over to England to report to his friend and patron the Secretary of State. He arrived at the crucial moment when the Committee of Foreign Affairs was bristling with indignation over the French project of alliance, and therefore was willing to hear counterproposals. Arlington and Bridgman entered heartilyinto De Witt's plan, the others agreed, and Temple was sent back to the Hague with power to treat.88 He had the King's permission to tell De Witt what had passed at the conference of December 2, when the league against the Dutch had been proposed, and to communicate the substance of that noncommittal statement which Ruvigny had so carelessly sanctioned.80 It would suffice to destroy any lingering delusions the Pensionary might yet be cherishing as to the protective value of the French alliance, and this is probably the purpose Arlington had in mind when he drew up the paper.

88 Carte MSS., 46, f. 583, Dec. 31, 1667.

"Temple, *Works,* I, 311, Jan. 27, 1668, N. S., Temple to Sir Orlando Bridgman, Lord Keeper.

Temple began his negotiation on January 8, 1668, and in five days had concluded with the States General and Sweden the treaties which were to preserve the barrier of the Netherlands. The parties engaged to force the belligerents to peace on the basis of the alternative, and to defend one another in case of attack by reason of their joint action.40

88 Ruvigny believed, for his own comfort, that the resolution to conclude the league was known to the King and Arlington alone, although Charles assured him that it was decided at a meeting of the whole Committee. (Arch. Aff. Etr., Angleterre, 91, f. 79, Feb. 2, 1668, N. S., Ruvigny to Lionne.) Temple's evidence, however, confirms the King's statement: " Upon all this, his Majesty came last night to a resolution of the greatest importance which has yet passed, I think, here in any foreign affair . . . in which the new Ministry, particularly my Lord Keeper and my Lord Arlington, have had a very great part." (.Temple, *Works,* I, 295, Jan. 2, 1668, N. S. Temple to his father, Sir John Temple.)

" Temple used this permission to hurry through his negotiations with the States. In his report to Arlington he says that he told De Witt and Isbrandt " what had passed between your Lordship and Monsieur Ruvigny three or four days after the date of my first instructions; upon which I told them frankly (as his Majesty gave me leave) what had passed in that affair. Monsieur de Witt asked me whether I could shew him the paper drawn up between you; and, knowing I had it not, desired earnestly I would procure it him, assuring me no use should be made of it, but by joint consent: but saying nothing would serve so far to justify them, in case of a breach growing necessary between them and France ". *Ibid.,* I, 300, Jan. 24, 1668, N. S.

40 *Ibid.,* I, 344-363.

In England, the report of the Triple Alliance gave the new ministry its first claim to respect, and evoked a quick, surprised approval." Ruvigny listened sourly enough to the rejoicings over his defeat. " The great applause which this new League first received has so tickled my Lord Arlington that he could not refrain from making known to his friends that he is the sole author, and his friends have published the fact, but perhaps he will repent of it soon, because people begin to seek the advantage which this union brings to England." 2

However tickled, the Secretary was by no means free of anxieties and misgivings. He had hastened through the treaties in the belief that they would have a conciliating effect upon Parliament when it should meet in February. Unless the Commons supported the league by a grant of money, the government would be discredited, the Alliance made ridiculous, and Louis XIV left free to pursue his conquests in Flanders. With this possibility haunting him, Arlington waited fearfully for the Parliament men to come up to town."

41 " It was certainly the masterpiece of King Charles's life, and, if he had stuck to it, it would have been both the strength and the glory of his reign. This disposed his people to be ready to forgive all that was passed and to renew their confidence in the King, which was much shaken by the whole conduct of the Dutch war." (Burnel, *Own*

Time, I, 456.) Pepys thought the Triple Alliance " the first good act that hath been done a great while ". (Diary, Jan. 20, 1667/8.)

42 Arch. Aff. Etr., Angleterre, 91, f. 90, Feb. 9, 1668, N. S., Ruvigny to Lionne.

" " As neare as wee are to the Parlament, wee cannot yet judge any better of the complexun it will bee likely to have then when wee parted last with them. All wee can promise ourselves of their temper is founded in the late Treatys wee have made with Hollande which everybody tells us will bee acceptable to them. His Majesty will put them upon the supporting them by a succour of five hundred thousand pounds at least; if they cheque at this, wee shall quickly see what wee may depende off from them." (Carte MSS., 46, f. 580, Jan. 28, 1667/8, Arlington to Ormonde.)

9

SECTION 9

CHAPTER VIII.
Rivalry With Buckingham.

On the tenth of February the House of Commons listened stolidly to the speech from the throne which set forth the program of the new ministry. There were but two important points: supply, to enable the King to sustain his part in the league by the equipment of a fleet, and a plan of comprehension which should unite all Protestant subjects.1 But the Commons clung still to the ill-humor which Clarendon's escape had engendered, and refused to be dazzled by the merits of the Triple Alliance into making a hasty vote of supply. Once they had granted money for a war, and the English fleet had been burned in port; now money was being demanded for a pretended, possible war, which no doubt would be spent in peaceful celebration by the Court. They called for the report of the committee appointed the previous autumn to inquire into the miscarriages of the war, and devoted themselves to that investigation, regardless of the needs of the Crown. Arlington was one of the first to receive their attention when the division of the fleet in 1666 was under discussion. The poet, Andrew Marvell, attacked him savagely: " We have had Bristols and Cecils Secretaries ", he told the House, " and by them knew the King of Spain's Junto, and letters of the Pope's cabinet;

and now such a strange account of things! The money allowed for intelligence so small, the intelligence was accordingly. A libidinous desire in men, for places,makes them think themselves fit for themlThe place of Secretary ill-gotten when bought with 10,0001. and a Barony." 2 But the Secretary's defenders were able to show that the two admirals, Rupert and Albemarle, had been informed of the rumor that the Dutch were out, in time to prevent the separation, had the report been credited. This brought the Commons to a vote which distributed the blame broadly among the ministers : " Resolved, That the not timely recalling the order for the division of the fleet, after the intelligence was given of the Dutch fleet coming out, was a miscarriage." '

1 Cobbett, *Parliamentary History,* IV, col. 404.

The beloved inquiries went on, and with them the introduction of many bills hostile or humiliating to the Court. Arlington, seeing Louis XIV still hesitating to admit the terms of peace prescribed by the allies, became very despondent: " God Almighty sett all our heades right", he exclaimed to Ormonde, " for there are few that are not verry giddy!"4 The giddiness subsided somewhat when at the end of February the Commons voted supply (though it was only $310,000instead of the *$500,000* for which Arlington had hoped), but revived once more when, before it was decided on what funds the supply should be fixed, the Commons bethought themselves of the King's proposal for uniting Protestants, and set everything aside to provide for the security of the Church.8 Religious affairs, as the Secretary remarked mournfully, " though admirable good in their places, are ill companions of money matters ".' The House was waiting to see whether Louis would choose peace or war before completing its gift; Louis was observing the actions of the House with equal attention. In the middle of March peace seemed so precarious that the Commons reluctantly finished their grant, and the government was obliged to anticipate it in order to make some preparation for war.7 The suspense came to an end in the first week of April, when Louis XIV accepted the alternative. This left the Commons free to continue their investigation of the mishaps of the Dutch War, but a quarrel with the Lords arose which put a stop to all business and brought about a prorogation May 1.

1 Grey, *Debates,* Feb. 14, 1667/8. When it was insinuated that intelligence was better managed in worse hands, meaning Thurloe's, Morice defended his office by declaring that he had never been allowed more than seven hundred and fifty pounds a year for intelligence, whereas Cromwell had spent seventy thousand. *(Ibid.,* Feb. 15, 1667/8.) If Morice spoke truly, then by far the major part of the intelligence money must have been spent by Arlington, for we learn that during the last year of Southampton's treasurership, from Easter, 1666, to Easter, 1667, the Treasury paid out $24,145 for intelligence. *(Cal. St. P., Dom., 1667-1668,* p. 288.) This should not have been inadequate, even for a year of war. When the committee appointed by the Commons to take account of the money expended for the war during the last year of its duration, reported to the House, Pepys records that " the first sum mentioned in the account brought in by Sir Robert Long, of the disposal of the Poll-bill money, is 5,000 /. to my Lord Arlington for intelligence; which was mighty unseasonable so soon after they had so much cried out against his want of intelligence ". *(Diary,* Feb. 21, 1667/8.)

8 Grey, *Debates,* Feb. 15, 1667/8.

4 Carte MSS., 46, f. 600, Feb. 18, 1667/8.

The Court had looked to Buckingham to quell the suspicions of Parliament, but his duel with the Earl of Shrewsbury, which had resulted in the latter's death, had cost the Duke much of his popularity. Moreover, it was reported he had boasted to the King that Parliament was as wax in his hands to be moulded at will.' This report Buckingham declared to be the work of Arlington, who, he said, had betrayed him.' Jealous ofthe credit which the Secretary had won by the Triple Alliance, he had begun to intrigue with Ruvigny, and with Madame, the Duchess of Orleans, sister of Charles II, for the dissolution of the league before the ink was fairly dry on Temple's treaties.10 He seldom attended the Committee of Foreign Affairs now, and its responsibilities devolved entirely upon Arlington and Bridg- man.

6 Cobbett, *Parliamentary History,* IV, col. 413-422.

Carte MSS., 46, f. 612, March 14, 1667/8, Arlington to Ormonde.

7 See Williamson's notes of the deliberations of the Committee of Foreign Affairs during March, 1668. Foreign Entry Book, 176.

8 Arch. Aff. Etr., Angleterre, 91, f. 130, Feb. 23, 1668, N. S., Ruvigny to Louis XIV.

Ibid.

The opposition of Buckingham to Arlington's foreign policy was purely personal and inconsequential, but the Secretary must also reckon on resistance from the mercantile class in England. The Dutch War had been waged in their interest, and they could not now concur in any agreement with the States General that did not concede commercial supremacy to England. The Royal African and East India Companies, whose political influence was great both at Court and in Parliament, demanded the support of the government in their quarrels with the rival Dutch companies. A marine treaty was set on foot between the two nations to settle outstanding commercial differences, but the discussions to which it gave rise seemed to increase the antagonism and showed no symptoms of compromise. It was of this rivalry that Arlington's friend, Sir Thomas Clifford, was thinking when, amid the first rejoicing over the Triple Alliance, he remarked: " Well, for all this noise we must yet have another war with the Dutch, before it be long." " Temple believed this was also the opinion of the other Commissioners of the Treasury, who knew that the expansion of trade would mean increased receipts from customs duties, and the simplification of their task of stretching the revenue to cover expenditure. But in spite of the Commissioners' opinion, Temple was confident that while the Triple Alliance had the support of Arlington and the Lord Keeper, it would endure."

10 See Buckingham's letter to Madame of Feb. 17, 1667/8, in Dalrymple'i *Memoirs of Great Britain and Ireland,* Appendix, pp. 8-9.

"Temple, *Works,* I, 434-438, July 22, 1668, N. S., Temple to his father.*Ibid.*

The most variable factor with which Arlington had to deal was Charles II. The King was disappointed that the Triple Alliance had not been more profitable to him financially, and was already crying his wares to France. Ruvigny, recovered from the discomfiture into which the news from the Hague had plunged him, fell into fresh bewilderment over the sweet reasonableness with which Charles offered himself and England to any uses Louis might have for them.18 But the ambassador was a wiser man than he had been the winter before, and he had his master's orders to listen and say nothing." While Charles angled in vain, promised secrecy in vain, Ruvigny ventured to sound the Secretary of State, who had wrecked his plans once before. At the suggestion of a union with France, Arlington assured him in general terms of the esteem in which he held his Most Christian Majesty's alliance, but added as his humble personal opinion that " the best way of making a good and sure alliance between his Majesty and the King his master, would be to complete the treaty of commerce begun long ago, which, being concluded to the satisfaction of the two states, would induce the English to unite with France; any other procedure would be like beginning a building with the roof. But he believed that France was far from the thought of such a union,since his Majesty " forbade his subjects' using the manufactures of the islands of Jersey and Guernsey."1 The very familiarity of this line of argument gave Ruvigny a feeling of depression.

" Mignet, *Negotiations,* III, 9-11; Dalrymple, *Memoirs,* Appendix, pp. 9-11.

"Mignet, *Negotiations,* III, 10, May 5, 1668, N. S., Lionne to Ruvigny.

Not only was this Arlington's personal opinion, but he contrived intermittently to make it the Ring's personal opinion also. Never had the unreliability of Charles been more disheartening, from the French point of view, than in the summer of 1668. At times in his talks with Ruvigny he seemed eager to sign a treaty with France before he slept; on the next occasion his conversation would be modeled after the arguments of the Secretary of State." Yet he thoroughly resented the supposition which he knew was current at the French Court, that he was under Arlington's thumb," and the Secretary, mindful of Clarendon's downfall, was no less anxious that such an impression should not get abroad: " Though my Lord Arlington labors with all art imaginable not to be thought Premier Ministre yet he is either so or a favorite, for he is the sole guide the King relyes upon ", is the opinion of the shrewd Lord Con- way."

While the Secretary was occupied at home in circumventing the King, the Duke of Buckingham, and the

'=/. c., Louis XIV.

18 Arch. Aff. fctr., Angleterre, 91, f. 282, June 7, 1668, N. S., Ruvigny to Lionne.

11 Mignet, *Negotiations,* III, 12, June 11, 1668, N. S., the same to the same; also pp. 14-18, July 8, 1668, N. S., Report of the Marquis de Ruvigny on his return to France.

18 " One thing I desire you to take as much as you can out of the king of France' head, that my Ministers are any thing but what I will have them, and that they have no parciallity but to my interest and the good of England." (Cartwright, *Madame,* 268, July 8, 1668, Charles II to his sister, the Duchess of Orleans.)

u State Papers, Domestic, Charles II, 235, f. 140, Feb., 1668, Lord Con- way to his brother-in-law, Sir J. Finch.

French ambassador, he was trying to strengthen the Triple Alliance abroad. France and Spain had reluctantly signed the Peace of Aix-la-Chapelle in April, but this, in the opinion of both Arlington and De Witt, by no means ended the work of the league: the peace must be guaranteed by England, the United Provinces, and Sweden; if possible, by the Emperor, the German princes, and the Swiss cantons. But the accomplishment of the Act of Guaranty proved extremely laborious, owing to the difficulties made by

Spain over payment of the subsidies promised to Sweden for her cooperation with the English and the Dutch. The latter powers declined to guarantee the Treaty of Aix-la-'"7 Chapelle until Sweden should be satisfied, and so matters remained at a standstill. To remove this obstacle, to keep the Dutch assured of England's firmness in the alliance, and to forward negotiations with Germany, Arlington sent Temple, whose heart was in the work, back to the Hague as ambassador, not without some opposition to the appointment from the Commissioners of the Treasury, and probably from Buckingham.10

In August, 1668, the Marquis de Ruvigny was recalled, and Colbert de Croissy, brother of the Controller- General of Finances, was appointed ambassador of France at the Court of St. James. Nothing can testify more clearly to the respect in which Arlington's influence was held in France than the instructions which Colbert carried with him. Buckingham, who believed that Louis XIV would be in despair without him, washardly mentioned, but to Arlington is dedicated page after page of the most painstaking analysis. He was *la plus delicate piece a faire jouer* in Colbert's prospective negotiation. "If the affairs of England were in other hands than this Lord's (as, on the contrary, they all are by the great confidence which the King his master has in him, who exercises no secrecy or reserve in his regard), the close alliance between their Majesties towards all and against all would be very easy to treat, and would almost conclude itself. But it happens, unfortunately for the good of the two states, that this minister is not only a good Spaniard, having conceived a strong affection for that country in a sojourn of several years at Madrid, and received divers favors there during the former misfortunes of the King, his master, but he is still more a good Dutchman, since he has married a Dutchwoman who has great influence over his mind....

10 After mentioning the opposition of the Commissioners of the Treasury, Temple says: " My Lord Arlington . . . takes part in it as a piece of envy or mal1ce to himself as well as to me, from some who are spighted at all that has lately passed between us and Holland, and at persons who have been at the head of those counsels." (Temple, *Works,* I. 437. July 22. 16e,8. To Sir John Temple.)

" The King has to-day an interest so considerable in breaking the Triple Alliance which is being negotiated,21 and in detaching England from Holland, to unite the former with him against the latter, that, if my Lord Arlington could be induced to act sincerely in it in favor of his Majesty, there is no recompense for this service that his Majesty would not esteem very well employed, even if it should be necessary to sacrifice 100,000 crowns paid down, and a pension of 10,000 crowns a year. The English nation is very mercenary, and the ministers of their kings have never scrupled to touch the money of France; it is only to be feared of this one, that his aversion to this Crown and his engagements with Spain and Holland still form in him a

M This refers to the negotiation of the Act of Guaranty.

more predominant passion than that for the great profit which he might obtain in serving the King. Nevertheless ... his Majesty desires that the Sieur Colbert make the trial. To this end three things must be done: the first, to make such a great offer that it overwhelms entirely his inclinations for Spain and Holland; the second, to relieve him of the shame of receiving a substantial gratification from the hand of a king other than his own, and whom he knows well, in his conscience, he has not invited to that; and the third, to give him confidence that we are speaking sincerely, and that he need not fear we are mocking him or laying a trap." "

There follow orders for the presentation of the bribe in a manner so delicate, so ingenious and respectable, that they are worthy of the experience of Louis XIV. Stripped of all its beauties, the offer amounted to this: on the day the ratifications of an offensive and defensive alliance between France and England are exchanged, Arlington shall receive silver plate to the value of 100,000 crowns.28

But in the interval that had elapsed between Ru- vigny's departure and Colbert's arrival, Arlington had managed to steady once again the shifting sands of Charles's nature. The ambassador was amazed at the coldness with which the King received him, so different from what he had been led to expect by Ruvigny's report. His first interview with Arlington was still more discouraging. The Secretary again thrust forward the unfinished treaty of commerce, and, with a confidence rarely displayed by him, told Colbert that before a league were made with France, one must be certain thatit would not prejudice the alliance with Holland, which England had a great interest in maintaining as ajhing most glorious to the King and to the kingdom. As for himself, that had always been his opinion, and he would still persist in it when his master should ask his advice. England must have peace, and to this end she must keep in good faith the treaty of the Triple Alliance." When Colbert harped upon the glorious results for royal authority of a union with France, Arlington replied gravely that " nothing could secure or increase the authority of a King of England except the affection of his subjects, and the more he tried to sustain himself by foreign alliances, the sooner would he fall into public hatred and the disgrace which must follow ". He spoke, declared Colbert, " as ingenuously and frankly as if I had been as good a Spaniard as himself "."

22 Mignet, *Negotiations,* III, 34-35, Aug. *2,* 1668, N. S., Instructions to Charles Colbert, Marquis de Croissy.

Ibid., 35-36. /

Louis XIV was astounded at this frankness, and furious at the warning he drew from it. " I certainly cannot complain of his sincerity", said he. " An abler man would have concealed his sentiments a long time ... but he did not wishlor did not know howlto keep me in doubt of his ill-will for a moment, or of the invincible aversion he feels to uniting the interests of the two kingdoms."2' Colbert received orders not to display his bribe as yet. In November, however, he was allowed to propose through an agent a " gratification " to Arlington's confidential secretary, Joseph Williamson. But Williamson had assimilated some of his master's discretion, and declined the present, saying hehad too little credit to be of the slightest use in advancing an alliance with France.27

M Mignet, *Negociattons, III,* 43, Aug. 20, 1668, N. S., Colbert to Louis XIV; als0, Arch. Aff. $tr., Angleterre, 92, f. 56, Aug. 24, 1668, N. S., the same to Lionne.

"Ibid., 92, f. 192-193, Nov. 26, 1668, N. S., the same to Louis XIV.

28 Mignet, *Negotiations, 111,* 45, Aug. 27, 1668, N. S., Louis XIV to Colbert.

To console him for the indifference of the Secretary of State, the ambassador had the assurances of Buckingham that by dark and devious ways he was struggling towards a league with France. Not caring to incur the notoriety of too frequent intercourse with the French ambassador, he used his satellite, Sir Ellis Leighton, as intermediary, and this man, who hoped something for himself from the *graces* of Louis XIV, proved more effervescent and extravagant than his master. He spoke in a slighting tone always of the Secretary of State, and confided to Colbert that the appearance of amity between the two ministers was entirely artificial, and that Buckingham was but awaiting a favorable opportunity to oust Arlington." The Duke, indeed, had several intrigues on his hands besides that with France, and these, being nearer home, interested him more. He must have six weeks, he told Colbert in November, in which to expel Clarendon's adherents from the Council, and from such places as they still held.TM A month later he demanded a year at least in which to break with the Dutch and prepare public opinion for the union with France."0 When the year 1668 came to an end without bringing England one step nearer the alliance so much desired by the French King, Louis made up his mind that the good-will of Buckingham would profit him nothing as long as Arlington remained in office.1 The Secretary couldhave repeated in December what he had written to Temple in October: " You must . . . take from Monsieur de Witt, and the rest of your Commissioners, all suspicion of Tergiversation in Us, in our Union and Triple Alliance, or hanging toward France; wherein I can assure you with all confidence, there is not the least step made since you left us." "

"Arch. Aff. fetr., Angleterre, 92, f. 181, Nov. 19, 1668, N. S., Colbert to Louis XIV.

n Ibid., 92, f. 22S, Dec. 24, 1668, N. S., the same to the same.

"Ibid., 92, f. 182, Nov. 19, 1668, N. S., the same to the same.

80 *Ibid.,* 92, f. 215-216, Dec. 17, 1668, N. S., the same to the same.

81 Mignet, *Negotiations,* III, 62-63, Dec. 26, 1668, N. S., Louis XIV to Colbert.

Arlington's faithfulness to the Dutch was commonly explained as the result of his wife's affection for the House of Orange, and the influence that she was believed to possess over her husband." Details of the Secretary's domestic life are scarce indeed, but it seems to have passed in harmony strange and bourgeois to the society in which he moved. The birth of his daughter and only child in the summer of 1667 had warmed and strengthened the somewhat conventional regard which he was prepared to give his wife at the time of their marriage. Yet it is impossible to credit Lady Arlington with authority over her husband in matters of business. She could never be provoked into a discussion of foreign affairs, to all appearances knew nothing about them, was polite to all the world and confidential to no one. It is true that she regarded the Prince of Orange as the head of her house, but that committed Arlington to nothing. In maintaining the Triple Alliance he was acting contrary to the Prince's interests, for the alliance was the conception of De Witt and redounded to his credit, thereby strengthening theparty in power which opposed the restoration of the House of Orange to its former honors."

" Arlington's Letters, I, 358, Oct. 23, 1668.

88 See Colbert's instructions, p. 144 of this biography. Buckingham explained to the ambassador that Arlington's tenderness for his wife was so great that he would never approve of a war with her country. (Arch. Aff. $tr., Anglcterre, 94, f. 171, May 2, 1669, N. S., Colbert to Louis XIV.)

The mutual distrust of Buckingham and Arlington was more evident in Court politics than in foreign affairs, particularly in the struggle each made to throw all available offices in the hands of his own friends. Arlington was undeniably the head of the diplomatic service. There was not a single representative of Charles II at any Court that did not owe his advancement to Arlington: Sir William Temple at the Hague, Sir William Godolphin at Madrid, Sir Robert Southwell at Lisbon, Sir John Trevor and Ralph Montagu at Paris, had all been appointed at his recommendation. In home appointments the patronage was almost evenly divided. The Mastership of the Horse was purchased by Buckingham for himself from the Duke of Albemarle, though the place was coveted by Arlington's friend the Earl of Ossory. The Duke was able to prevent the admission of two of the Secretary's supporters, Lord Andover and Sir Thomas Lyttelton, to the Council.25 But Arlington succeeded, after some delay, in effecting a bargain between Morice and Sir John Trevor for the other secretaryship of state.2 Trevor was a sturdydefender of the Triple Alliance and his accession to the Committee of Foreign Affairs gave weight to the party of Arlington and Bridgman.

M In September, 1668, the Prince was admitted to the Estates of Zealand as first noble of the province. Arlington displayed the liveliest anxiety to convince De Witt that Charles II had no hand and no interest in *the* incident. *(Arlington's Letters,* I, 35o, Sept. 14, 1668; *ibid.,* 352, Sept. 18, 1668, Arlington to Temple.)

88 Arch. Aff. $tr., Angleterre, 91, f. 36, Jan. 12, 1668, N. S., Ruvigny to Louis XIV.

" The Duke of York writes that " Buckingham and Arlington joined to bring in Trevor, a creature of theirs " (Macpherson, *Original Papers,* I, 41), but Ruvigny says that Buckingham tried to defeat the appointment of Trevor, and succeeded in delaying the change almost a year. (Arch. Aff. $tr., Angleterre, 91, f. 35, Jan. 12, 1668, N. S., Ruvigny to Louis XIV.) As Trevor was a sincere advocate of Arlington's Dutch policy, it seems more probable that Ruvigny is right.

The place most seriously contested was that of Lord Lieutenant of Ireland, still held by the Secretary's oldest friend, the Duke of Ormonde. It is not likely that Buckingham ever contemplated forsaking the Court to govern Ireland in person, but he may have cherished a passing fancy for the title of Lord Lieutenant, an honor which would not be incompatible with the appointment of one of his friends as deputy to bear the actual burdens of government. An attack upon Ormonde for malversation of funds had been threatened before the last prorogation of Parliament"lunjustly enough, for although the revenue of Ireland had been shamefully plundered, it had not been by Ormonde's advice or encouragement. Realizing that Buckingham would not be likely to await the next session in order to press the charge, but would try to obtain his dismissal from the King, Ormonde had come to England to fight his own battles in the spring of 1668.

He found Charles wavering and Arlington torn between his affection for his " Brother Ossory ", as he always called Ormonde's son, and his suspicion that the Lord Lieutenant would embrace any opportunity for procuring the recall of the Earl of Clarendon. When Ormonde reassured him on this point, the Secretary promised his best efforts to preserve him in the government of Ireland, in spite of the Duke of Buckingham.88 This Ormonde wanted to believe in the

"Carte MSS., 46, f. 610, March 7, 1667/8, Arlington to Ormonde; Arch. Aff. Etr., Angleterre, 91, f. 235, April 30, 1668, N. S., Ruvigny to Lionne.

K Carte, *Life of Ormonde,* Appendix, LXXX, June 30, 1668, Ormonde to Ossory.

trying time that followed, but Arlington was so uncommunicative and the circumstances so perplexing that the Lord Lieutenant sometimes doubted whether he were really his friend after all.88 The situation was complicated by the fact that an attack upon Ormonde could hardly fail to involve the Earl of Anglesey, formerly Vice-Treasurer of Ireland. Anglesey cordially disliked the Secretary of State, and was disliked in return, which may have been the reason why the Duke of Buckingham professed a warm affection for him 0 and was determined to keep him in the office he then held of Treasurer of the Navy. If the power of the two ministers balanced nicely, both Ormonde and Anglesey might be savedlor the compromise might work the other way and both be lost.

The struggle continued through the summer of 1668 with increasing rancor on both sides. In July, when Arlington was at Bath, Buckingham won from the King the appointment of a commission to inquire into the Irish accounts." In September he obtained an order stopping payment of money due Ormonde by the Explanatory Act, but Arlington was able to secure the reversal of the order.4"

M " I have not been able to keepe lookers on from beleeveing my lord Arlington to be lesse my frend then I am confident he is and will be found at last. I am not easyly brought to suspect, nor to think it reasonable to impose a methode to my frends in their proceeding concerning me. I have patience enough to see the event and cannot despaire to be enough considerable then to recompence good turnes with the like." *(Ibid.,* LXXXII, Aug. 15, 1668, the same to the same.)

"Arch. Aff. $tr., Angleterre, 92, f. 137, Oct. 15, 1668, N. S., Colbert to Louis XIV.

41 " You may remember your Lordship told me your goeing to the Bath was sayd to be to avoid the difficulty of givcing your hand to something like this, or the inconvenience of endeavouring to prevent it." (Carte MSS., 51, f. 427, July 18, 1668, Ormonde to Arlington. Copy.)

Carte, *Life of Ormonde,* Appendix, LXXXIV, Sept. 26, 1668, Ormonde to Ossory.

Both ministers were now considering the probabilities of the meeting of Parliament in November. Arlington, having unhappy memories of the last time the " multitude of counsellors " came together, feared for Ormondelperhaps also for himselfland urged a prorogation to some distant date, or better still, a dissolution.8 Buckingham was clever enough to work upon his fears and opposed postponing the meeting. At the end of October, the beginings of an agreement ominous to Ormonde glimmered through the fray: Parliament was prorogued to October, 1669, and Anglesey was deprived of the treasurership of the navy, the charge being assigned to a commission of two, Sir Thomas Osborne, one of Buckingham's partisans, and Sir Thomas Lyttelton of Arlington's faction. It was reported that the Secretary of State drank the health of the new commissioners with every evidence of joy." December saw Buckingham and Arlington much together, with all signs of understanding and good- fellowship.'18 The Lord Lieutenant's friends shook their heads over this development, and were not surprised when in February, 1669, Ormonde was finally obliged to surrender the sword. It was generally reported and believed that the Secretary had abandoned his friend out of subservience to Buckingham, and the choice of the Duke's adherent, Lord Robartes, as

"Arch. Aff. $tr., Angleterrc, 92, f. 228, Dec. 24, 1668, N. S., Colbert to Louis XIV.

44 *Ibid.,* 92, f. 184, Nov. 19, 1668, N. S., the same to the same.

48" Cependant je vois toutes les apparences possibles d'une parfaite reconciliation entre ce Due et Milord Arlington, et je les trouvay encore heir tous deux enfermez ensemble ..." *(Ibid.,* 92, f. 222, Dec. 20, 1668, N. S., the same to i.innnr.)

I C.U tii-a. iX"V

deputy, made this the most obvious conjecture." With much greater probability, however, one can look upon the reconciliation with Buckingham and the withdrawal from Ormonde as parts of a far-reaching readjustment of the Secretary's personal relations and political aims which he was obliged to make early in the new year, for his own preservation. It was pressure from the King, not from Buckingham, however the latter may have flattered himself, that forced Arlington to yield. Something of the despondency with which he made this submission is apparent in a letter to Ossory written soon after the removal of the Earl's father. Speaking of Ormonde, the Secretary said: " The suspence of this matter so long, and, as it were, from day to day, has made mee a greater Stranger to him than I wish or ought to be to such persons, and so related to my lord of Ossory; and I feare this conclusion will put mee into a worse state with them than I deserve to be. But this must be a matter of time and length to justify mee in. I conjure you to keepe one care for mee when you have heard all tales, and to believe I am, as I ought to be, most unfainedly and most faithfully yours."47

w The Duke of York explains that Buckingham " sent Ralph Montague to Arlington, to let him know he would have nothing to do with him, unless that affair was done in a day or two. Arlington went immediately to the King; and it was declared the next day, February the fourteenth." (Macpherson, *Original Papers,* I, 51.) But a little later he declares " The ladies, Hervey and Trevor bullied Arlington to give up the duke of Ormonde; and got Roberts made lord lieutenant." *(Ibid.,* I, 55.) Both of these stories were probably current at Court, but neither seems well founded. Montagu was always far more the ally of Arlington than of Buckingham, as was always his sister, Lady Harvey. And it is difficult to think of the Secretary as being bullied by ladies.

"Carte MSS., 51, f. 433, Feb. 13, 1668/9. (Copy.)

10

SECTION 10

CHAPTER IX.
The Treaty Of Dover.

When Sir John Trevor became Secretary of State, Dutch affairs were transferred to him, but the senior Secretary assured Temple that his interest in the latter's negotiation would in no wise decline on this account. " Besides ", he wrote, " *utrumque nostrum incredibili modo consentit astrum:* and I am resolved never to leave you till I have made you able to make my own fortunes."1 Yet at the moment of writing he had already deserted Temple and their stars were never more to shine in the same quarter of the political firmament.

On the twenty-fifth of January, 1669, Charles II, in the presence of the Duke of York, Arlington, Lord Arundel/ of Wardour, and Sir Thomas Clifford, announced his conversion to the Catholic faith, and discussed with them the possibility of recovering all England for that Church. Since such a project could not be accomplished without money, Charles and his confidants resolved to turn to France, the paymaster of Europe, for assistance in the holy cause.2

With the sincerity of Charles in his conversion we have properly no concern, save as his attitude influenced Arlington. Had the King been free to choose on whatChurch he would confer the responsibility of his salvation, no doubt he would have chosen that of Rome at any time in his career. But if one grants him thus much spiritual prompting, it is nevertheless difficult to believe that other considerations, more definite and more valuable, had not the greater share in his resolution : the desire to rule in less limited sovereignty than his Protestant people seemed disposed to permit, and the conviction that for the conversion of England large sums of money would be forthcoming from France, and possibly from the Pope and Spain.

1 Temple, *Works,* II, 192, Jan. 19, 1668/9. 2 Clarke, *James II,* I, 441-442.

Of the men whom the King honored with his confidence, two were Catholics, the Duke of York as yet in secret, Lord Arundel avowedly. Clifford, who had been hovering on the frontier of doubt, was swept across by the royal example. Of Arlington one cannot speak positively. In spitelor perhaps becauselof the rumors that had been current ever since his return from Spain that he was at heart a Roman Catholic, he had pinned himself ecclesiastically to the Established Church, and would have done the same, no doubt, had that Church been Mohammedan. He was as unconcerned now about doctrine as in the days when he had been prospective parson of Harlington, and would have been glad to set religion aside as a bit of individual psychology, free from political entanglement. His soul had never been an assertive organ. But though he was by nature a tolerationist, he had not owned such principles since the failure of the Declaration of 1662, and occasionally, to remove suspicion from the government, enforced the persecuting acts with a severity that made him detested of the Catholics. But he loved persecution no more than his master, and was glad to layit aside when political exigencies permitted." When a debate arose in the Committee of Foreign Affairs touching the advisability of a proclamation for the enforcement of laws against Dissenters, Arlington opposed it as resolutely as Buckingham, the acknowledged protector of the " fanatics ", on the ground that it was imprudent to make the nonconformists desperate. " There is a wisdome in all Governments above Lawes ", he concludes owlishly.4

The Secretary would have been indignant had any one accused him of unbelief, or of indifference in spiritual matters. " Few men so often upon their knees", says Clarendon, " or so much desired to be thought a good Protestant by all the parties which professed that Faith, and could willingly comply with all of them, and yet took time of the Roman Catholics to be better informed."5 If he had varied secretly from thisopen-mindedness in the direction of the Church of Rome, he did not admit it even to the King himself, and long afterwards he avowed to the French ambassador that he had never liked the " Grand Design " as Charles had christened the plan for the conversion of England.' It is probable that, instead of affording him religious gratification, the King's revelation gave the Secretary a purely mundane shock, since it meant the destruction of a policy in whose wisdom he believed, and which had brought him all the credit he had enjoyed as a minister. It was certain that Louis, Most Christian as he was, would not open his purse solely for the sake of converting the heretic. His price would be that league against the Dutch for which Colbert had hitherto hinted in vain. The Triple Alliance had taught the French King who were his most constant and most unpurchas- able opponents; with the patience that distinguished him he put aside his greater ambitions, and prepared to crush from his path *Messieurs les marchands.* The first step was to make sure of England, and England was now ready to be bought. No doubt Arlington tested the strength of his master's resolution before he yielded to the necessity of assisting him in it. The alternative of withdrawing entirely from affairs was impossible to a man of his strong ambition and easy principles. Charles, reading his old servant well, seems never to have doubted his compliance.

8 " He was believed a papist . . . Yet in the whole course of his ministry he seemed to have made it a maxim, that the king ought to shew no favour to popery, but that all his affairs would be spoiled if ever he turned that way, which made the papists become his mortal enemies, and accuse him as an apostate and the betrayer of their interests." (Burnet, *Own Time,* I, 18o.) The purely political nature of Arlington's point of view in religious matters is shown by two letters to Ormonde. The first was written apropos of the trial of some Irish Catholics: " I was verry glad to understande from your Grace how lucky the first poore men weare in their triall before the Commissioners. I cannot but wish many more may meete the same, supposing them to bee for the most part verry Innocent papistslat least I am sure their proceedings for the most part shew them to bee soe if folly and Innocence bee the same." (Carte MSS., 221, f. 22, Jan. 24, *1662/3.)* The other letter replied to one from Ormonde asking the King's leave to connive at the private practice of the Catholic religion in certain cases. The Secretary, after stating the King's consent, continued: " I conclude there must either be a way found out of making them live comfortably to themselves, and with security to the Government, or, being such Numbers, they ought in Reason of State to be forced out of it, and the former end will I hope be attained by the way your Grace has now before you." *(Miscellanea Aulica,* 4o3, May 26, 1666.)

4 Foreign Entry Book, 176, April 15, 1669.

5 *Clarendon State Papers,* III, Supplement, Ixxxii.

Arch. *AS.* litr., Angleterre, 108, f. 114, Nov. 20, 1673, N. S., Colbert to Louis XIV. Though Charles once drew upon his imagination so far as to say that the Duke of Buckingham inclined to Catholicism *(ibid.,* 95, f. 182, Nov. 14, 1669, N. S.), he never made that statement about Arlington. It seems probable that had the Secretary been secretly a Catholic at this time, the King, in defending him to Madame, would have mentioned the fact.

If Arlington had some premonition of the King's resolve before its formal communication on January 25,7 that would explain why, on December 27, he entertained the French ambassador at dinner, and took that opportunity to assure him that he had no affection either for Spain or for Holland, but, on the contrary, inclined to a good union with France." Lord Crofts made a point of seeing Colbert at Whitehall on January 20, in order to testify to the Secretary's enthusiasm for the French alliance." Lady Arlington made haste to second these advances by her amenities to the ambassador's wife.10 Colbert was lost in wonderment, especially when, in February, the Secretary showed a disposition to take up the treaty of commerce in good faith, making it, as he said, the approach to a league. " I found him very much changed ", wrote Colbert, " and I do not doubt that the affair of the Duke of Ormonde has affected him greatly." " Of the true extent of the Secretary's trouble at this time, the ambassador was ignorant.

In view of all these circumstances, it is difficult to accept Ormonde's removal as an effect of Buckingham's power. The King, who was momentarily in earnest inhis resolve of Catholicism, wanted a man less firmly attached to the Established Church in the government of Ireland, and Arlington, who had submitted to the whole plan, had not the spirit to contest this development of it.u The reconciliation with Buckingham, which Ormonde's retirement completed, was probably a measure of protection. The Duke of York, finding the Secretary prepared to accept the Grand Design, reinstated him in his friendshipIan honor which Arlington had not enjoyed since the fall of ClarendonIand informed him of the correspondence which Buckingham was carrying on with Madame." Arlington, fearing, perhaps, lest his rival should so prejudice him in the opinion of the Duchess that he would be excluded entirely from the all-important negotiation with France, thought it wisdom to be friends. Therefore he set about distracting the Duke's attention from foreign affairs, and succeeded so admirably that Colbert was disgusted at the falling away of the one ally he had thus far found in the English Court. " I believe ", declared the ambassador, " that he does not show enthusiasm for a union except when he is at odds with Arlington. But as the latter knows how to win himback easily by holding forth bright hopes, and by the pleasures which their good friend, Lady Harvey, knows how to furnish abundantly ... he escapes us when we believe him most engaged, and thus my Lord Arlington, who is the less clever of the two, does not fail, by application, to govern according to his inclinations and caprices." "

On Dec. 27, 1668, Charles, writing to his sister, speaks of his plan as being known but to himself and to ' that one person more ". (Cartwright, *Madame,* 275.) This was evidently not the Duke of York, for on March 22, 1669, the King wrote to Madame: " Before this comes to your hands, you will cleerly see upon what score 363 [the Duke of York] is come into the businesse ", which intimates that the Duke was not his original confidant. *(Ibid.,* 284.) It might have been Arundel or Clifford, but is, I think, more likely to have been Arlington, since the change in foreign policy would have to be accomplished through him.

8 Arch. Aft. $tr., Angleterre, 94, f. 5. Jan. 7, 1669, N. S., Colbert to Louis XIV.

"*Ibid.,* 94, f. 36, Jan. 31, 1669, N. S., the same to the same.

Ibid.

11 *Ibid.,* 94, f. 1o2, Feb. 28, 1669, N. S., the same to the same.

11 The King wrote to his sister in regard to this change: " I see you are misse informed 1f you thinke I trust my Lord of Ormonde lesse than I did. There are other considerations which made me send my Lord Robarts into Ireland, which are too long for a letter." (Cartwright, *Madame,* 282-283.) Lord Robartes, who was a Presbyterian, would naturally be, if not more tolerant, at least less insistent on conformity, than Ormonde. After a year Robartes was recalled, and Lord Berkeley was sent over in his place, and showed much favor to the Catholics. (See the account of Berkeley by J. M. Rigg in the *Dictionary of National Biography.)* The dismissal of Coventry at this time, March, 1669, from the Council and the Treasury Commission, on the pretext of a quarrel with Buckingham, was perhaps another instance of the change of personnel which Charles contemplated in regard to the ministry, but did not persist in.

18 Clarke, *James II,* I, 444-445.

Having thus diverted his rival, Arlington sought the favor of Madame, the Duchess of Orleans, for, knowing how tenderly the King loved this sister, he could not doubt that her dislike would be very damaging to him. Charles himself undertook to convince her of his Secretary's fidelity,18 and Arlington wrote her a letter in June, 1669, in which he strove to make clear how entirely he had accommodated himself to the royal will:

If Your Royal Highness complains of the general terms in which my letter is written, I have, with submission, much more reason to complain of the particular terms of yours; and assuredly your correspondents in this Court must have given a false description of me to your Royal Highness, otherwise you would never have thought of treating me in this way. I have been all my life a good servant of the King, my master, and such I will die, by the grace of God, and I would not, for all the wealth of the world, act any other part than that of a

14 Arch. Aff. Etr., Angleterre, 94, f. 147, April 8, 1669, N. S., Colbert to Lionne.

11 " I will answer for Arlington, that he will be as forward in that matter as I am, and farther assurance you cannot expect from an honest man in his post, nor ought you to trust him, if he should make any other professions then to be what his master is for." (Cartwright, *Madame,* 288, June 6, 1669, Charles to Madame.) Two weeks later, the Princess being apparently of the same opinion, the King wrote again, rather irritably: " And for Arlington I can say no more for him than I have already done, only that I thinke, being upon the place and observing every body as well as I can, I am the best judge of his fidelity to me, and what his inclinations are and, if I should be deceived in the opinion I have of them, I am sure I should smarte for it most." *(Ibid.,* 292, June 24, 1669, the same to the same.)

good Englishman. Moreover, the King will bear me witness, that in two or three remarkable conjunctures I have pleaded the part of France more earnestly than any of his ministers, but it was when I thought its friendship would be the most useful to him. I have done the same, in other cases, for Spain and Holland, when the same reason seemed to necessitate it, but always (thank God!) without expecting or receiving any benefit for myself. You now see, Madame, my temper, and if such a man can be agreeable to Your Royal Highness, I entreat you most humbly to accept me as your most humble and most obedient servant, who honours you with profound veneration, as being the beloved sister of my master, and also, as I firmly believe, the most accomplished Princess in the world. I might add to this my interest in serving Your Royal Highness well, knowing how much the King loves you, and how he prizes your affection. I conclude by reminding Your Royal Highness that His Majesty has been so good as to answer for me, and that thus all other cautions would be not only superfluous, but derogatory to the royal warrant which you have already received for me.

ARLINGTON.1'

It was probably not this letter, which showed almost defiantly the Secretary's dislike of the new policy, that induced the Duchess of Orleans to accept Arlington's participation in making the league she so much desired, but rather her brother's evident determination to trust him with it. Thereafter she was careful to speak very kindly of the Secretary, who confirmed her goodwill by persuading the King to make her a present of five hundred pounds."

Charles, fearful that his secret would come unseasonably to light, conducted the negotiations with France personally through his correspondence with Madame,who in turn communicated with Louis XIV. The French ambassador, Colbert, was entirely unaware of what was going on until November, 1669, and until that time Arlington, too, had no active part in the negotiation, though he probably advised the King privately.

18 *Ibid.,* 290.

"Hist. MSS. Comm., *MSS. of the Duke of Buccleuch, I,* 435, Aug. 26, 1669, N. S., Ralph Montagu, ambassador to France, to his sister, Lady Harvey.

In foreign affairs|particularly in those pertaining to the Triple Alliance|the Secretary had to flounder along as best he might, having to allow for the secret negotiation and yet conceal it. It was important to avoid all appearance of an understanding with France before the meeting of Parliament in October. On the other hand, Charles was averse to engaging himself further in the Triple Alliance; therefore, to the despair of Temple, Arlington began on various pretexts to draw England away from the Dutch. The guaranty of the Treaty of Aix was signed by the three allies on April 27/May 7, but the Secretary hung back from an agreement projected by Temple and De Witt which stipulated the forces each ally should furnish in case the Peace were violated, or one of the allies molested. With encouragement from the East India Company, he obstructed the marine treaty in process of negotiation with the Dutch, and cultivated a difference arising from the provisions of the Treaty of Breda with regard to the right of the English inhabitants of Surinam, until it developed unworthily into a quarrel.

The autumn of 1669 brought Parliament together, and with it a fresh outbreak of hostilities between Buckingham and Arlington. The immediate cause was Buckingham's resentment of the Secretary's understanding with the Duke of York, and the renewal of his friendship with Ormonde, in which Buckingham readthe beginnings of a combination against himself.19 " I could not well omit the condoling with you for the loss of my Lord Duke of Buckingham ", wrote Montagu from Paris. " I can only comfort you as the divines use to do for the loss of the good things of this world, which whilst we did enjoy, were so uncertain, that we ought never to have set our hearts much upon them." " The history of the disagreement is succinctly told in a series of letters written by an onlooker:

July 28. " Bucks and Arlington seem to be a little eclipsed and not as gracious as formerly."

Sept. 20. " Bucks and Harlington cannot set their horses together. Arlington, as is muttered, sits very uneasy."

Sept. 22. " Arlington sits fast still."

Oct. 13. " Bucks and Arlington are still pecking one at the other."

Nov. 10. " Bucks and Arlington were made friends on Saturday last, and long it will last."

Nov. 16. " Bucks and Arlington are broke out again.20

To this account the addition of a few particulars is necessary. The King had done his best to patch up a peace, but the farce of a reconciliation to which he obliged them had no real effects. The quarrel practically monopolized the attention of Parliament, for Buckingham used all his influence in the Commons to promote an attack upon Arlington's friend, Sir George Carteret, who had been Treasurer of the Navy at the time of the Dutch War.21 By way of reprisal, Arlington joined the Duke of Ormonde in an attempt to impeach the Earl of Orrery, who belonged to the Buckingham party and was Ormonde's inveterate enemy.12 " Each party ", wrote Colbert, " professes to wish sincerely the satisfaction of the King, but rather than allow the opposing faction the advantage of having contributed most towards it, would prefer to form all possible obstacles to what the King ardently desires." M It was Buckingham, naturally, and not Arlington, who overshot himself. Charles did not like the affectation of pity for the poor defrauded people of England with which the versatile Duke hounded on the prosecution of Carteret."4 He liked still less the rumor said to have been started by Buckingham, that $800,000 of the money voted for the war could not be accounted for by Carteret and had been expended on the royal diversions. Deeply annoyed at so dangerous an interruption to the business of supply which was all he desired of Parliament, Charles prorogued on December 11 to February 14, 1670, thus cutting short proceedings against both Carteret and Orrery.

MHist. MSS. Comm., *MSS. of the Duke of Buccleuch, I,* 441, Sept. 28, 1669, the same to Arlington; also Clarke, *James II, I,* 436, 444. "Hist. MSS. Comm., *MSS. of the Duke of Buccleuch,* I, 441.

20 *Ibid., jth Report,* 487, MSS. of Sir H. Verney, Bart., extracts from letters of Sir John Verney to Sir R. Verney.

21 Arch. Aff. $tr., Angleterre, 97, f. 71, Feb. 3, 1670, N. S., Colbert to Louis XIV.

Arlington's hands were now full with the French negotiations. The King's correspondence with Madame had resulted in certain general conclusions accepted on both sides as the basis of a treaty: there was to be a war with the Dutch, undertaken jointly by the two kings; Louis XIV was to assist Charles with subsidies to enable him to carry on the war, and was alsoto give such aid, financial and military, as should be necessary to the fulfilment of the Grand Design of the conversion of England. At this point Charles consented to admit the French ambassador, Colbert, to the secret, and the negotiation was handed over to him and to Arlington. Colbert cheerfully put out of his mind all the suspicions and resentment that he had hitherto conceived of the Secretary, and the two set to work very amicably. But somehow the treaty did not seem to advance. Arlington made extravagant demands for his master's cooperation in the war,28 and it was plain that he intended to insist upon the King's public declaration of his conversion preceding the breach with the Dutch, in which case, as Colbert saw, the latter would be subject to indefinite postponement, and might never take place at all." He could not detect that Arlington was in the least stirred up against the Dutch, notwithstanding assurance from Charles himself that the Secretary, though married to a Dutchwoman, was eager to abate the pride and power of that nation.18 Probably Arlington still hoped that the difficult arrangement would never be perfected, and that the King would yet revert to the policy of the Triple Alliance before any harm was done. He seemed not ill satisfied when the negotiation came to a halt over the amount of the subsidies, and even suggested to Colbert that should Charles II be unable to join in the war against the Dutch, he would none the less expect theassistance of the King of France to the accomplishment of the Grand Design.2' Colbert's anger over the audacity of this proposal disturbed him not at all. Conference followed conference; the bargaining continued through the winter and spring of 1670, Louis XIV making many concessions only to have another thorny point or unreasonable demand raised against him. Perhaps the whole fabric of the treaty|Grand Design and all|would have vanished into thin air, had not a more artful diplomat than Colbert taken it in hand.

22 Arlington was believed to be jealous of Orrery's credit with the King. (Hist. MSS. Comm., *MSS. of the Duke of Buccleuch,* I, 437-438, Sept. 6, 1669, N. S., Montagu to Arlington.)

28 Arch. Aff. $tr., Angleterre, 97, f. 19, Jan. 6, 167o, N. S., Colbert to Louis XIV.

21 *Ibid.,* 97, f. 71, Feb. 3, 167o, N. S., the same to the same. *Ibid.*

39 See the first project of the league, drafted by Arlington, and delivered to Colbert on Dec. 8, 1669. (Mignet, *Negotiations,* III, 117-123, Dec. 18, 1669, N. S.)

" *Ibid.,* Ill, 117, Dec. 5, 1669, N. S., Colbert to Louis XIV.

88 Arch. Aff. ktr., Angleterre, 97, f. 62, Jan. 29, 167o, N. S., Colbert to Louis XIV.

Madame, the Duchess of Orleans, out of personal affection for the two kings, had long hoped to see the conclusion of the league between them. Louis XIV now played her as his trump card. In the latter part of April she came to Dover to pay her brother a long- promised visit. Charles, whose eagerness for the French alliance and for Catholicism had languished of late, was fired afresh by her enthusiasm; the last difficulties were smoothed away, and the Treaty of Dover was signed on May 22/June 1.

It engaged both kings to a war against the Dutch, and stipulated the forces each should provide, the naval command being left to England, while the disposition of the land forces was given to France. Of the conquests to be made from the Dutch, England was to have the islands of Zeeland, and, while the war continued, Charles II was to receive three million francs a year. By a vague article Charles agreed to aid in making good any " new rights " upon the Spanish monarchy which should devolve on the King of France, but it was also stipulated that the treaties of the Triple Alliance and of Aix-la-Chapelle should not be violated. For

Arch. Aff. fetr., Angleterre, 97, f. 67.

assistance in the Grand Design Louis promised to pay two million francs; it was agreed that Charles should declare his conversion before the kings joined their arms against the Dutch, but the choice of the moment proper for this announcement was left to him.M

This last point was disadvantageous to Louis, since it might easily be used to delay the war, but Madame brought her powers of persuasion to bear so effectively upon her brother that he promised to make war whenever the King of France should be ready, even if the moment suitable for the declaration of his conversion had not yet arrived.81 Madame also obtained the consent of Arlington and Clifford, who had conducted the treaty through its final stages, to this arrangement.1 But though the Secretary, noting her power over the King, yielded thus easily to her wishes, she was keen enough to perceive his real disinclination to the war," and exerted herself to make his adherence to her foreign policy valuable to him. She had brought with her a ring for Lady Arlington, the gift of the King of France, but Charles, fearful lest the jewel arouse suspicion in some acute observer of the transactions at Dover, forbade her to offer it.'4 In a matter muchnearer Arlington's heart she was entirely successful, for she obtained the King's consent to the betrothal of the Secretary's daughter, a baby of three years, to Henry Fitzroy, Charles's second son by the Countess of Castlemaine." Perceiving that the embers of the last quarrel between Buckingham and Arlington were still smouldering, she brought the two ministers together, and by her gentle authority made them assume the appearances of friendship once more." Buckingham had been of late in the shadow of his master's displeasure for his activities in Parliament against Carteret, but Madame was unwilling to leave behind her any ill feeling or disagreement that might upset her plans, so she made Buckingham's peace with the King," and kindled once more that nobleman's enthusiasm for an alliance with France, he being, of course, in entire ignorance of the treaty that had been signed under his very nose.

80 The treaty is printed in full in the appendix to volume IX of Lin- gard's *History of England,* 503-510.

81 Clarke, *James 11,* I, 449-450.

22 *Ibid.*

88 Charles, warming to the war, had expressed the wish that Turenne had accompanied Madame to England, as he would like to discuss with him the method of attack by the joint forces. Madame suggested to the ambassador Colbert, that Turenne be sent for on the pretext of conducting her home, but begged him not to mention the plan to Arlingtonlan incident which implies that she still distrusted his sincerity in the French alliance. (Mignet, *Negotiations,* III, 186, May 30, 1670, N. S., Colbert to Louis XIV.) f j

M Arch. Aff. Etr., Angleterre, 97, f. *266,* June 10, 1670, N. S., the same to the same.

The French ambassador showed himself less adept than Madame in his efforts to cultivate Arlington's affection for the French league. No sooner was the treaty signed than he confided to the Secretary that he saw with joy that nothing could longer restrain the King of France from demonstrating his recognition of Arlington's part in promoting the alliance, and that besides the present which was destined for him as oneof the signers of the treaty, the King wished to distinguish him from the others by a particular mark of his esteem. And thereupon Colbert glided over the subject of a pension with winged words. But the Secretary replied soberly that, although he thanked the King of France for the honor intended him, and would apply for his protection if any reverse of fortune should oblige him to withdraw from England, he had never received presents from any prince except his own master, and begged in all humility that his Majesty would not think of conferring gifts either upon himself or upon the other commissioners who had signed the treaty,88 since without the express order of Charles II they could not accept them.88 Colbert was at first inclined to suspect the genuineness of this refusal, but when, in August, 1670, he proposed a pension of 10,000 crowns a year, the Secretary again declined in almost the same words." Arlington was too cautious to touch the money of France, nor is it too much to say that a sense of honorlseventeenth-century honor that dictated discriminations not always appreciable to a later agel entered into this decision. It did not prevent him later from accepting, with his master's consent, presents of considerable intrinsic value which convention allowed to the plenipotentiaries who had signed treaties.41 Andif Arlington declined pensions for himself he did not despise them as motive power for others, and did not hesitate to propose a pension for the Countess of Shrewsbury, Buckingham's mistress, as a method of making the Duke more pliable to the wishes of Louis XIV.42

88 I believe it is to this that Montagu referred when he wrote to Arlington on June 21, N. S., congratulating him on " the honour Madame tells me the King intends you ". (Hist. MSS., Comm., *MSS. of the Duke of Buccleuch, I,* 474.) On her death-bed Madame spoke of Arlington to Montagu, saying: "... tell the King my Brother I hope he will for my sake, do for him what he promised, Car c'est un home qui l'ayme, et qui le sert bien." *(Arlington's Letters,* I, 444, July 15, 1670, Montagu to Arlington.)

" Clarke, *James II,* I, 451.

Ibid.

28 The other commissioners were: Lord Arundel of Wardour, Sir Thomas Clifford, and Richard Sellings.

" Arch. Aff. fetr., Angleterre, 97, f. 267, June 10, 1670, N. S., Colbert to Louis XIV.

i *Ibid.,* 98, f. 112, Aug. 25, 1670, N. S., the same to the same.

a Presents for all the commissioners who had signed the Treaty of Dover reached Colbert in December. *(Ibid.,* 100, f. 15, Jan. 1, 1671, N. S., the same to Lionne.) Although they were not in the form of money, Arlington declined to accept his, and was still declining at the end of October, 1671. *(Ibid.,* 101, f. 106, Nov. 9, 1671, N. S., the same to Louis XIV.) It seems to have been commuted, finally, to a pearl necklace for LadyArlington, which was at last accepted. *(Ibid.,* 103, f. 185, April 11, 1672, N. S., the same to the same.) After the embassy of Buckingham and Arlington to the French camp in the summer of 1672, each of the ambassadors received from Louis XIV a jeweled snuff-box, and Arlington in addition a diamond ring. (Mignet, *Negociations,* IV, 49.)

Madame went back to France and to the sudden, tragic death that overtook her a fortnight after her return. The English Court returned to London, and Arlington fell to work again on the difficult task of destroying the Triple Alliance while he pretended to build it up. He had to restrain the eagerness of Temple who, seeing the preparations for war begun in France, worked to cement the union between the English and the Dutch in every way possible. He had to combat the suspicions of Van Beuningen, the Dutch ambassadorl" a prying, talking, pressing man ", the Secretary describes him"lwhom De Witt had sent over to persuade Charles to a closer league with the United Provinces.44 He must endure the keener scrutiny of the Prince of Orange who visited England in October and came every day with little ceremony toGoring House." He had to deny, with such feeble arguments as the circumstances permitted, the admission of the Emperor to the Triple Alliance, for which Lisola was importuning him by letter.48 He had also to elude the envoy of the Duke of Lorraine, whose duchy was seized by Louis XIV in August, and who thereupon implored the protection of the Alliance." In the Committee of Foreign Affairs the Lord Keeper Bridg- man, Secretary Trevor, and the Duke of Ormonde were still faithful to the old policy; to override them three new members were added to the Committee: the Duke of Lauderdale, who was content to accept anyprogram which found favor in his master's eyes; and Clifford and Ashley, Commissioners of the Treasury, who were eager for another war with the Dutch. They did much to assist the Secretary in his task of keeping the Triple Alliance in a state of harmless inactivity while the two kings completed their preparations for the war.

4JArch. Aff. $tr., Angleterre, 98, f. 119, Aug. 28, 1670, N. S., Colbert to Lionne.

48 Foreign Entry Book, 176, April 4, 1669.

44 The innocent assurances of Bridgman and Trevor that England would abide by the Alliance to some extent blinded Van Beuningen to the real situation in England, but nevertheless the conduct of Arlington aroused his suspicions: " I cannot help remarking ", he wrote to De Witt, " that Arlington, who until now had appeared to me to remain steadfast in his favourable disposition, is seeking for quibbles, as if he were desirous to transfer his affections." (Lefevre-Pontalis, *John de Witt,* II, 52.)

Colbert wrote afterwards of ' la grande familiarite avec laquelle le Prince d'Orange vit chez luy, y mangeant tous les jours ". (Arch. Aff. E"tr., Angleterre, 1oo, f. 74, Feb. 18, 1671, N. S., Colbert to Louis XIV.)

Lisola, who was now Leopold's agent at the Hague, had first proposed the admission of the Emperor to the Triple Alliance in 1669. (State Papers, Holland, 185, f. 91, Oct. 25, 1669, N. S., Lisola to Arlington.) Having received no reply, he wrote again in March, 167o, saying that Louis XIV was preparing for another war, this time against the Dutch, and that the inclusion of the Emperor in the Triple Alliance must be hastened. He inclosed the project of a treaty which he said was approved by De Witt and by the Swedish ambassador at the Hague, and asked that Arlington send a power to Temple to sign it. *(Ibid.,* 186, f. 113, March 14, 167o, N. S., the same to the same.) The Committee of Foreign Affairs discussed the matter on April 1o, and the French party dominating, resolved that orders should be sent to Temple not to enter into any negotiation for any prince's admission to the Alliance. (Foreign Entry Book, 176, April 1o, 167o.) During the latter half of 167o, Lisola bombarded Arlington with arguments and projects. (State Papers, Holland, 186, *passim.)* On November 18, Arlington finally replied that there was nothing to prevent his Imperial Majesty from guaranteeing the Treaty of Aix-la-Chapelle whenever he cared to do so, but he said nothing about a defensive league, which was the working basis of the Triple Alliance. *(Ibid.,* 186, f. 1o1, Nov. 18, 167o. Copy.) It is not likely that Lisola needed further enlightenment as to what was to be expected from England.

7 State Papers, France, 13o, ff. 194, 196, Nov. 6, 167o, N. S., Charles of Lorraine to Charles II and to Arlington. Temple had already assured the Secretary that the Dutch were willing to act jointly with their allies in favor of the exiled Duke. (Temple, *Works,* II, 162, Sept. 2, 167o, N. S., Temple to Arlington.)

In September Temple was called home on the pretense of urgent need of his advice in the matter of Lorraine. His first interview with Arlington confirmed all the fears that the equivocal conduct of the government had awakened in him: " When I came to town, I went immediately to my Lord Arlington, according to custom. And whereas upon my several journeys over in the late conjunctures, he had ever quitted all company to receive me, and did it always with open arms, and in the kindest manner that could be, he made me this last time stay an hour and half in an outward room before he came to me, while he was in private with my Lord Ashley. He received me with a coldness that I confess surprised me; and after a quarter of an hour's talk of my journey and his friends at the Hague, instead of telling me the occasion of my being sent for over, or anything else material, he called in Tata48 that was in the next room, and after that my Lord Crofts, who came upon a common visit; and in that company the rest of mine passed, till I found he had nothing more to say to me, and so went away." " Poor Temple! The personal slight made the treachery to the Alliance look even blacker. He could never like the Secretary of State again.

48 This was Arlington's pet name for his little daughter, Isabella. 'Temple, *Works,* II, 173-175, Nov. 22, 167o, N. S., to Sir John Temple.

Arlington was at this time unostentatiously guiding another tortuous negotiation with France. Only he and Clifford, of the English ministers, were aware of the existence of the Treaty of Dover, and, because of its frankness on the subject of the Grand Design, it could not well be communicated to Protestants like Buckingham and Ashley. To enable the King to avow the league, and to flatter Buckingham into believing that his was the leading role in European politics, he was allowed the glory of negotiating a treaty with France. It was begun by him alone when he went to Paris in August, 1670, to acknowledge on the part of Charles II the condolence of the French King upon the death of Madame. After his return Charles appointed four other commissioners to assist him in the sham negotiation with Colbert: Ashley, Arlington, Lauder- dale, and Clifford. Buckingham fancied that he was accomplishing the league in spite of the most strenuous opposition from Arlington but behind the scenes the Secretary, with the assistance of the ambassador and Clifford, shaped the new treaty to coincide with the earlier one. Only, the Grand Design was omitted, and the subsidy for that purpose was added to the amount destined for the war.TM

With convincing gravity the Secretary played his part in the farce, dragging out the negotiation on one pretext or another until Buckingham suspected him of having received a bribe from the Dutch,51 while Lauder- dale in exasperation swore that the treaty should be finished in spite of Arlington, since neither Buckingham, Ashley, nor himself had married a Dutchwoman, and therefore they were free to wish the prosperity of the King of France.52 It required much time and much manipulation to bring the articles into agreement with the Treaty of Dover, but it was done at last, and on December *21,* Buckingham triumphantly signed the new treaty, not dreaming that its every provision had been dictated by the man he seemed to have outwitted.55The Cabal Ministry.

50 The exact nature of the sham treaty was decided before Buckingham's departure for France, by Colbert, Arlington, and Clifford. (Arch. Aff. Etr., Angleterre, 98, ff. 84-86, July 28, 167o, N. S., Colbert to Louis XIV.)

M Dalrymple, *Memoirs,* Appendix, pp. 69-76.

a Arch. Aft. $tr., Angleterre, 98, ff. 197-199, Oct. *23,* 167o, N. S., Colbert to Louis XIV.

58 The text of this sham treaty is printed in Mignet, *Negotiations,* HI, 256-267. England's share of the expected conquests was slightly increased from what the Treaty of Dover stipulated. On the same day that the sham treaty was signed, Charles signed a declaration confirming the provisions of the earlier treaty in regard to the Grand Design, and promising to employ the subsidies as arranged in that agreement. This declaration was countersigned by Arlington. The other commissioners with the exception, perhaps, of Clifford, knew nothing of it. *(Ibid.)*

While the commissioners were quarreling over the sham treaty, Parliament was engaged in providing supply for the maintenance of the Triple Alliance.1 When the Houses adjourned for the Christmas holidays, the Court could congratulate itself on a session of rare amiability. Unfortunately in this interval several incidents occurred which irritated the Commons on the dear point of their privileges.2 Also, it began to be noticed that although France was arming for some large undertaking, that fact seemed to be causing no uneasiness to the English ministers.2 The rumor of atreaty with France was so circumstantially and persistently circulated, that the Duke of York and Arlington, knowing that Buckingham was given to " blabbing " as Burnet says, accused him of revealing the secret. " The bitterness is so great among those who share the secret", wrote Colbert, " that is to say, between the Duke of Buckingham and his friends, and my Lord Arlington and his, that they will have difficulty in preserving unity sufficient to carry through what they have resolved."8 Lauderdale and Ashley could always be found in agreement with Buckingham, while the Duke of York and Clifford supported Arlington. So even a division naturally produced many a deadlock in the Committee of Foreign Affairs and complicated the interplay of faction in Parliament. Neither of the ministers was-sorry to see his rival an object of suspicion to the Commons, but each was eager to establish his own innocence. Buckingham, careful of his popularity in the House, made haste to explain everywhere his aversion to a French alliance, declaring that if such perfidy had been, he was not a party to it, and that the good faith and well-being of England demanded that she abide by the Triple Alliance.' He went so far as to say that such an accusation might more properly be preferred against the Secretary of State.7 Arlington was not to be outdone in protestations and, in order to make them with better grace, introduced in the Committee of Foreign Affairs a project for the inclusion of the Emperor in the TripleAlliance on the same basis with the original allies." Colbert was horrified beyond measure at such backsliding in the man on whom he most relied, and even the rejection of the project by the Committee, and Arlington's excuse that he had presented it purely for the sake of diverting suspicion from himself, hardly restored the ambassador's peace of mind. He proposed to his master that a pension, augmented now to four thousand pounds a year, be once more offered to Arlington. " Whether it be accepted or not", said Colbert sagely, " it will have a good effect."10

1 Bridgman, in his opening speech, had with entire sincerity exalted the noble results of the Triple Alliance, called attention to the French preparations, and asked for money that England might fulfil her responsibilities to the league as the Dutch were making ready to do. So flagrant was the contradiction in this speech to the actual design of the government, that Arlington vainly tried to prevent its being printed. (Marvell, *Works,* II, 335, Nov. 1, 167o, Marvell to the mayor and aldermen of Kingston upon Hull.) Parliament, misled by the innocent Bridgman, promptly voted to supply the King proportionally to his occasions. (Cob- bett, *Parliamentary History,* IV, col. 456-459.)

2 Sir John Coventry, a member who had dared a contemptuous reference to the royal diversions, had been attacked on the street one night, and his nose had been slit. Also, an obvious attempt to manage a by-election in favor of the Court candidate, had been discovered. *(Ibid.,* col. 46o.)

8 Colbert mentions the prevalence of this suspicion (Arch. Aff. Etr., Angleterre, 1oo, f. 147, April 13, 1671, N. S.), and it figures in some doggerel lines by Marvell written about this time under the title, " Farther Instructions to a Painter. 167o."

" Change once again, and let the next afford
The figure of a motley council-board
At Arlington's, and round about it sat
Our mighty masters in a warm debate.
Full bowls of lusty wine make them repeat,
To make them t'other council-board forget
That while the King of France with powerful arms,
Gives all his fearful neighbours strange alarms,
We in our glorious bacchanals dispose
The humbled fate of a plebean nose; "

(Marvell, *Works,* I, 323.)

4 Burnet, *Own Time,* I, 478; Arch. Aff. far., Angleterre, 1o0, f. 55, Feb. 2, 1671, N. S., Colbert to Louis XIV.

8 *Ibid.,* 100, f. 77, Feb. 18, 1671, N. S., the same to the same.

' *Ibid.,* 100, f. 131, April 2, 1671, N. S., the same to the same.

7 *Ibid.,* 1o0, f. 77, Feb. 18, 1671, N. S., the same to the same.

An agitation begun in the House for the enforcement of the laws against popish recusants, afforded the Secretary a welcome pretext to adjourn indefinitely thefulfilment of the Grand Design. For some time he had been ostensibly at work on instructions for the priest who was to arrange at Rome the reception of England into the bosom of the Church. These instructions he apparently constructed and demolished like the web of Penelope while he observed the temper of the House and the subsidence of such fervor as Charles may once have thought that he felt in the cause of Catholicism." When Colbert asked to know the date on which the King proposed to announce his conversion, Arlington replied Scripturally that " the heart of the King must be converted before his mouth shall declare it ", though he did not omit in this same interview to demand the second payment due for the Grand Design.12 He was perfectly aware that Louis would not forego the practical advantages of the league out of religious disappointment.

The project for the Emperor's inclusion in the Triple Alliance was drawn up by Williamson according to orders given orally by Arlington and jotted down by the under-secretary on a paper which he indorsed: " The Emperor to be received into the Warranty. 167o/1. My Lord Arlington's first thoughts in order to the Instrument." (State Papers, Archives, 1oo, f. 635.) The following is Williamson's note as to the clause of mutual defense: " 3. and give him that V. Article of the Triple allyance for a Warranty towards one another." The instrument which Williamson prepared in consequence of these orders, and which Colbert saw, is also in the Record Office. *(Ibid.,* ff. 649-657.)

Arch. Aff. Etr., Angleterre, 1oo, ff. 45-47, Jan. 25, 1671, N. S., Colbert to Louis XIV; *ibid.,* 1oo, ff. 52-55, Feb. 2, 1671, N. S., the same to the same. To satisfy Colbert, Charles called a meeting of the Committee of Foreign Affairs, the project was read, and the objectionable clause condemned. (Foreign Entry Book, 176, Jan. 15, 167o/1.) A new draft was made omitting the provision for mutual defense, and this was sent to Lisola with a letter from Arlington, basing the omission on the impossibility of mutual assistance between the Emperor and Charles II, their estates being so remote one from the other. (The revised draft is in the Record Office, State Papers, Foreign, Archives, 1oo, f. 671.) Lisola was at this time acting in concert with De Witt rather than in harmony with orders from Vienna. In this year the Emperor was attracted into negotiations with France, and on Nov. 1, 1671, N. S., he signed a treaty, by which he promised to remain neutral in any war between France and the United Provinces. (Mignet, *Negotiations,* III, 548-552.)

10 Arch. Aff. Etr., Angleterre, 1oo, ff. 74-76, Feb. 18, 1671, N. S., Colbert to Louis XIV.

Delays in the completion of the money bills prolonged the session well into the spring of 1671. Seeing the anti-French sentiment of the Lower House steadily increasing, Buckingham and Ashley showed a disposition to fall in with it, and even endeavored to reduce the duties provided by one of the bills of supply. This led to a quarrel between the two Houses over the right of the Lords to amend money bills. As Charles could not advance his plans for a breach with the Dutch while Parliament was in session, he was finally obliged to prorogue on April *22,* although two of the bills ofsupply were yet to pass. The loss of these grants was severely felt by the needy King, and he was very angry at the meddling of Buckingham and Ashley. The Secretary of State did not allow him to forget his just resentment."

11 See Colbert's letters on this subject: Arch. Aff. $tr., Angleterre, 98, f. 2oo, Oct. 23, 167o, N. S., Colbert to Lionne; *ibid.,* 98, f. 222, Nov. 6,

167o, N. S., the same to the same; *ibid.,* 1oo, f. 39, Jan. 19, 1671, N. S., the same to the same. The priest to whom Charles seemed resolved to entrust this matter was the rector of the English college at St. Omer or

I)uu;ii, and may have been Charles's illegitimate son, James de IJ Cloche.

12 *Ibid.,* 1oo, ff. 81-84, Feb. 23, 1671, N. S., the same to the same.

The vanishing of Parliament left Buckingham in eclipse. To strengthen himself in the Committee of Foreign Affairs he planned to have Bridgman removed and the seals given to his friend the Earl of Anglesey. " He enjoined me secrecy", wrote Anglesey in his diary, " for the Lord Arlington, if it were known, would tell it as news to the King to disappoint it."" But it needed no effort of Arlington's to defeat this plan, for Bridgman still represented to the public eye the health of the Triple Alliance, and the moment for his removal had not come.

In the summer of 1671 Buckingham had the pleasure of vanquishing his rival in a contest for the chancellorship of the University of Cambridge,15 but a grave political discomfiture which followed hard upon this victory left him small satisfaction in it. The Duke had set his heart on the command of the four thousand English troops which, by the treaty he had signed, were to be furnished to the land forces of Louis XIV. Now he learned that by the instances of Arlington andMontagu the French King had been persuaded to forego the English contingent for the first year's campaign. Buckingham was convinced that the Secretary's sole intention in so acting was to preclude him from acquiring military fame. He burst out in angry expostulations to the King, but Charles reminded him coldly of the " millions " *he* had lost in the last session of Parliament through the Duke's demagogism, which made it impossible for him to support the expense of maintaining the troops; then, growing angry at the Duke's insolence, he added that when the latter's interest conflicted with the public welfare, he considered him no more than his dog. Finally, he said that he wanted all who had signed the treaty with France to act in harmony, and that if they did not he should know whence the trouble proceeded, and should banish the guilty parties from his confidence, admitting others who better deserved it. This warning he took occasion to repeat to Ashley and Lauderdale, whose mortification was not displeasing to York, Arlington, and Clifford." The Secretary had now leisure to perfect a very delicate bit of domestic diplomacy in which he was deeply interested, the installation of Louise de la Kerouaile in his master's affections. " Madame Carwell ", as the English managed her difficult name, had been admired by Charles II when she came to Dover as one of the Duchess of Orleans's maids of honor. After the death of her mistress, she was preferred to a similar post in the household of the Queen of England, " and then ", as Burnet says, " lord Arlington took care of her "." All the flattery he had once paid to the Countessof Castlemaine, all the good advice which Mistress Stewart had wisely flouted, he now offered to the French beauty who seemed to have the susceptible heart of the King in her keeping. He was most anxious to promote her fortunes in counterpoise to the influence of Buckingham's protegee, Nell Gwyn, and discussed the matter quite frankly with the French ambassador. " My Lord Arlington told me recently ", reported Colbert, " that he was very glad to see the King his master attached to her, for although his Majesty is not disposed to communicate his affairs to women, nevertheless as they can on occasion injure those whom they hate, and in that way ruin many affairs, it was much better for all good servants of the King that he was attracted to her, whose humor is not mischievous, and who is a lady, rather than to comediennes and the like, on whom no honest man could rely, by whose means the Duke of Buckingham was always trying to entice the King, in order to draw him away from all his Court and monopolize him . . . That the young lady must be counseled to manage well the good graces of the King, not to speak to him of affairs, and not to show any aversion to those who are near him, and, in short, to let him find only pleasure and joy in her company." He proceeded with the utmost candor to recommend to the young lady through Colbert the conduct which he and Lady Arlington thought advisable for her."

u The circumstances which occasioned this prorogation are far from certain. Buckingham told Colbert that it was resolved by the persuasion of Arlington, without his [Buckingham's] knowledge, and contrary to the King's assurance to him and to Ashley the day before. *(Ibid., 1o0, f.* 214, July 14, 1671, N. S., the same to Louis XIV.) Several months later Charles reminded Buckingham of the " millions he had been the cause of his losing in the last session of Parliament". (Dalrymple, *Memoirs,* Appendix, p. 87.) See also Christie's *Life of Shaftesbury,* II, 27, and Cnbbett's *Parliamentary History,* IV, col. 495-496.

" Hist. MSS. Comm., *13th Report,* part VI, 266, MSS. of Lieut.-Gen. Lyttleton-Annesley.

" Gardner, *George Viltiers,* 247-249.

a Dalrymple, *Memoirs,* Appendix, p. 88, Nov. 9, 1671, N. S., Colbert to Louis XIV. (Translated.) 17 Burnet, *Own Time, I,* 599.

In October, the French ambassador and his wife, accompanied by Mademoiselle de la Keroualle, came to visit Lord and Lady Arlington at Euston Hall in

"Arch. Aff. $tr., Angleterre, 1o1, ff. 66-68, Oct. 8, 1671, N. S., Colbert to Pomponne. This passage is quoted in part in Forneron's *Louise de Keroualle,* 48.

Suffolk, while the Court was at Newmarket only a few miles away. Charles divided his time between Euston and Newmarket, drawing with him always a throng of courtiers whom Arlington received and entertained with a splendor which the King himself had never equaled. " Came all the great men from Newmarket, and other parts both of Suffolk and Norfolk, to make their court, the whole house filled from one end to the other with lords, ladies, and gallants; there was such a furnished table, as I had seldom seen, nor anything more splendid and free, so that for fifteen days there were entertained at least 200 people, and half as many horses, besides servants and guards, at infinite expense."1' The house-party lasted three weeks, and in that time Louise de la Keroualle confirmed her ascendancy over the King, as Arlington had meant that she should, but, in a larger sense, the scheme failed after all, for she never felt either gratitude or liking for the Secretary, and her coldness became more dangerous to him than the shrewishness of the Countess of Castle- maine or the mockery of Nell Gwyn.

At the wish of Louis XIV, the outbreak of hostilities against the Dutch had been timed for the spring of 1672, and so with deliberation during the winter of 1671-1672 Arlington pursued the causes of quarrel that came to hand, for, as he explained to the Committee of Foreign Affairs, " our businesse is to breake with them, and yet to lay the breach at their doore "." A third treaty with France, a replica of Buckingham's, was signed in February by the same commissioners, and was to be made public when war should be declared, to convince the world that no previous agreement was in existence." It was not intended to open hostilities before April, but an accident initiated the war abruptly in March.

10 Evelyn, *Diary,* Oct. 16, 1671.

20 Foreign Entry Book, 177, March 8, 1671/2.

The Committee had discussed on March u the advisability of hastening the declaration of war, in order to make prize of home-faring Dutch vessels. Lauder- dale, with his habitual indifference to the practices of civilization, advised the King to " declare by action rather then words" until the fleet should be ready. But, it was objected, the Dutch ambassadors would be certain to demand by what order their ships were seized. What could be said to them if war had not been formally declared? Lauderdale saw no need of any explanation. " Nothing is yet caught", he remarked cannily. " Surprize 5 or 6 dayes and you will see whether the Prizes be worth it or not." Arlington thought notice of embargo or detention, at least, should be given the ambassadors, and the King and Ashley inclined rather uncertainly to this point of view, but Lauderdale, with the concurrence of the Duke of York and Prince Rupert, overruled them." In pursuance of this policy, an English squadron under Sir Robert Holmes fell upon the Dutch Smyrna fleet as it passed through the Channel on its way home, but the merchantmen defended themselves so bravely that only two of their vessels were made prize. The shame and the failure of this engagement forced the Committee to publish a Declaration of War on March 17."

n Mignet, *Negociations,* III, 700-701.

12 Foreign Entry Book, 177, March 11, 1671/2.

28 " Il ne fut pris qu'un ou deux vaisseaux mediocrement riches, et cette infraction, sans nulle denonciation precedente, fut assez g$neralement improuvee." (Mavidal, *Memoires du Marquis de Pomponne,* 485.)

It is somewhat more difficult to determine Arlington's share of the responsibility for two other unpopular war measures. On January 1, all payments from the Exchequer, due to various bankers who had advanced money to the government, were stopped for one year, and the funds thus seized, amounting to more than a million pounds, were used for the fleet. The resulting distress and excitement though severe were of brief duration, but the shock to the government's credit made itself felt through the remainder of this reign. The step had been proposed and urged by Clifford and Ashley; Arlington, though not bold enough to originate the plan, did not condemn it, and when he was questioned in the House of Commons long afterwards, would only say that the ministers were united in that advice."

The other war measure was the suspending of all penal laws in regard to religion. This was proposed in the Committee of Foreign Affairs as a means of keeping " fanatics " quiet while the government was occupied with the war, but to York and Cliffordlpossibly to the King and Arlington, as welllit may have been looked upon as a step in the direction of Rome. Clifford spoke confidently of the repeal of the penal laws when Parliament should meet. He was the most enthusiastic, but Lauderdale, Ashley, and Buckingham seconded him warmly, and as if there could be no doubt of the prerogative in ecclesiastical matters. The King hung back a little, and expressed the fear that

conventicles would increase if the toleration were not

M See p. 233 of this biography. For the responsibility of Ashley and Clifford, see Evelyn's *Diary,* March 12, 1671/2; Temple's *Works,* II, 184; Clarke's *James II, I,* 488.

limited: they should, he said, be tolerated and regulated " at one chopp ", but Clifford exclaimed against the delay that this complication would cause. The Secretary of State, in so far as we may judge from the minutes of the meeting, listened to the discussion and said not a word himself.28 Whether he disliked the plan because it seemed a reversion to the Grand Design, or whether the fate of his Declaration of 1662 was in his mind, he held his peace. Clifford triumphed, and the Declaration of Indulgence was published on March 15, two days before the Declaration of War. The dissenting sects hastened to avail themselves of it, but among orthodox Anglicans it seemed but a prelude to popery, and received gloomy significance from the fact that the Duke of York was now persistently absenting himself from communion. Their protests could avail nothing, however, before the next meeting of Parliament.

The stop on the Exchequer, the Declaration of Indulgence, the abandonment in effect, if not in theory, of the Triple Alliance, and the unwelcome league with France, brought the personnel of the ministry into unenviable prominence. The five men in whose hands the power now lay were popularly known as " the Cabal", from the pleasing chance that their initials could be so arranged as to spell that word: Clifford,

Arlington, Buckingham, Ashley, and Lauderdale. The Lord Keeper, invalided by the gout, and aware of his exclusion from the King's confidence, ceased to attend the meetings of the all-powerful Committee of For-

M Williamson's notes of the debates in the Committee upon this subject are unusually full. As he was devoted to Arlington's interests at this time, I believe he would have recorded any remarks by the Secretary, had such been made. (Foreign Entry Book, 177, March 6 and 9, 1671/2.)

eign Affairs. Secretary Trevor died in May, and a successor was not immediately appointed. Ormonde was made a baron, Lord Clifford of Chudleigh; Ashley tribution of honors in April pointed out unmistakably the men who now served the King's wishes. Clifford was made a Baron, Lord Clifford of Chudleigh; Ashley became Earl of Shaftesbury; Lauderdale ascended to the rank of duke in the peerage of Scotland. Buckingham could not be further exalted as he already enjoyed the highest title it was possible for his master to bestow. Arlington's rewards were most extensive of all: he was created Viscount Thetford and Earl of Arlington," and in June he realized a long-cherished ambition in being installed Knight of the Garter.27 August saw the marriage of his five-year-old daughter to the King's son, Henry Fitzroy, a boy of nine, the best-loved of the Countess of Castlemaine's children.TM Buckingham had exerted himself to break off the match, and had promised instead the hand of an heiress, the Earl of Northumberland's daughter, for young Harry. But Charles, thinking perhaps of his promiseto the sister he had loved, replied briefly that it was too late to change the arrangement already made.20

" Cokayne, *Complete Peerage,* Arlington title.

7 " Concerning my Self, I am sure you rejoice in all my good Fortune; I must not omit to tell you that His Majesty, the last Week, was pleased to Honour me with a blew Ribbon." *(Arlington's Letters,* II, 375, June 17, 1672, to Sir William Godolphin.)

M Colbert refers to him thus. (Christie, *Life of Shaftesbury,* II, Appendix, xiii.) From a letter of the Earl of Sunderland, then ambassador to Spain, to Arlington, it seems probable that the Secretary had once thought of marrying his daughter to Sunderland's son and heir: As for Tata ", wrote the ambassador, " she was alwayes too much in jest to be accused of Infidelity or Inconstancy, but if that matter had beene as serious as it was the Contrary, I hope your Lordship does not thinke me so voide of sence as not to know the difference betweene her gallants nor so little your servant as knowing it not to consent to her choice. But I ever said she was Coquette and that you will give me leave to doe a little longer." (State Papers, France, 134, f. 117, July 2, 1672.)

To a worldly courtier like the Secretary of State such a marriage was all that he had ever hoped for his daughter. He adored the vanities of life and his pride increased as he grew older. " That Lord", Ormonde once remarked, " expects to be treated as if he had been born with a blue ribbon, and forgets Harry Bennet, that was but a very little gentleman." " The little Isabella was a " pretty babe " as even Buckingham admitted," and Arlington loved her with a tender devotion which was the wonder and the jest of the Court.

" For tho' to us he's stately like a king
He'll joke and droll with her like anything." "

Yet even for her he was content with dross and show. Sir John Evelyn, who could see the boy's unpromising heritage as Arlington, infatuated by his nearness to royalty, could not, looked on sorrowfully at the ceremony that bound the children to each other: " I was at the marriage of Lord Arlington's only daughter (a sweet child if ever there was any) to the Duke of Grafton, the King's natural son by the Duchess of Cleveland; the Archbishop of Canterbury officiating, the King and all the grandees being present. I had a favour given me by my Lady, but took no great joy at the thing for many reasons." TM

w Macpherson, *Original Papers,* I, 67.
80 Carte, *Life of Ormonde,* bk. VIII, par. 193.
81 Buckingham, *Works,* II, 163.
" *Ibid.*

"*Diary,* Aug. 1, 1672. Henry Fitzroy was Earl of Euston at this time and did not become Duke of Grafton until 1675.

From an English point of view the campaign of 1672 was far from satisfactory in its results. To be sure, Louis XIV had conquered the better part of three provinces rapidly and easily, and at sea the allies had defeated the Dutch in the battle of Southwold Bay, but these successes were profitable to France alone; none of that part of the United Provinces allotted to England had been conquered, and it began to be doubted whether Louis XIV wished it to be conquered. Spain, seeing the trend of events more clearly now than in 1667, was lending her forces in Flanders to garrison Dutch towns, and this deeply alarmed the Cabal, who knew that if the French alliance drew them into a breach with Spain, the war would become too unpopular to continue and they themselves would be " travelers to Montpelier ", as Shaftesbury once said in allusion to the refuge of Clarendon."

Most serious of all, the Exchequer was empty, and the ministers did not know where to look for money, it being inexpedient to call upon Parliament until the success of the war had been clearly demonstrated. Aldington in desperation turned over the Grand Design, hoping to extract some pecuniary profit from its revival. By his advice Charles communicated his intention to bring England back to Catholicism to the Queen of Spain, but, bigot as she was, her reply afforded no encouragement to expect subsidies." Then Arlington, with much tactful circumlocution, approached Colbert: he suggested that an " able doctor of theology thoroughly acquainted with ecclesiastical history, the Councils and the Fathers " be sent over

" Christie, *Life of Shaftesbury,* II, 47.

"Arch. Aff. Etr., Angletcrre, 1o3, f. 138, March 14, 1672, N. S., Colbert to Louis XIV.

from France to satisfy the King's thirst for information on such matters, and to advise him about the conversion of his subjects." Charles assured the ambassador that in a few days he would send a priest to Rome to take counsel with the Pope touching the spiritual welfare of England." The situation being relieved, by this preface, of all mercenary taint, the Secretary impressed upon Colbert that since it would not be prudent to call upon Parliament for help, the King must have money from the Holy See, or from the clergy of France." He did not add " or from the King of France ", but Colbert understood him perfectly, and, to avoid the embarrassment of a more explicit demand, suggested that Charles could obtain money by the sale of Tangier, which he had obtained from Portugal with the hand of Catharine of Braganza. But Arlington remembered too well the odium heaped upon Clarendon for the sale of Dunkirk, to welcome this proposal.80 Things were at this pass when, on June 10, two deputies arrived from the Dutch to discuss terms of peace, and at the same time the ministers heard that the King of France was already talking over conditions with

"Ibid., 103, f. 146, March 21, 1672, N. S., the same to the same. Louis complied by sending an Italian abbot, Balati *(ibid.,* 103, f. 186, April 11, 1672, N. S., the same to Lionne) who does not appear to have gained the confidence of the King, but we learn that " Abbot Balletti lived four years in the house with Lord Arlington, and lives now [1676] in the city." (Hist. MSS. Comm., *nth Report,* part VII, p. 17, MSS. of the Duke of Leeds.) Evidently Arlington felt responsible for him, but it is odd that if the abbot actually lived in his house, the fact was not known and used when the Secretary's enemies in the House of Commons were seeking material of that very sort to justify an impeachment. His intimacy with Father Patrick, the Queen's almoner, was severely noticed, but no one knew of Balati. (Grey, *Debates,* Jan. 16-20, 1673/4.)

"Arch. Aff. Etr., Angleterre, 103, f. 213, May 9, 1672, N. S., Colbert to Louis XIV.

K Christie, *Life of Shoftesbury,* II, Appendix II, pp. xii-xx, June 7, 1672, N. S., the same to the same. (Translated.)

Ibid,

other deputies whom the States General had sent to his camp." The Cabal was startled at the thought that even then Louis might be concluding a peace which would leave England in the lurch. Buckingham, who had cooled towards the French Alliance as his rival had warmed, advised treating with the deputies, or, as he said, " aske them what they will doe for us ". But the King silenced him sharply: " No, by no means! Aske no such question. Onely aske what have they to say to us." Arlington, who was never rash either to trust or to distrust, took a middle ground: it would do no harm to keep the deputies in England until it was known whether the King of France was thinking of peace." Accordingly, Viscount Halifax was hastened away to the French camp to hold Louis to his treaty, and the Dutch deputies were kept in strict seclusion at Hampton Court to await his return." But, it happened,only a few days after the departure of Halifax, Colbert received a despatch from his master in which it was proposed that the King of England send some one to the French camp empowered to treat for peace. Buckingham, who had found no chance to distinguish himself in the war and now longed to win credit by making the peace, at once urged and obtained his own appointment as plenipotentiary for this mission. His annoyance was great when he learned that Arlington, fearing to hazard this important negotiation in the Duke's hands and jealously guarding his own supremacy in foreign affairs, had engaged the King to join him with Buckingham, though his departure left England without a Secretary of State."

40 Sidney Godolphin, Charles's agent in the French camp, reported the arrival of the Dutch deputies sent to Louis XIV, and expressed some doubt of the good faith of France. (State Papers, France, 134, f. 75, June 23, 1672, N. S., Sidney Godolphin to Arlington; *ibid.,* 134, f. 94, June 26, 1672, N. S., the same to the same.)

41 Foreign Entry Book, 177, June 13 and 16, 1672.

41 Not so strict, however, but that Buckingham managed to communicate with them. He tried to extract from them proposals for peace, and a paper came mysteriously into being setting forth certain conditions as the basis of a treaty. There is a copy of it in Williamson's hand, undated, bearing the indorsement: " My Lord Duke of Buckingham's paper (as it is called) i. e. which was pretended to be sent from the States' Deputyes at London to his Grace by Mr. Howard." (State Papers, Archives, 101, f. 27.) The paper was disavowed by both the Duke and the Dutch deputies, and Buckingham's agent, William Howard, afterwards Lord Howard of Escrick. admitted that it had been drawn up by himself with the connivance of Kingscot, the secretary of the deputies. But Howard's confession intimates that the substance of the proposals came from Buckingham, which is highly probable as they allowed all the demands the English were prepared to make. (Arch. Aflt. iftr., Angleterre, 104, ff. 14-15, July 3, 1672, N. S., Colbert to Pomponne; *ibid.,* f. 25, Declaration de Mr. Howard . . . de tout ce qui s'est passe entre moy et les depute?, d'Hollande qui sont a Hamtoncourt.)

Many were the hints that Colbert hurried off to his master on the handling of the rival plenipotentiaries. Buckingham's disaffection for France, he advised, must be cured by a gift of money and a show of complete confidence from Louis XIV, who should not make too much of Arlington in his presence. " It will be difficult enough to content both of them, for although in appearance they are amicable, at bottom they hate each other bitterly, and the Duke of Buckingham will be very jealous of the caresses which the King may bestow on my Lord Arlington." But the latter would be sure to know the real intentions of Charles II in regard to a peace, and therefore should be interviewed separately. " The King of England, in sending my Lord Arlington to the King our master, sends, if one may be permitted to say it, an other self, for this minister knows his most secret intentions and designs and possesses his confidence, his esteem and his friendship in the highest

"Ibid., 103, f. 275, June 30, 1672, N. S., Colbert to Louis XIV. 44 *Ibid.,* f. 278, June 30, 1672, N. S., the same to Pomponne.

degree that a good subject could desire . . . You have in his person the law and the prophets of England; he has more honor and merit than any one else I have met in this country, and his credit is established on almost as solid foundations as the Crown itself."" From this eulogy it is plain that whatever doubts of the Secretary's sincerity in the French alliance Colbert may once have entertained, he was certain of his allegiance now.

The instructions that the ambassadors carried with them looked rather to the continuation of the war than to peace, for even in the present straits of the government, the ministers dared not consider terms that would not justify the war in public opinion; therefore their demands were as high as if they as well as Louis XIV had an army in the heart of the Provinces. Ali Dutch vessels must honor the English flag by striking their own and lowering their topsails. The States General must pay the King a yearly tribute for the right to fish off the coasts of England and Scotland, and must also pay a sum of money for the expenses of the war. Three or four towns, as Flushing, Sluys, and Brill or some other, must be ceded to England in full sovereignty. The Prince of Orange and his heirs male must be created Princes of Holland, or at least restored to the stadholderate. The East India trade must be regulated along the lines desired by England, and the rights claimed for English subjects in Surinam accorded. In a final conference before the ambassadors' departure, it was decided that if neither these terms northose stipulated in the treaty with France were obtainable, then the war must go on."

45 Foreign Entry Book, ff. 28o-282. The latter part of this letter to Pomponne is quoted in Christie's *Life of Shofteibury,* II, 85.

The plenipotentiaries landed at Maeslandsluys on June 23, and there learned that the Louvestein party, of which De Witt was the head, had fallen from power, and the Prince of Orange was now Stadholder of the United Provinces. The inhabitants of Maeslandsluys were celebrating this occasion, and the arrival of the ambassadors, who, they thought, were bringing peace, completed their joy. " The towne was all drunke ", wrote Arlington to Clifford, who was performing the duties of Secretary of State in his absence, " and saluted us with the complement: God blesse the King of England, God blesse the Prince of Orange and God confound the States! " "

The inflammable Buckingham was in transports of delight over this revolution and the enthusiasm with which his presence was hailed. Of Maeslandsluys he said: "If that place had been worth keeping, wee might certainely have maintained it", and of Brill: " I believe I might have taken that Towne my selfe." His imagination pictured the abased States General accepting thankfully any conditions of peace the King of England might impose, and he concluded his report to Clifford by saying: " If the Prince of Orange could be perswaded to send in the Dutch Fleete to the Duke,48 and deliver up some Townes into our hands, it would be in my opinion not only the best way for us, but alsothe surest for him to finde his accownt in this busi- nesse." "

48 This conference, at which the King, the Duke of York, Prince Rupert, Buckingham, and Arlington were present, took place on the Duke's flagship, the *Prince,* lying at the Nore. (Foreign Entry Book, 177, June 22, 1672.)

47 State Papers, Holland, 189, f. 2o6, June 25/July 5, 1672.

/. e., of York.

At the Hague the ambassadors learned that the States had put the negotiation of peace with both kings in the hands of the Prince of Orange, who was then with the Dutch army; therefore they remained but one night in the town, and the next morning proceeded to his camp on the Old Rhine.

The States of Holland, far from the despair that Buckingham fondly imagined, had grasped the truth that the ambassadors were not happy over the dazzling success of Louis XIV, nor desirous of seeing the whole of his demands granted, nor too secure in the conviction that he would not make peace when it suited his convenience, regardless of his ally. Therefore the terms which the Prince was empowered to offer were conciliatory but not submissive. He might allow a sum of money for the costs of the war, andlif the peace hung upon itla yearly payment for the right to fish; but the surrender of any towns or men-of-war was prohibited, and if England accepted these terms, she must at the same time agree to an offensive and defensive alliance with the States.80

William III, Prince of Orange, was a young man. The English ministers made the error of treating him with a fatherly patronage that aroused all his obstinacy. When the cession of towns was mentioned, though, as Arlington said, "to make our termes goe down the more easily, we called it Cautionary Townes, for the performance of what should be promised us ", William declared that the States would never do it, nor could he

State Papers, Holland, 189, f. 101, June 25/July 5, 1672. 80 Hop and Vivien, *Notulen,* pp. 180-181, July 5, 1672, N. S.

advise them so. In vain the two men to whom sovereignty seemed the sweetest, most desirable thing in life, dangled its temptations before the Prince, offering the province of Holland for his kingdom if he would procure satisfaction for England and reasonable terms for France. William replied that he liked better the honor of Stadholder which his people had given him, and that he could not prefer his personal advantage to his duty. " We found all the young men about him of a contrary mind ", wrote Arlington, " and whether we would or noe we heard them wishing there were a dozen of the States hanged, soe the Country had Peace and the Prince were Soveraigne of it."81 But William knew the role he must play better than the young hotbloods who surrounded him. He did all he could to strengthen the English distrust of France, succeeding so well with Buckingham that if it had not been for his phlegmatic colleague, a peace might have been struck up then and there. The Duke was sure that Charles would be content with reasonable terms, and that he would compel Louis XIV to similar reasonableness, or break the alliance. Buckingham even charged himself with the responsibility of obtaining a moderation of the French terms. Arlington, on the contrary, said frankly that the two kings could not be separated, and that it was useless to expect Louis to forego the advantages to which his conquests entitled him. The Prince's angry arguments could no more move Arlington from this stand than Arlington's dissertation upon sovereignty could move the Prince, and sothe ambassadors took their leave and drove to the camp of Louis XIV near Utrecht.52

81 State Papers, Holland, 189, ff. 226-234, June 28/July 8, 1672, the plenipotentiaries to Clifford.

The French King received them graciously and made them feel that their master's concerns were as dear to his heart as his own. Buckingham, who took color from his surroundings, chameleon-like, forgot all his assurances to the Prince of Orange and basked in the flattery of the Roi Soleil. *" Les Francois sont honestes gens ",* he said, " *il faut faire les affaires avec eux. "* Nevertheless, a faint, lingering suspicion on both sides, however concealed and denied, induced the French and English ministers to agree that the two kings should pledge themselves anew not to treat or conclude anything with the Dutch, without mutual participation and consent. This act, which was drawn up and signed in the French camp on July 6, is known as the Treaty of Heeswick.54 With the consent of Louis XIV, Arlington made one more effort to bribe the Prince of Orange with the offer of kingship. He drew up an act for William's signature in which it was promised that if he would procure the cession of the places required by England, the allied kings would make him sovereign of the United Provinces, with the exception of such parts as should be yielded to France by treaty.55 But the messengers who carried this proposition to the Prince came back with no more satisfaction than Buckingham and Arlington had had. William'sreply was to ask once more that the kings would inform him of the lowest conditions acceptable to them."8

82 Wicquefort, *Histoire des Provinces-Unies,* IV, 441-442.

58 Hop and Vivien, *Notulen,* 2o9, July 12, 1672, N. S.; Wicquefort, *Histoire des Provinces-Unies,* IV, 446-447.

M A copy of the treaty is in the Record Office. (State Papers, Holland, 19o, f. 46.)

MThe original draft of this contract in Arlington's hand *(ibid.,* 19o, f. 316) is undated.

Accordingly both French and English conditions were put on paper and sent to him with a copy of the Treaty of Heeswick to convince him that the allies could not be separated. Louis's territorial demands comprised roughly all of Flanders and Brabant belonging to the States General, with that part of Guelders lying on the left bank of the Rhine. To this must be added humiliating commercial concessions, freedom for the exercise of the Catholic religion throughout the United Provinces, and the yearly presentation of a medal whose inscription should admit that the Provinces enjoyed liberty by grace of the King of France.57

The English ambassadors differed widely over the extent of the English demands. Buckingham wanted to claim all Zeeland in the presumption still that whatever they asked, the States would have to yield. Halifax, who had arrived at the French camp somewhat later than the plenipotentiaries, and now occupied an anomalous position on the outskirts of their embassy, advised that the demands be moderated as much as possible for the sake of peace, of which, he was certain, England stood in need. Arlington's opinion lay midway between these extremes, adhering rather more closely to the instructions, which probably emanated from him in the first place.58 Eventually he compromised with Buckingham: the delivery of the islands of Walcheren, Cadsand, Goree, and Woorne, and the city of Sluys, was required, but as " cautionary " to the fulfilment of the treaty|a phrase of which Arlington was fond because it committed the government neither to the redelivery of the places nor to their retention. For the rest, the instructions were observed, the sum for the expenses of the war being placed at one million pounds, and that for the right to fish at ten thousand pounds a year.TM

M *Ibid.,* 19o, f. 46, July 7/17, Arlington to Clifford; State Papers, Archives, 1o1, f. 16, letter undated, from the Prince of Orange to Buckingham, Monmouth, and Arlington. (Copy.)

87 Mignet, *Negotiations,* IV, 33-34.

08 State Papers, Holland, 189, f. 315, " Some unperfect Memoires of passages in the Lords Ambassadors Journey to the French Camp, 1672 etc." These notes are by Williamson, who was secretary to the ambassadors. Part of the passage here referred to is quoted in Foxcroft's *Life of Halifax,* I, 92-93.

So little did the ambassadors expect the States to yield these terms without further fighting, that they did not wait for the Prince's answer, but made their adieux to the King of France and started on their homeward journey through Flanders, intending to interview the Spanish governor, the Count de Monterey, at Antwerp and frighten him, if possible, into withdrawing the forces he had loaned the Dutch. Twice they were delayed by messages from the Prince of Orange, who seemed to be wavering and half-inclined to yield to the English terms if they were moderated but a little. But his real purpose was tc discover what passed between the ambassadors and Monterey, and, to gain time by pretending indecision.TM His advances made the ambassadors hesitate and think of returning to the French camp to resume pourparlers, but, having consulted with the French ministers by letter, they continued their journey, advising the Prince to send deputies fully em-

" Mignet, *Negociations,* IV, 48-49.

M Wicqucfort, *Histoire des Provinces-Unies,* IV, 452-453; State Papers, Holland, 190, f. 94, July *11/21,* 1672, Buckingham, Arlington, and Halifax to Clifford, from Antwerp; *ibid.,* 190, ff. 320 *et seq.,* Williamson's journal, July 11/21-July 18/28; State Papers, Archives, 101, f. 37, July 15/25, 1672, Arlington to Charles II. (Copy.)

powered to sign the peace to both London and Paris. At Antwerp the Governor-General turned a deaf ear to their threats, though he entertained them at supper where, it is written, all was " great and noble and healths went round a pace ".' 1

Arlington was so far deceived by the Prince's semblance of yielding that he believed the peace was very near. Writing to Charles II from Antwerp, he said: " To-morrow we part from hence, and shall make all hast we can home. But that your Majesty may not be without some faire prospect of your buisness I will presume, by way of advance, to lay before you some points of it, of which I thinke you may be secure. I That a peace may be speedily made with honor and advantage to your Majesty. 2' That the Prince of Orange will remaine soveraine of the Dutch Low Countries. 3ly That the maritime force of it will not be in the French hands of which your Subjects have expressed so much Jealousy that they cannot take pleasure in your success. God continue it to your Majesty all the days of your life and make them long." 2

In this comfortable conviction, not ill-pleased with the circumstances of his negotiation, the Secretary returned to England and took up the routine of his office.

nlbid., 101, f. 48, July 8/18-July 11/21. (Copy of Williamson's journal.)

"*Ibid.,* 101, f. 37, July 15/25, 1672, Arlington to Charles II. (Copy.)

11

SECTION 11

CHAPTER XI.
Parliament And The Cabal.

During the latter half of 1672 Arlington's state of mind gradually changed from confident expectation of the peace to passionate desire for it. The cause was the financial difficulties of the government coupled with his personal fear of Parliament. The Houses were to meet on October 30. If the Commons declined to support the war, it would be impossible to maintain the fleet through another campaign, and, on the other hand, the Dutch would be emboldened to refuse terms of peace that would enable England to withdraw from the war with credit. Unfortunately William of Orange realized this as well as the Secretary of State. Several agents commissioned by the Prince appeared successively in England, ostensibly to make proposals for a separate peace between England and the Dutch. Their real errand, as the Committee of Foreign Affairs began to suspect, was to discover the state of public opinion in regard to the French alliance, perhaps to bring influence to bear on members of Parliament, and certainly to create the impression that the Prince was making every effort to restore peace, while England was hanging back at the bidding of France.1

1 The first of these agents was the Princess Dowager's physician, Doctor Rompf, who arrived in London the latter part of July with proposals for a separate peace. The next was the Prince's secretary, Van Reede, who came about the middle of September, similarly commissioned. The final attempt of the sort was made by a lawyer named Zas, accompanied by a notary of the Hague, called Arton. They arrived in January, 1673, Zas having a credential letter from Fagel, who had succeeded De Witt asGrand Pensionary of Holland. By this time the patience of the King and his ministers was exhausted, and the nearness of the date set for Parliament's meeting, made them suspect that the Dutchmen had come with some design to influence that body. (See the minutes of the Committee of Foreign Affairs, Foreign Entry Book, 177, Dec. 11, 1672; Jan. 25 and Jan. 26, 1672/3.) The two men were thrown into the Tower, were shown the rack, and tried as spies by court-martial. They were still in the Tower in May, 1673, and probably remained there until the peace was signed.

At his return, Arlington had expected that deputies fully empowered by the States General to treat for peace would follow him to London, while others were sent at the same time to Paris. Disappointed in this, he still hoped to end the war before Parliament should assemble. In the Committee of Foreign Affairs he contended with his more belligerent colleagues to obtain a moderation of the English demands. On his advice, and contrary to Buckingham's, the King offered to accept the coveted towns for a period of ten years instead of in perpetual sovereignty.2 On his advice, too, and contrary to that of the rest of the Committee, Charles conceded the point of treating in a neutral place, instead of obliging the Dutch to send their plenipotentiaries to London and Paris." But the Prince was deaf to these and to other blandishments. His aloofness, and the suspicion that he was tampering with Parliament men in order to embarrass the government, was more than Arlington could endure with philosophy. Under the pressure of his official anxieties the suave courtesy and self-possession for whichhe was distinguished, dropped away, and when, shortly after the assassination of De Witt, the Prince's secretary, Van Reede, came to England with a letter of barren compliment to the King, and proffers of a peace apart from France, Arlington lost his temper. He gave Van Reede to understand that it would be a simple matter, if the King of England so desired, to have the Prince served as De Witt had been. It was the worst mistake he could have made in dealing with the Stadholder. William replied at once without dissembling the cold, disdainful rage that the threat had aroused: " Do not believe", he wrote, " that your menaces of having me torn to pieces by the people frighten me greatly. I am by nature not very timid."' Colbert noticed with apprehension that the King and the Secretary were becoming more and more eager for peace as the time of Parliament's meeting drew near.' On August 19, Arlington confided to him that if the peace were to be made, it must be in three weeks, in order to defeat the intrigues already forming among members of Parliament; he seemed in almost feverish haste to begin a treaty, and spoke of going himself as plenipotentiary.7 At the meeting of the Committee the day before, he had urged a prorogation until after Christmas, as it was unlikely that money would be granted before that time anyway, and the delay might oblige the Dutch to treat. But Shaf tesbury argued thatunless it were certain a treaty could be set on foot, the postponement would be worse than useless.' On September 5, Arlington applied in desperation to Colbert for the loan ac a million pounds over and above the subsidy due in Octoberlrelief that would enable the King to prorogue, but the ambassador assured him that his master's resources, already taxed by the war, would not permit of the loan, and refused to report the Secretary's proposition.'

2 Rompf had offered terms acceptable to England save as to the cess1on of places. In that point, he offered Sluys to be held only until the other conditions had been fulfilled. (Mignet, *Negotiations,* IV, 52, Aug. 8, 1672, N. S., Colbert to Louis XIV.) It was decided in Committee to encourage this negotiation by offering to accept two places, as Brill and Helvoetsluys, or Flushing and the island of Goree, for a term of ten years. As Charles still declined a separate peace, Rompf's advances came to nothing. (Foreign Entry Book, 177, July 31, 1672.)

8 *Ibid.,* Aug. 18, 1672.

4 Temple, *Works,* IV, 85. For the nature of Van Reede's mission, see in Fruin's *Verspreide Geschriften,* IV, 355, the article entitled, " Willem III en zijn geheime Onderhandelingen met Karel II van Engeland in 1672 ".

8 State Papers, Holland, 191, f. 225, Oct. 7, 1672, N. S., the Prince of Orange to Arlington. (French.)

Arch. Aff. far., Angleterre, 104, f. 67, Aug. 11, 1672, N. S., Colbert to Louis XIV.

7 *Ibid.,* 104, f. 87-92, Aug. 29, 1672, N. S., the same to Pomponne.

Nevertheless the Cabal finally made up its mind to try the effect of a prorogation to the beginning of February. This was decided on September 16 in the Committee, and, in order that the step should not seem to have been taken conspiratorily, the Privy Council was called on the seventeenth to hear the King's reasons.10 It was hoped that before February a treaty of peace would be signed, and this seemed highly probable when in November the combatants agreed to a truce in order that negotiation might begin.

The English ministers made ill use of the breathing space that the prorogation allowed them, by wrangling with one another. This time the fault was Arlington's. In the middle of November the King took the seals from Bridgman, who had long been but a shadow in affairs, and bestowed them on Shaftesbury with the title of Lord Chancellor. This left a vacancy in the Treasury Commission, and public opinion at once jumped to the conclusion that a new Lord Treasurer would be chosen. Surmises divided between Arlingtonand Clifford for the post.11 The Secretary longed to enjoy the title and the honor, but he feared the danger to which such a charge might expose him in Parliament, and did not care to make himself conspicuous by advancement before the next session at least. While he pondered and hesitated, the Duke of York, whose friendship for Clifford had thriven on a common fervor for the Catholic faith, proposed that Arlington join him in recommending Clifford for the place. Arlington and Clifford had been intimate friends for ten years, a relationship which the Secretary still regarded as that of patron and protege, for it was under his wing that Clifford had first made his appearance at Court, and Arlington's favor had made his advancement rapid. He was a member of the Treasury Commission and also Treasurer of the Household; thus he had had considerable experience in finance which the Secretary entirely lacked. But neither Clifford's fitness nor the long friendship was proof against Arlington's jealousy. He answered the Duke of York coldly, saying that he believed the King had no intention of altering the administration of the Treasury. At the same time, he endeavored to obtain the nomination of his brother-in-law, Sir Robert Carr, to Shaftes- bury's place on the Commission.12

8 Foreign Entry Book, 177, Aug. 18, 1672.

o Arch. Aff. Etr., Angleterre, 104, ff. 117-118, Sept. 15, 1672, N. S., Colbert to Louis XIV.

10 Foreign Entry Book, 177, Sept. 15 and 16, 1672; Arch. Aff. for., Angleterre, 104, f. 128, Sept. 26, 1672, N. S., Colbert to Louis XIV.

But the Duke of York was not to be turned aside; he went alone to the King and proposed that Clifford bemade Treasurer. As Charles himself had much liking for a man whom he knew to be honest and courageous as well as capable, he readily gave his consent. He added that Lord Arlington had a mind to have that staff, but he was not fit for such an office which would surely be his ruin by exposing him to the malice of his enemies. He, the King, had told him that he had too much kindness for him to grant his wish." So, on November 28, the white staff was put in Clifford's hands, and Arlington made no secret of his disappointment, complaining bitterly to his friends of the other's ingratitude." The good-natured King, noticing his favorite's glum looks, bade the Duke of York remonstrate with him and bring about a reconciliation, but, though both men submitted to his endeavors, the old friendship was broken past mending.15

u " Great speeches of a new Treasurer. Earl of Arlington some. Lord Clifford others." (State Papers, Dom., Charles II, 319 A., Williamson's Journal, Nov. *21,* 1672.) "The Treasury yet continues to be managed by the old commission but it's thought my Lord Arlington or Lord Clifford will soone be declared Treasurer. Most think my Lord Clifford." *(Hatton Correspondence,* I, 1o2, Nov. 21, 1672, Charles Lyttelton to Lord Hatton.)

u Clarke, *James II,* I, 481.

This humiliation and the failure of certain well- defined hopes he had been cherishing that his master would make him a duke, brought the year gloomily to an end for the Secretary of State.1 It was whispered at Court that his great power was waning, and he did not lack enemies to rejoice." In the Committee ofForeign Affairs Clifford now acted with Shaftesbury and Lauderdale, leaving Arlington isolated, for Buckingham was playing the country gentleman at Cliveden, preparatory to embracing the popular causelwhatever that might belwhen Parliament should meet. Charles II now turned often for advice to his more audacious counsellors, and was less anxious for peace than he had been. When Arlington pressed him to agree to one of the places suggested by the Dutch as suitable for the meeting of the plenipotentiaries, instead of insisting on his own choice of Dunkirk, the other ministers convinced the King that the concession was unnecessary. " It's your Majestys interest in Parliament to show all willingnesse to a Peace ", the Secretary said. Shaftesbury replied that Parliament would not like to see the King of England yield everything, and the King of France nothing. Then Arlington asked: " Will not Holland upon this refusall, prosecute their Tricks of sending ambassadors hither?", referring to an offer from the Dutch to treat at London, where, the ministers suspected, their ambassadors would endeavor to cultivate anti-French sentiments in Parliament men. " Let them", responded the King hardily, " and appoint them the Isle of Wight or Jersey." 18

"*Ibid.*

" He talked at length to Colbert on the subject. (Arch. Aff. $tr., Angleterre, 1o4, f. 21o, Dec. 8, 1672, N. S., Colbert to Pomponne.)

" Clarke, *James II, I,* 481.

18 On the day that Clifford became Treasurer, Colbert wrote to Pomponne: " Je sc.ais aussi de bonne part que le Roy Son Maitre a dessein de le faire bien tost due sous le titre de Berri, et de luy donner du bien con- siderablement pour soutenir cette dignite." (Arch. Aff. Etr., Angleterre, 1o4, f. 21o-211, Dec. 8, 1672, N. S., Colbert to Pomponne.) The ambassador's " reliable source " was probably Arlington himself. " Berri " no doubt means Bury St. Edmunds, in whose neighborhood (at Saxham) Arlington had been born, and near which his country seat of Euston was situated.

17 " Lord Arlington is defeated in all his pretensions ... he speedeth no better in that than in his hopes of a dukedom. Chancellor, Treasurer, and Lauderdale keep firm, and seem to resolve to let him have nothingthey can hinder him of. Buckingham is the last man of the nation, out with the King and everybody else." (Christie, *Life of Shaftesbury,* II, 98. Quoted from a letter of Thomas Thynne to Sir W. Coventry, Dec. 4, 1672, among the Longleat Papers belonging to the Marquis of Bath.) 18 Foreign Entry Book, 177, Jan. 30, 1672/3.

The influence of the three ministers who now possessed the royal confidence is apparent in the masterful speech from the throne with which Charles opened Parliament on February 4, 1673. The Lord Chancellor's discourse was a still more daring defense of thewar, and concluded with the uncompromising allusion, " *Delenda est Carthago!"* At first it seemed that the policy of boldness was to be entirely successful, for the Commons voted a handsome supply promptly and unanimously, though they evaded expressing approval of the war. But the atmosphere changed suddenly when, taking up the Declaration of Indulgence, they addressed the King for its withdrawal. 10 Before the address reached his hands Charles called his ministers together to discuss what reply should be made.20 Shaftesbury, Clifford, and Lauderdale were in favor of inducing the House of Lords to object to the presentation of an address by the Commons without the Lords' concurrence. It was thought that in the defense of their privileges, the Upper House could be brought to assert the King's prerogative in ecclesiastical matters that the Commons had denied. Arlington, on the contrary, was anxious to avoid a quarrel between the Houses until the money bill had left the Commons. His opinion was shared by the other Secretary of State, Henry Coventry, but the Chancellor, the Treasurer, and Lauderdale declared that to have the Lords maintain the King's power in ecclesiasticals would be better than the money. Arlington inquired: " Whatif the House of Lords should deceive your expectations and vote as the House of Commons did? " The King became a little uncertain : " Upon the whole matter that the Money Bill be first gott. What is the discretion for a man to be angry to his owne hurt . . . Have a care not to be left without a Fleet this Spring." 21

M Cobbett, *Parliamentary History,* IV, col. 5o3-533. MAt the first debate on this subject in the Committee, the Ministers came to the following decisions: " Resolved.

1. To keep the House Sweet.
2. To endeavor to gett the Lords sent to for their consent.
3. To endeavour to drive to a Bill of the matter of the Declaration.

4. If the addresse be drawne sweet and gentle, so as onely to acquaint the King with their resolves and desires to frame a Bill etc., and not to bring and throw the Vote in the King's face, then not to have it goe to the Lords, but let it come directly to the King."

(Foreign Entry Book, 177, Feb. 12, 1672/3.)

But the Commons had no intention of parting with the money bill until the King had satisfied them in regard to the Declaration of Indulgence. Charles was obliged to reply to the address, which he did on February 24, offering to agree to any bill which should be presented to him for the relief of Protestant Dissenters, without, however, abandoning his position in regard to the prerogative in ecclesiastical matters. The Commons easily detected the subterfuge and demanded a more satisfactory answer. While awaiting it they worked on a bill to prevent the growth of popery, to be known later as the Test Act. It provided that all persons refusing the Oaths of Allegiance and Supremacy, and declining to receive the sacraments according to the rites of the Church of England, should be incapable of public employment, military or civil.

In the meantime the King had once more taken counsel. Shaftesbury, Clifford, Buckingham, and Lauder- dale, supported by the Duke of York, advised him to maintain the Declaration and dissolve Parliament. Arlington alone argued for the withdrawal of the Declaration on the ground that while the King had a great war on his hands, the matter of first importance was to draw an aid from his people that should enable him to make an advantageous peace. After that Parliamentmight be dissolved.28 But Charles was not in a mood to relish this prudent advice. Failing to obtain encouragement from the Lords, he made up his mind to dissolve Parliament, and would have done so had not Louis XIV, to whom as to Arlington the money bill was more important than the Declaration, pressed him to yield." On March 8 the Houses learned that the Declaration had been canceled.25

u Foreign Entry Book, 177, Feb. 16, 1672/3. 12 Cobbett, *Parliamentary History,* IV, col. 54

546-5S5-

The House of Lords now became the storm-centre. Clifford felt himself inspired of God to make a long impassioned speech against the Test Bill, thereby startling all the Ministers, angering the Commons, and once more endangering supply.28 But Shaftesbury's conduct caused a greater sensation, for he suddenly deserted the Court party and spoke in favor of the Test." The usual explanation of his abrupt about-face is the supposition advanced by the French ambassador: that Arlington, bent on the Treasurer's ruin, communicated the Grand Design to Shaftesbury, and also to Ormonde at this time.28 Colbert was even disposed to credit anassertion of Saint-Evremond, that Shaftesbury and Arlington together devised the Test, knowing that Clifford's conscience would not allow him to take it." But it is difficult to believe that the Secretary ever communicated the existence of the Treaty of Dover to any one, being far more implicated in its negotiation than Clifford. If Shaftesbury was enlightened as to the religious predilections of the Court, it was more probably by the Lord Treasurer's fondness for the Declaration, his speech against the Test, his intimacy with the Duke of York whose conversion to Catholicism was scarcely in doubt, and the favor he enjoyed with the King. When the Test was being devised in the House of Commons, the Chancellor was working with Clifford to fortify the King in maintaining his prerogative in matters of religion, while Arlington would clearly have sacrificed every one of the Thirty- nine Articles for the bill of supply. Is it likely that at the time of this disagreement the Chancellor and the Secretary of State were plotting the Test in entire harmony? It was a simple matter for Shaftesbury to change horses in mid-stream when once he was satisfied that he could run a better race in another saddle. Probably the events of the session convinced him that the government was doomed to eventual defeat by the unpopularity of both its foreign and domestic policies. With characteristic prescience he transferred himself to the winning side before it had realized that it was the winning side.

28 Dalrymple, *Memoirs,* Appendix, p. 13o, March 9, 1673, N. S., Colbert to Louis XIV; also, Arch. Aff. Etr., Angleterre, 1o6, ff. 133-135, the same to Pomponne, of the same date. These letters were written just after the ambassador had listened to Arlington's explanation of his attitude in the matter.

24 Dalrymple, *Memoirs,* Appendix, p. 95, March 2o, 1673, N. S., Colbert to Louis XIV.

25 Cobbett, *Parliamentary History,* IV, col. 561. 25 Christie, *Life of Shaftesbury,* II, 138-139. *"Ibid.,* II, 136.

28"... je n'ay que trop d'Indices que pour perdre le feu Milord Cliffort, il donna cognoissance au due Dormont et au Chancellier, et par eux au Parlement du premier dessein qu'il m'a advoue luy mesme n'avoir jamais aprouve dans 1'atne, et ne s'y est rendu que pour eviter sa perte." (Arch. Aff. litr., Angleterre, 1o8, f. 114, Nov. 2o, 1673, N. S., Colbert to Louis XIV.) This letter was written eight months after the event, and at a time when Colbert no longer trusted Arlington's attachment to the French alliance. The accuracy of the guess is therefore open to doubt.

The Cabal had never enjoyed public esteem, but of late it had become more than ever an object of hatred and suspicion. Just a week before Parliament met,the Secretary received a pamphlet published anonymously at the Hague, entitled *England's Appeal from the Private Cabal at White-Hall, to the Great Council of the Nation, the Lords and Commons in Parliament Assembled. By a true Lover of his Country™* In spite of Arlington's efforts to keep the book out of England, a consignment was smuggled into the country in March, and the comment it evoked was highly damaging to the French alliance and to the English ministry." The author intimated " the wonderful Effects the French King's Liberality had (almost four years since) in converting the strongest Opposers of his Interest". Certain aspects of Arlington's hospitality were dwelt upon: " I suppose it is not usual to see so great a familiarity (as hath been observed long since) between Ambassadors and first Ministers of State, continual Treatings, and frequent going to Country-houses, there to stay several days and weeks, is a new thing in the world: and an Ambassador using so Noble a House with so much freedom, gave a just cause to all observing men to conclude he had paid dear for it." The death agonies of the Triple Alliance were rehearsed:the rejection of overtures from the Emperor and the Duke of Lorraine; the metamorphosis of the Committee of Foreign Affairs, by which Bridgman, Ormonde, and Trevor were forced into the background on account of their Dutch sympathies. Next the author turned to the embassy of Buckingham and Arlington to the French camp the preceding summer. He accused them of sacrificing the interests of England to the aggrandizement of France, by refusing to treat unless the impossible demands of Louis XIV were also satisfied; by making the Treaty of Heeswick; by excluding Halifax from the secrets of the negotiation. The pamphlet concluded with a series of twenty questions propounded to Parliament for an investigation of the basis of the French alliance. The twentieth sums up the crimes of the Cabal: " And Lastly, How faithfully our Ministers have discharged their Trust in these great Emergencies. How free they have been from dependences upon Foreign Courts . . . Their industrious Endeavours and various Stratagems to engage his Majesty and the Nation in this War, their Ingrossing all business of concernment, and concealing the most Important Debates and Resolutions from his Majesty's Privy Council. Nay, their keeping it unseasonably from his great Council, and putting off their Sessions, lest they might cross their designs. Lastly, The carriage of some of them in Holland, and of the care they took of the Interest both of England and of the Protestant Religion."

2S Christie, *Life of Shaftesbury,* II, 138-139.

80 Arlington mentioned to Colbert that he had received a copy of the book on Jan. *28,* 1672/3. (Arch. Aff. Etr., Angleterre, 106, ff. 78-79, Feb. 7, 1673, N. S.) *England's Appeal* has been reprinted among the *State Tracts.*

11" Ce projet qui tend, comme Votre Majeste peut juger, a revolter les sujets cOntre le Roy leur Maistre, a fort irrite ledit Roy." (Arch. Aff. Etr., Angleterre, 106, f. 79.) " Les Holandois ont trouve moyen de respandre Icy un des Libels Intitulez *Appel de VAngleterre* . . . Milord Arlincton m'a dit qu'il estoit extremement Injurieux a la france et tres dangereux dans la conjoncture presente de 1'assemblee du Parlement." *(Ibid.,* 106, f. 169, March 27, 1673, N. S., Colbert to Pomponne.) "This book vexes the English extremely." (*Cal. St. P., Dom., 1673,* p. 127.) " The Dutch deputies say this pamphlet does wonderfull effects in England." (Additional MSS., 34342, f. 67, April 4, 1673, Baron de Vique to Sir Robert Southwell.)

What this book lacked in literary finish it more than made up in crude, forthright vigor. It was the work of one Pierre du Moulin, who had gained in Arlington's office some of the information he now gave to theworld. He was at present in the employ of the Prince of Orange, who may have supplied the facts touching the embassy of Buckingham and Arlington." A personal grudge that Du Moulin cherished against the Secretary of State added to the ardor of his attack. Fortunately for Arlington the pamphlet made its appearance too late in the session to be assimilated by Parliament. The Test Act had passed the House of Lords, so in good faith the Commons completed the bill of supply, and the King was able to prorogue on March 29 to the following October.

The summer was a period of change both of persons and policies in the government. York and Clifford resigned from their places; the Admiralty was put in commission, while the Treasurer's staff was bestowed on Sir Thomas Osborne, Buckingham's protege, the King again ignoring Arlington's advice to reestablish the Treasury Commission." Shaftesbury, by his championship of the Test Act, was completely outof favor with the King and the Duke of York, and was regarded by them as a dangerous renegade. The Chancellor was rapidly drifting away from the French policy that he had so lately endorsed, in the direction of the popular preference for Spain and Holland."

Moreover, the Duke of York suspected him of a plan to dissolve the King's marriage and conclude another by which Charles might have legitimate issue to succeed him.85

u Pierre Du Moulin, grandson of the renowned Huguenot controversialist of that name, was a figure of some minor political importance. He had been secretary to the English embassy at Paris until Montagu, unable to endure his intrusiveness, insisted upon his dismissal. At the solicitation of the Countess of Horn, Lady Arlington's cousin, Arlington then appointed him secretary to the Committee of Trade and Plantations. He was, however, too much of a busybody to keep out of mischief. In 1672 he was caught endeavoring to communicate with the Dutch deputies at Hampton Court, and, to escape imprisonment in the Tower, fled to Holland. The Prince of Orange took him into his service, and tried, through his knowledge of persons and parties in England, to keep in touch with discontented members of Parliament. Du Moulin's authorship of *England's Appeal* is asserted by Colbert de Croissy (Arch. Aff. Etr., Angle- terre, 106, f. 78, Feb. 7, 1673, N. S., Colbert to Louis XIV) and by the Baron de Vique in a letter to Sir Robert Southwell (Additional MSS., 34342, f. 67, April 4, 1673, N. S.). The suspicion that Lisola collaborated in the writing is, I think, unfounded, for the piece is wholly lacking in the elegance of his style.

"Arch. Aff. $tr., Angleterre, 107, f. 49, June I, 1673, N. S., Colbert to Louis XIV.

Arlington, too, was shortening sail in expectation of a shift of the wind, but he acted with such caution that neither his friends nor his enemies could be sure of his position. Whatever had been his attitude in regard to the Test Act, it had not prejudiced him with the King, who, though he saw fit to deny him the Treasurer's staff, still displayed great affection for him." The King and Queen were entertained at Goring House in August, and it was again reported that Arlington was to be made a duke." Yet it did not escape observation that while the Secretary exerted himself to maintain his influence over his master, he was at the same time progressing well in an intimacy with Shaftesbury, and was once more the close friend of Ormonde, whobelonged to the party opposed to the French alliance.58 Colbert noticed these new affiliations with some uneasiness, as also a more marked inclination on the Secretary's part to consider the interests of the Prince of Orange.20 But his suspicions were quieted by assurances from Charles, as well as from Arlington himself, of the latter's good faith towards France." The ambassador could not extract much comfort, however, from Arlington's exposition of the situation. The Grand Design, said the Secretary, must be entirely abandoned, for in an enterprise so odious to the kingdom the most powerful assistance that Louis XIV could give would be useless; one must think now only of re-establishing the King's credit by an advantageous peace.41 It would be impossible for England to break with Spain, in case that power, joining the Dutch, should declare war on France. Arlington went so far as to say that his master would be obliged to separate from France, rather than incur a war with Spain.41 Charles was now no less solicitous than his minister that the Grand Design be buried and forgotten, and that a good peace be obtained before he need meet his Parliament again."

" "Le Chancelier d'Angleterre . . . s'est declare depuis la Cessation du parlement d'estre tout a fait Hollandois ..." (Arch. Aff. Etr., Angle- terre, 1o7, f. 39, May 18, 1673, N. S., the same to Pomponne.)

85 *Ibid.*, 1o6, f. 213, April 17, 1673, N. S., the same to Louis XIV.

s" My Lord Arlington keepes his own very well, I assure you." (HoKon *Correspondence,* I, 1o7, June 24, 1673, Charles Lyttelton to Lord Hatton.) On June so/July 1o, Colbert wrote of Arlington: " Ce dernier a tousjours la plus grande part dans la Confiance du Roy son Maistre et acquerre en mesme temps beaucoup d'estime et de Credit dans le Parlement." (Arch. Aff. Etr., Angleterre, 1o7, f. 9o.)

87 *Letters to Sir Joseph Williamson,* I, 156, Aug. 11, 1673; *ibid,,* p. 59, same date. (News-letters.)

88 Arch. Aff. $tr., Angleterre, 1o7, f. 63, June 22, 1673, N. S., Colbert to Louis XIV; *Letters to Sir Joseph Williamson,* I, 31, June 13, 1673; *ibid.,* II, 25, Sept. 23, 1673; *ibid.,* II, 29, Oct. 3, 1673. (News-letters.)

"Arch. Aff. Etr., Angleterre, 1o7, f. 35, May 15, 1673, N. S., Colbert to Louis XIV.

"Ibid., 1o8, f. 33, Oct. 5, 1673, N. S., the same to the same.

41 *Ibid.,* 1o6, f. 195, April 3, 1673, N. S., the same to the same; *ibid.,* 1o6, f. 214, April 17, 1673, N. S., the same to the same.

albid., 1o8, f. 32, Oct. 5, 1673, N. S., the same to the same.

48"... le Roy d'Angleterre et Milord Arlincton desirent si pas- sionnement que la paix se fasse avant I'assemblee du Parlement qui doit estre au commencement du mois d'octobre, que je suis persuade qu'aussi- tost qu'ils croiront la pouvoir conclurre a des conditions qui n'atirent pas a sa Majeste Britanique ou ausdits Ministres les reproches de la nation, ils y consentiront avec Joye." *(Ibid.,* 1o7, *f. 79,* July 6, 1673, N. S., the same to the same.)

Weary as Arlington undoubtedly was of the French alliance, he still felt unable to extricate himself or his master from it until the war had justified itself and peace were made. If he had an understanding with Shaftesbury and Ormonde, it was probably to secure their assistance in keeping Parliament amenable until this should be accomplished, though it may have comprehended a reversion to the policy of the Triple Alliance as soon as the King could disengage himself from France. Arlington believed that he could manage Shaftesbury,4 and he thought to make use of the Chancellor's newly-won popularity in the House of Commons. The King, who understood Arlington if any man did, insisted that the Secretary was sincere in his desire to fulfil the treaty with France, and he told of a bribe of forty thousand pounds offered by Spain to Arlington, who refused it.45 During the summer Arlington spared no pains to gain over to the Court party all the members of the Commons whose adherence might prove valuable, and in the autumn he flattered himself that the docility of the House could be relied upon.4

44 Both Charles and Arlington assured Colbert that they were certain of Shaftesbury's good behavior, as if they had some engagement from him to that effect. (Arch. Aff. ftr., Angleterre, 1o8, f. 34, Oct. 5, 1673, N. S., Colbert to Louis XIV; *ibid.,* 1o8, f. 77, Nov. 6, 1673, N. S., the same to the same.)

48 *Ibid.,* 1o7, f. 147, Aug. 1o, 1673, N. S., the same to the same. At the end of November, Charles told Colbert that the only persons who wanted to maintain the alliance with France were himself, the Duke of York, and Arlington. *(Ibid.,* 1o8, f. 149, Dec. 4, 1673, N. S., the same to Pom- ponne.)

48 " Ledit Mylord continue d'employer tous ses soins a asseurer au Roy son Maistre tous les principaux mcmbres du Parlement, et il y a desja sy bien reussi auprez de quelques uns des plus suivis qu'il me tesmoigne avoir beaucoup moins d'Inquietude qu'auparavant du succez de la seance pro- chaine, et sur tout il me pria fort hyer d'asseurer positivement sa Majeste que quelques fortes que puissent estre les Cabales, elles ne seront pas capables d'obliger le Roy son Maistre a contrevenir a son Traitte." *(Ibid.,* 1o8, f. 41, Oct. 19, 1673, N. S., the same to Pomponne.)

But the campaign of 1673 did nothing to cultivate a national fondness for the war or for the alliance with France. Since April the plenipotentiaries of the belligerents had been quarreling over terms of peace at Cologne, without coming in hailing distance of agreement. In the meantime the war went on but brought no advantage to England. The loss of a naval battle in August was attributed by Rupert, who commanded, to the cowardice of the French squadron, which the English were very ready to believe. This defeat made impossible the " descent " on the coast of Holland that the government had long been planning, and the troops that Charles had raised at great cost for this purpose were useless. Arlington, with his thoughts always on the meeting of Parliament, had moments of panic when he wanted to recall the English ambassadors from Cologne, rather than face the Commons still in uncertainty between peace and war." He would have persuaded the King to dissimulate his intention to abide by the French league, in order not to excite opposition, but Charles laughed at his fears.48 All five members of the Cabal were shaken by the vogue of *England's Appeal,* and hearing rumors of impeachment of this one and that, took the precaution of obtaining pardons of the King in the course of the summer and autumn.1Arlington, however, became somewhat more confident as he believed he saw results of his attentions to the Parliament men, and he upheld his master in a determination not to prorogue.50

47 " Nothing can be more prejudiciall to his affaires then coming to the Parliament in October with an uncertainty between Peace or War." (State Papers, Archives, 221, p. 183, Aug. t8, 1673, Arlington to the ambassadors at Cologne.)

"Arch. Aff. $tr., Angleterre, 1o7, ff. 161-162, Aug. 17, 1673, N. S., Colbert to Louis XIV.

Clifford's pardon is dated July 3, 1673 (Co/. 5. *P., Dam., 1673,* p. 418); Lauderdale's, Oct. 3 *(ibid.,* p. 567); Shaftesbury's, Nov. 7 *(ibid.,* 767.3-7675, P- "); Buckingham's, Nov. 19 *(ibid.,* p. 26). Arlington's pardon is not calendared, but one of his clerks wrote ta-Williamson: " My Lord Arlington, the people say, would not be as good as his word to trust them,for this day his pardon was also sealed as ample as any of the others." *(Letters to Sir Joseph Williamson,* II, 46, Oct. 17, 1673, Henry Ball to Williamson.)

M" Milord Arlinton ne m'a pas paru moins oppose que le Roy son Maistre a l'esloignement de l'assemblee de son Parlement." (Arch. Aff. $tr., Angleterre, 1o7, f. 2oo, Sept. 11, 1673, N. S., Colbert to Louis XIV.) In a letter of October 8 to the ambassadors at Cologne, Arlington wrote very cheerfully: " Wee are preparing here to see the Parliament assemble att the day appointed wherein wee doe not despayre of seeing His Majesty enabled to prosecute the War, notwithstanding the great aversion and dissatisfaction in the generallity of the People against the Allyance with France. But the point of Treatyes, Allyances with Forreigne Princes, the making of War and Peace, being so indisputable in the Crown, I can not perswade my self, that a Parliament so well complexiond as this towards Monarchy, and so particularly addicted to His Majesties Person, will abandon Him and his Honor in such an exigent, which I mention here to you, to fortify your discourses with the French Plenipotentiaries and the Mediators respectively, that the vulgar reports so artificially fomented by our adversaries may not dishearten them, especially His Majesty being resolved to maintayne the honour of His Treaty against all opposition whatsoever." (State Papers, Archives, 221, p. 332.)

12

SECTION 12

CHAPTER XII.

At The Bar Of The House Of Commons.

Whatever hopes the leaders of the House of Commons had encouraged in the Secretary of State, proved themselves delusive without delay when the Houses met on October 20. The Court had decided at the last moment to prorogue for a week, in order to observe the temper of the members. But before Black Rod could summon the Commons, they had hurried through an address upon their nearest grievance, the marriage recently arranged for the Duke of York with a Catholic princess, Maria of Modena. In spite of this ominous beginning, Arlington persisted during the week's respite in believinglor in pretending the belieflthat if the Houses were given a free hand in religious matters, they would not encroach on the prerogative in foreign affairs.1 He did not yet realize that hatred of popery and hatred of the French alliance were one in the public mindlthe effect in no small degree, perhaps, of *England's Appeal.*

Shaftesbury saw nothing to be gained by sacrificing his popularity in a hopeless cause, nor is it likely thathis best efforts would have availed to save the government from the storm that now broke. Refused satisfaction in regard to the marriage, the Commons resolved not to consider further supply before the expiry of that last granted,2 unless the obstinacy of the Dutch should make it necessary; nor before grievances were redressed, and the kingdom secured against popery, popish counsels and counsellors. On November 4, it was moved to consider the business of evil counsellors, and the Duke of Lauderdale's name had been mentioned, when proceedings were cut short by another prorogation, this time to January 7."

1 On October 26, Arlington wrote to the ambassadors at Cologne: " If wee may believe the asseverations of particular men that are the most leading in the House, or the Generall complexion of it, when His Majesty shall have given them satisfaction in matters of Religion, it is confidently presumd they will gratify him in all His other desires, and more ex- pressely abstayne from enquiring into the motives of the War, but on the contrary afford him a competent succour for the prosecution of it." (State Papers, Archives, 221, p. 373. Copy.)

This dismal end of his expectations filled the Secretary with terror and despair. " I found my Lord Arlington in the deepest dejection at this result", wrote Colbert the day before the session ended, " seeing clearly that his ruin is attached to the fall of the French alliance . . . My Lord Arlington fears greatly, too, that he will be accused this afternoon as an evil counsellor." 4 His timidity increased beyond possibility of concealment. Although the Princess of Modena had already been married to the Duke of York by proxy and was now at Paris, in the last stage of her journey to England, Arlington intimated to the French ambassador that it would not be convenient to have the lady come at this shameful crisis, and that her best plan would be to retire of her own accord into Italy.5 He would have disposed of the bridegroom no less summarily for, with the support of Shaftesbury and Ormonde, he advised the King to send the Duke away from Court until the popular obsession of the prevalence of popery had somewhat subsided. Charles was ready to take any advice that might placate Parliament, and so allowed them to suggest withdrawal to the Duke. But James rejected the proposal so angrily that they dared not pursue it, having every reason to believe that he would never forgive them.'

2 *I. e.,* Sept., 1674.

a Cobbett, *Parliamentary History,* IV, col. 585-61o.

Arch. Aff. fitr., Angleterre, 1o8, ff. 95-96, Nov. 13, 1673, N. S., Colbert to Louis XIV.

' *Ibid.,* 1o8, f. 75, Nov. 6, 1673, N. S., the same to the same. The Duke of York says: " Arlington advised the King to stop the Duchess in France." (Macpherson, *Original Papers,* I, 7o, Nov., 1673.)

The two months' recess was spent by the King and his ministers, first, in purifying the Court of all outward and visible professors of Catholicism except the Duke of Yorklin which work Arlington displayed a vigor that measured his anxiety; second, in trying to settle upon a tenable foreign policy. It happened that a Spanish ambassador, the Marquis del Fresno, had recently come to England with certain proposals in charge from the Dutch for a peace that should exclude France. While Arlington had hoped for the support of Parliament, he had evaded making any answer, but a few days after the prorogation he told Colbert that it was impossible for the King of England to continue the war; he must listen to the Spanish ambassador, and before Parliament should reconvene the peace must be signed. Colbert argued in vain for a further prorogation to the end of 1674. The Secretary was immovable.7 Nor could Charles, when appealed to, reassure the ambassador. Though he still insisted that he would not make peace without France, he confessed almost in the same breath that he could not continue the war.8Having no plans himself he was waiting for some one to solve the situation for him, and Colbert knew that he would yield to strong pressure from whatever direction it came. Pressure from Arlington was what the ambassador chiefly dreaded. " My Lord Arlington ", he wrote, " tries to save his fortune by an entire compliance with the wishes of Parliament."' Colbert believed that he was arranging a treaty with Fresno, and would have it ready to sign when Parliament met, expecting that the King would then be forced to give his hand to it.10 He was not surprised when, at the end of December, Arlington asked for Louis XIV's consent to a separate peace for England."

' Burnet, *Own Time, II,* 42; Temple, *Works,* II, 294-295. "Arch. Aff. iftr., Angleterre, 108, ff. 107-112, Nov. 20, 1673, N. S., Colbert to Louis XIV. *Ibid.*

Though the Secretary was taking the only course left open to him, it was one that entailed grave risk. Charles was sincerely anxious to keep faith with the King of France, and he wanted advice to that end, but Arlington could only suggest a surrender at discretion to Parliament. Impatient of such timorous counsel, Charles put himself in the hands of Buckingham and the new Treasurer, who at least had something to propose. They were quick to use this advantage to discredit the Secretary, whose influence with the King seemed to decline day by day while theirs increased."As they were now championing the French alliance to gratify their master, Arlington, for his own preservation, was obliged to throw himself into the arms of the popular Dutch party more unreservedly than he probably would have done otherwise, and to claim the protection of its leaders, Shaftesbury and Ormonde.81 The former was now in open revolt from the Court party, having been summoned to deliver up the seals early in November. In his place, Sir Heneage Finch, a man in the confidence of the Treasurer and Buckingham, was appointed Lord Keeper. Arlington had vainly opposed the change, and even after it was made he still cherished the hope of reconciling Shaftesbury with the King." But the other faction took care that he should not succeed, and it is not apparent that the Earl cared very much to be reinstated.

Arch. Aff. $tr., Angleterre, 108, ff. 114-115.

10 *Ibid.,* 11i, f. 24, Jan. 1, 1674, N. S., the same to the same.

11 Mignet, *Negotiations,* IV, 256.

12 " Le credit du due de Bouquinkam auprez du Roy son Maistre semble augmenter et celuy dudit Milord [Arlington] diminuer, ce qui luy donne beaucoup de Chagrin. Mais comme il est fort utile et affectionne au Roy son Maistre, il ne faut pas douter que ce Prince ne luy rende bientost sa confiance." (Arch. Aff. $tr., Angleterre, 108, f. 128, Nov. 23, 1673, N. S., Colbert to Pomponne.) " Treasurer hath infinitly eclipsed Arlington with King." *(Essex Papers,* I, 150, Dec. 6, 1673, Lord Conway to Essex.) " King is firme to the Interest of France; . . . Treasurer and Duke push hard at Arlington." *(Ibid.,* I, 153, Dec. 20, 1673, the same to the same.)" Buckingham gains ground every day of Arlington with King and Duke. Hee and Treasurer and Speaker are, I thinke, at this time the persons of greatest power ..." *(Ibid., I,* 155, Dec. 25, 1673, Sir William Temple to Essex.)

Buckingham was busy with plans to prop up the French alliance. At his suggestion Louis XIV recalled Colbert, who could put no faith in Buckingham, and sent over Ruvigny once more. Buckingham's first plan had been to buy a majority in the House of Commons with the money of France," but he abandoned this in favor of another less difficult and less dangerous. The Commons were suspicious that the Court had an agreement with France to overthrow the Established Church and bring in popery. To allay their fears, Buckingham, the Treasurer, and Ruvigny joined in advising the King to offer the treaty of December 21, 1671, which Buckingham still believed to be the original agreement with France, for the inspection of the House as evidence of the purely political nature of the league. Charles gave his consent, and it was decided not to inform the other members of the Committee of Foreign Affairs of the proposed step. At the last moment, however, the King's resolution began to fail, and he wanted to consult the whole Committee. His advisers were discomfited, but were obliged to yield, seeing him on the point of abandoning the plan entirely.1' So, the day before the Houses were to meet, the Committee, now composed of York, the Keeper, the Treasurer, Buckingham, Ormonde, and the two secretaries, heard the proposal. " It was approved by all", says Ruvigny, " except my Lord Arlington and the Duke of Ormonde, who opposed it absolutely." " Arlington knew that another treaty had preceded that of December, 1671, and no doubt he saw danger in the practice of exhibiting treaties to the House. Nevertheless, the King was once more persuaded to the plan.

18 One of Lord Conway's correspondents wrote on December 11: " These are the two partyes at Court, the Duke of Ormonde, Lord Arlington, Lord Shaftesbury, and Secretary Coventry; the Duke of Buckingham, Lord Treasurer, Mr. Speaker, and the Lord Latherdale, if he were there." *(Letters to Sir Joseph Williamson,* II, 92, a letter signed M. P., but indorsed " Roger Jones to Lord Conway ".)

" " Quoy qu'il soit amy de Milord Arlinton, ce Ministre ne m'a pas paru fort satisfait de ce changement." (Arch. Aff. Etr,, Angleterre, 108, f. 119, Nov. 20, 1673, N. S., Colbert to Louis XIV.) "II [Arlington] est mesme persuade qu'il a ramene le Chancelier a son devoir, et que ce Ministre est resolu de regaigner les bonnes graces du Roy son Maistre, travaillant a sa satisfaction conjointement avec tous ses amis." *(Ibid.,* 108, f. 132, Nov. 27, 1673, N. S., the same to the same.)

It had absolutely no effect. The Commons, ignoring the King's offer to display the treaty, went back to theirgrievances, and on January 13 began what threatened to be a thorough annihilation of the government, by attacking the Duke of Lauderdale, whose arbitrary administration in Scotland, and the despotic advice which he had offered the King, made him the most cordially detested of all the ministers. An address was voted for his removal from all employment, and from the King's person and counsels forever."

"Gardner, *George yilliers,* 280-281; Mignet, *Negotiations,* IV, 238-239.

"Mignet, *Negotiations,* IV, 257, Jan. 15, 1674, N. S., Ruvigny to Pomponne.

11 Arch. Aflf. $tr., Angleterre, 111, f. 101, Jan. 18, 1674, N. S., the same to the same.

It is possible that the Duke of Buckingham would have been reserved for another day if, in his eagerness to hasten Arlington's punishment, he had not introduced himself by a letter to the Speaker, desiring to be heard on " some truths relating to the Public "." The Commons called him in, pleased at this tribute to their power and hoping to extract some information that would incriminate the other ministers. But the Duke, when he actually stood at the bar, suddenly lost his self-possession and spoke with clumsy incoherence. He declared that he had had as great a hand as any man in the making of the Triple Alliance, but that he did not want to see a war in which France had everything and England nothing, and if his advice had been followed all would have been well. *He* had not advised asking ships of the Dutch instead of towns. *He* was not of those who had received four, five, or six hundred thousand pounds, although he had spent an estate in the King's behalf. He referred pathetically to his sufferings for his devotion to the House in the astrological affair, when witnesses had been bribed to swear against him. Sneering at the incapacity of his colleagues, he said: " I can hunt the Hare with a pack of Hounds, but not with a pack of Lobsters." M He concluded by asking leave to sell his place of Master of the Horse if his removal was voted, and then withdrew in much confusion.21

18 Grey, *Debates,* Jan. 13, 1673/4.

10 *Ibid.; Letters to Sir Joseph Williamson,* II, 62, Nov. 5, 1673, Thomas Derham to Williamson; *ibid.,* 103-106, Jan. 2, 1673/4, Sir Gilbert Talbot to the same.

The House was ill-satisfied with the indefinite nature of this discourse. One member not inexcusably wondered that the Duke " should interpret the weighty affairs of this House to be his own private affairs "." The Duke, too, felt he had not done himself justice, and intimated that he desired to be heard again. The next day, therefore, the Commons drew up a list of questions on the points in regard to which they desired enlightenment, and then called him in. This time he spoke more connectedly and more boldly. It had been the opinion of himself and Shaftesbury, he said, to ask the advice of Parliament before war was declared, but this was contrary to Arlington's opinion. He had opposed using French ships in the war, and had wanted France to give money instead; Arlington wanted ships. Shaftesbury and he wished to engage the French to conquer and hand over to England certain of the Dutch towns. Arlington wanted no towns delivered for oneyear, so the French got all and England nothing. " Consider who it was locked up with the French Ambassador ; my spirit moves me to tell you. When we are to consider what to do, we must advise with the French Ambassador."

20 Grey, *Debates,* Jan. 13, 1673/4. Burnet says "a brace of lobsters" *(Own Time,* II, 44), and interprets the metaphor to mean the King and the Duke of York, though he adds: " He had used that figure to myself but had then applied it to prince Robert and lord Arlington." *(Ibid.)* But the way the expression is quoted in Grey, and the fact that it follows an allusion to Arlington, make it seem probable that he still referred to that Minister, and possibly to Ormonde and Rupert. Another account, by a member of the House, bears this out: " His discourse was ffull of distraction, and sayd he was weary of the company he was joyned with, and knew how to kill a hare with hounds but could not hunt with lobsters." *(Letters to Sir Joseph Williamson,* II, 115, Jan. 16, 1673/4, Sir Christopher Musgrave to Williamson.)

81 Grey, *Debates,* Jan. 13, 1673/4.

Ibid.

When he had ended his harangue, the Speaker asked him the questions agreed upon. They elicited only further accusations of the Secretary: Arlington had obtained the appointment of the French general, Schomberg, to command the English forces recently raised for the descent upon Holland. He had been informed that Arlington wanted government by an army. Arlington had advised the attack on the Smyrna fleet without declaration of war. It was Arlington and Ormonde that had got the vast sums he had named the previous day. As to his own activities, the Duke again claimed the credit of the Triple Alliance, showing forgetfulness of the fact that the treaty had been signed in Holland: " Lord Arlington and I were only employed to treat, and finding the danger we were in of being cheated, pressed the Ambassadors to sign before they had powerlIt was an odd request to the Ambassadors, yet they did sign." To the question, " Who made the first Treaty with France, by which the Triple League was broken?", he answered: "I made no Treaty." He disclaimed advising the Stop on the Exchequer, though he would not say who didlproof positive that Arlington had no hand in it. He avowed guardedly his approval of the policy of Indulgence, " but no farther than what might be done by the Declaration by Law ". He assumed responsibility only for the Treaty of Heeswick, which he defended as thebest measure possible under the circumstances. This was the net result of the examination."

Buckingham had protested overmuch. No one who heard him was so blind as not to see that his answers had been dictated by personal hatred and not by love of parliamentary government. The House did not fall tooth and nail on Arlington, but discussed the quality and insufficiency of the Duke's revelations. One member declared that no one man could have carried through all the measures attributed to the Secretary, and therefore others must be implicated. The debate came to an end with an address for Buckingham's removal similar to that resolved in Lauderdale's case."

In other quarters the Duke suffered for his ill- considered defense. The House of Lords was displeased because he had presented himself before the House of Commons without permission from the Upper House.28 The King was offended because Buckingham had broken his privy councillor's oath and revealed matters transacted at the board.5' Therefore the Duke, who a few weeks before had seemed the most powerful man in England, now found no protectors. He vanished from Court in obedience to the Commons' address, and his place of Master of the Horse was given to the Duke of Monmouth.

Arlington, whose case came next before the House, profited by the mistakes of his enemy. He was aware that an impeachment was preparing against him andhad even seen the heads of *it."* On the morning of the fifteenth of January the attack was begun by Sir Gilbert Gerrard in a fashion so clumsy and inept that it gave the Secretary an advantage at the outset. Gerrard had, he said, " no prejudice to him or disobligation from him", but must do his duty. Arlington was " the great conduit-pipe " through which all affairs passed, therefore he was responsible for the Declaration of Indulgence, and for the newly raised forces, and was meditating the destruction of the liberties of the House. Then in anti-climax to the broad wickedness thus alleged, Gerrard instanced: first, that Arlington with thirty others had voted for a proviso to the Conventicles Act, allowing the dispensing power of the King; second, that the licenses to conventicles consequent upon the Declaration of Indulgence, had passed through the Secretary's hands.28

28 Grey, *Debates,* Jan. 14, 1673/4; Cobbett, *Parliamentary History,* IV, col. 630-649; Ashmole MSS., 807, f. 5.

24 Grey, *Debates,* Jan. 14, 1673/4.

"Essex Papers, I, 162, Jan. 17, 1673/4, Lord Aungier to Essex.

28 *Letters to Sir Joseph Williamson,* II, 130-131, Jan. 23, 1673/4, Sir Robert Southwell to Williamson.

This was the oral accusation. Gerrard also presented a written charge in several articles grouped under the three heads following:

" 1. That the said earl hath been a constant and most vehement promoter of Popery and Popish Counsels.

" 2. That the said earl hath been guilty of many and undue practices, to promote his own greatness, and hath embezzled and wasted the treasure of this nation.

" 3. That the said earl hath falsely and traiterously betrayed the great trust reposed in him, by his majesty, as counsellor and principal secretary of state." 1J

21 His brother-in-law, Carr, would naturally furnish him with this information. In his speech before the House, Arlington took up in order the points which his enemies were prepared to present in their accusation.

18 Grey, *Debates,* Jan. 15, 1673/4.

4Ibid.

The House had hardly entered in debate on these matters when a note from Arlington was read by the Speaker. He had heard that the Honorable House was informing itself of public affairs, wherein he humbly conceived what he could say might be of use and satisfaction and he begged to be admitted.20 As the Commons really enjoyed minister-baiting, they made no difficulty about admitting him, and resolved to put the same questions that Buckingham had answered.

Arlington had obtained the consent of both the King and the House of Lords to make his defense, and for the last hour had been waiting in the lobby of the Commons. The faithful Ossory accompanied him as far as the door. Now that the long-dreaded impeachment actually confronted him, he displayed a firmness and serenity that surprised all who witnessed it, and that is difficult to account for. It is possible that he had some assurance from Shaftesbury that all would go well with him. Certainly the beginning of the session had not alarmed him, and he had even expressed a belief that it would end well for the King." He faced his accusers now with entire composure, bowed to the Speaker and to the four quarters of the House, and drew forth a paper from which he read his remarks, excusing this procedure on the ground of a poor memory.

Beginning with the point of religion, he said he had never deviated from his education in the Church ofEngland, nor had he ever attended mass or confession. He was present when the Declaration of Indulgence was debated, but was not the author of it. " I did at that time believe the King had an inherent right in him in such matters, but when I knew the Contrary, and that it was not Consistent with law, I was the first Man that perswaded the King against it." As to his having shown particular favor to papists: " I have promiscuously obliged all persons I could, without nicely enquiring theire Religion."

0 Grey, *Debates,* Jan. 15, 1673/4.

11 " The Parliament now begins to sitt close to their work, and have yet declard no profess'd Severityes against any but the Papists. Wee Ministers are more then a little threatend. God knowes what will become of us. Notwithstanding which I cannot but promise my self this will prove a good session to the King our Master and Kingdome." (State Papers, Archives, 221, p. 537, Jan. 12, 1673/4, Arlington to the ambassadors at Cologne. Copy.)

Turning then to the political charges, he explained that he had ever been against any violation of the Triple Alliance, but that Buckingham had wished to destroy it. The treaty with Francelhere the Secretary became rather vaguelhad followed Buckingham's embassy of condolence to the French Court after the death of Madame. He, no less than Buckingham, had tried to obtain money instead of ships from France, but had been unable to prevail. " As to my being domestic with the French ambassador, I only received him with good Manners, and have used the same some time to Spaine, some time to Holland, and they have all been angry enuf with me since to have declared it if I had any pension from them long before now." He defended the appointment of Schomberg on the ground of his military skill, mentioning that he was a Protestant, born of an English mother, and had commanded the English troops in Portugal four years without any objection being made in England. The Treaty of Heeswick had been a precaution which the circumstances made necessary, though he and Halifax would have preferred to offer the Dutch more lenient terms than Buckingham would agree to. " Tis urged I wasagainst having of townes. Tis true. What could we have done with them ? Should we have rais'd an army only to defend them?" Parliament had not been acquainted with the King's intention to declare war, it being unnecessarylhere he intimated the prerogative lto do so. The Commissioners of the Treasury had assured the King that he had the money for it. The Secretary had never advised government by an army, nor the use of troops to overawe Parliament, and he had never heard any one else so advise.

Lastly, the Secretary took up the more personal crimes of which he was charged: " As to my having vast grants from the King, Tis true I have a very indulgent Master, who hath been very kind to me, yet till of late I never got any thing. I have now an estate given me but for my own life: the Reversion is to others,82 and what I have is not halfe enuf to support the honor and dignity the King hath given me. I never had any Mony out of the treasury of England. Ten thousand pound I had out of Ireland, and twas payd me only as what I had for Secret Service. The Estate given me in Ireland was forfeited; it is about 1000 *l*. a yeare,lI am sure not 1100 *l*.

" As to my engrossing all affairs, those that know me, know tis not my humor so to do, and that I would thinke my selfe happy could I with Convenience retire." "

52 That is, to his son-in-law, the Earl of Euston. See p. 102, footnote 18.

88 The fullest version of Arlington's defense, from which the quotations in the text have been made, is in the Additional MSS., 28045, f- 21 ? It has been in part abstracted in the *Cal. St. P., Dom.,* 1673-7675, p. 103. It follows closely though more

amply the summary in Grey's *Debates,* Jan. 15, 1673/4, and the account in Cobbett's *Parliamentary History,* IV, col. 653-656.

The questions served to make clear that the Secretary was strongly entrenched behind the argument of collective ministerial responsibility, and could not be dislodged. He assured the House that the French alliance, the Stop on the Exchequer, the Declaration of Indulgence, the attack on the Smyrna fleet, and the recent prorogations of Parliament were measures in which the whole ministry agreed.84

By his speech Arlington made an impression entirely unlocked for in the House, of intelligence and capacity for affairs. Hitherto his participation in all the frivolities of the Court and his pandering to the King's mistresses had shown him in a disagreeable, and in some respects a mistaken light. Public opinion would have agreed with the Count de Grammont, that by means of his Spanish solemnity and his mysterious expression he " had given himself the character of a great politician ; and no one having leisure to examine him, he was taken at his word, and had been made minister and secretary of state, upon the credit of his own importance *".2* His speech before the Houselthe only one, apparently, that he had ever madelwon surprised recognition of mental qualifications that few had supposed he possessed.'8 It contained a large number ofimpeccable truths in the radiance of which certain reservations and imperfections passed unnoticed, and it struck a dignified mean between arrogance and servility. He had admitted his participation in every decision the government had taken, but denied a monopoly of authority by himself or any other man. He had not incriminated any one, for though Buckingham's name had several times been mentioned, it had not been in an accusing manner, whatever the intention. He had shown respect for the House, but he had maintained the prerogative. ,

84 Additional MSS., 28045, f a1.

" *Memoirs of the Court of Charles II by Count Grammont,* 143.

88 "... never man behaved liker a gentleman and a just servant to his master, and for his abilities showed himself worthy his master's choice of him to that place. Whereas he went in with the great ill impression the House had given them of his guilt, he came out with their great applause." (Co/. *St. P., Dom., 1673-1675,* p. 108, Sir Nicholas Armorer to Williamson.) " My Lord Arlington hath been these two days *sur le tapis.* He spoke yesterday to the House very long and very weli and with an Universal1 applause, for his Frankness and Generosity not lightly criminating others, with great decency towards the House, and yet without any servile Submissions . . . thus much I dare surely say, That though the two former Presedents may draw him into the Mischief, yet he will have in the worstof Events this Advantage of his Narrative, that his Enemies will Confess him much more fitting for the Charge he hath so long exercised then they had ever acknowledged before." (Additional MSS., 25123, f. 13, Jan. 16, 1673/4. Sec1etary Coventry to Sir Leoline Jenkins. Copy.) For the impression made by Arlington's speech, see also: Sheffield, *Works,* II, 85; *Essex Papers,* I, 163; *Cal. St. P., Dom., 1673-1675,* pp. 114, 119; *Letters to Sir Joseph Williamson,* II, 112, 115, 119; Burnet, *Own Time,* II, 44-45.

When the Earl had withdrawn, debate was resumed in a tone far more favorable to him than it had manifested before. Nevertheless, his enemies were not disposed to let him escape, and for that day and four days thereafter his case occupied a large share of the attention of the Commons. Finally on January 20, the House divided on the question whether an address should be made for his removal, and it was found that one hundred and sixty-six had voted against the address, and one hundred and twenty-seven for it." After this triumph, Arlington's friends did not oppose a motion to refer Gerrard's articles to a committee, to discover whether there were ground for an impeachment.'8 The history of the committee is soon told. OnFebruary 16 its chairman reported that the committee was uncertain of just what it was expected to do. The House thereupon instructed that it should report" What proof or inducements shall be offered to the Committee fit for an impeachment upon every head of the said Articles "." So the Committee continued its meetings but, as one observer remarked: " Haveing not hopes to ruine him they are very slow in meeteing, and when they doe 'tis onely to adjourne."" By this method of procedure they had accomplished nothing, made no report, when the session came to an end on February 24"

87 Grey, *Debates,* Jan. 20, 1673/4.

" *Ibid.; Letters to Sir Joseph Williamson,* II, 127, Jan. 23, 1673/4, Sir Gilbert Talbot to Williamson. Arlington's friends had not opposed an impeachment from the first, seeing the flimsiness of Gerrard's articles, and his inability to produce witnesses to prove them. (Grey, *Debates,* Jan. 16-20, 1673/4.)

The failure of the attempted impeachment cannot be ascribed wholly to the eloquence with which the Secretary defended himself. It happened that at the moment of the attack he enjoyed the support of two parties.The misbehavior of Buckingham had brought the King back to his old dependence upon Arlington," which gained for the latter the suffrages of all adherents of the Court. At the same time, he could count on every vote that Shaftesbury or Ormonde could influence. This almost accidental combination was the chief factor in the Secretary's preservation. Even during the five days of suspense he seems to have felt reasonably confident that he was saved," and was preoccupied with plans for the peace which it was no longer possible to defer.

" *Commons' Journal,* Feb. 17, 1673/4.

i *Letters to Sir Joseph Williamson,* II, 138, Feb. 6, 1673/4, Thomas Derham to Williamson.

41 The list of the committee does not show that Arlington was particularly favored in its formation. Of his friends, it included Sir Robert Carr, Mr. Howe, Sir John Talbott, Sir Charles Harbord, Lord Aungier, Sir Thomas Lyttelton, Sir Henry Capel, and William Harbord. Of his enemies, there were: Sir Thomas Meres, Sir George Downing, Colonel Birch, Lord Cornbury, Mr. Sacheverell, Sir Gilbert Gerrard, Sir Charles Wheeler, Mr. Thynne. There were, however, twenty others on the committee, whose attitude it is difficult to determine from Grey's *Debates,* or from personal or party associations. *(Commons' Journal,* Jan. 20, Jan. 26, Feb. 11, Feb. 17, 1673/4.) After the prorogation it was rumored that Arlington had induced the King to end the session because he feared the committee was about to report an impeachment. (Arch. Aff. Ktr., Angle- terre, 112, f. 37, March 8, 1674, N. S., Ruvigny to Louis XIV.) But from the evidence of a member of the committee it is probable that the prorogation forestalled a report to the House in Arlington's favor: " Had the Parliament sate longer I am confident the Committee who were to consider of the Articles against my Lord Arlington would have pronounced him innocent, to which they had a greate inclination

last night, but Sir Robert Carres modesty cooled it, for when it was moved and so well seconded that there was but very little opposition, Sir Robert cryed Adjourne; so they breake up and adjourned till Fryday." *(Letters to Sir Joseph Williamson,* II, 155, Feb. 24, 1673/4, Lord Aungier to Williamson.)

On January 22 Arlington announced to the French ambassador that the King of England must use all means to facilitate peace, and therefore could not refuse the conditions which the Marquis del Fresno was empowered to offer; he besought Ruvigny once more to obtain his master's consent to a separate peace.4 The ambassador hastened to the King, who soothedhim with the assurance that Fresno's proposals would not be accepted," but Arlington had not devoted in vain a lifetime of study to the character of Charles II. In two weeks the treaty of peace was signed.

" " Your Excellency will easily imagine how much wee have rejoyced in my Lord Arlington's good hap, for whom his Majesty was much con- cern'd, and as much displeased against the Duke of Buckingham for his behavior in the Houseldisclosing his councills, and telling things not agreeable to the truth." *(Letters to Williamson,* II, 130, Jan. 23, 1673/4, Sir Robert Southwell to Williamson.) " King sticks very close to Arlington." *(Essex Papers,* I, 164, Jan. 24, 1673/4, W. Harbord to Essex.)

48 The following is Arlington's dry account of what had taken place, written on January 19, to the ambassadors at Cologne: " Understanding I should be brought on the Tapis on thursday I gott leave of the House of Lords to goe to the House of Commons in person, where speaking long and ingenuously (as I thought) to them, great advantages are taken (as they call it) from my confession, which remains now my single charge in effect, after a long and well worded impeachment seemes in effect to be layd aside; my buisnesse alone hath entertayned the House, much to my grief, four full dayes, and candles having been refused to be brought in this evening, they have adjourned the debate till tomorrow when in all probability they will come to the decisive question, as they did in the Dukes of Buckingham and Loutherdales cases, wheather I shall be removed from His Majesties Counsells and presence." (State Papers, Archives, 221, p. 554, Jan. 19, 1673/4. Copy.)

44 Mignet, *Negotiations,* IV, 264.

The House of Commons had a share in this denouement. After relegating Arlington to the limbo of a committee, they had voted on January 24 to consider the state of the nation and the grievances arising from the war. To divert them from this fruitful theme, it was decided in the Committee of Foreign Affairsl perhaps on Arlington's suggestion, and certainly with his approvallto communicate to the Commons the conditions offered by the Dutch through Fresno, and to ask the advice of the House." On the twenty-seventh of January it was voted to advise his Majesty " to proceed in a Treaty with the said States in order to a speedy Peace ".7 Having asked for advice, Charles was obliged to take it, however reluctantly, and, the Spanish ambassador having powers from the States General to conclude, the Treaty of Westminster was signed on February 9. By it, England received the honor of the flag from Finisterre to Norway; permission for English subjects in Surinam to depart with their property; and eight hundred thousand crowns for the costs of the war. The regulation of the EastIndia trade was to be left to a joint commission which should meet at once in London. At the last moment Charles was inveigled by the Spanish ambassador and the Secretary of State into allowing the inclusion of an article by which each party agreed not to assist the other's enemies."

Ibid.

46 Arlington wrote to the plenipotentiaries at Cologne in regard to this step: " This communication hath wrought wonderfully upon the minds of both Houses, and disappointed the violentnesse of them for the present in the desires they had of pressing His Majesty strangely in many important points of the Government." (State Papers, Archives, 221, p. 568, Jan. 26, 1673/4. Copy.) I doubt if Arlington would have spoken so cordially if the proposal had been made by the Treasurer. But Lord Conway says: " This bone was cast before Parliament by advice of Treasurer, but I think Arlington broke the French Allyance." *(Essex Papers,* I, 168, Jan. 27, 1673/4, Conway to Essex.)

41 Grey, *Debates,* Jan. 27, 1673/4.

Thus ended the French alliance, and with it the rule of the Cabal. Clifford had died soon after his retirement; Buckingham was in disgrace; Shaftesbury had associated himself with the " country party " in opposition to the Court; Lauderdale's race was not yet run, in spite of the Commons' address, for as Secretary of State for Scotland he was practically out of reach of the English Parliament. Arlington, saved from Parliament and still trusted by the King, stood half- committed to both the Court and the Opposition, and must now choose between them.

M Mignet, *Negotiations,* IV, 269-271, Feb. 22, 1674, N. S., Ruvigny to Louis XIV; Burnet, *Own Time,* II, 48-49.

13

SECTION 13

CHAPTER XIII.
Retirement.

The joy with which the Treaty of Westminster was hailed in England celebrated not so much the return of peace as the abandonment of France. It pointed out emphatically the foreign policy which would be most grateful to the English people. It was a policy most grateful, too, to the Secretary of State, notwithstanding the fact that he had strayed very far from it in deference to the King's fondness for France. He was obliged to reckon with that fondness still, although it had been thwarted by the failure of the war and the revolt of Parliament. Charles would consent to no alliances with the enemies of France, and thus prohibited a return to the measures of the Triple Alliance as long as the war should last. The negotiations at Cologne had proved ineffectual, and in the spring of 1674 the powers recalled their ambassadors and prepared to go on with the war. Spain and the Emperor had joined the Dutch, who, thus strengthened, were by no means disposed to come to a peace before the aggressive power of France was humbled. To the difficult task of overcoming this disinclination Arlington now applied himself. As soon as England had withdrawn from the war, Charles offered his mediation to the belligerents; it was accepted gladly by France, politely by the

Prince of Orange, and reluctantly by Spain, who hoped to force Louis XIV to admit oncemore the limits of the Peace of the Pyrenees. Such a reception augured small success to the pacific efforts of England, and, indeed, no progress was made.

What could not be accomplished by formal mediation, Arlington attempted by way of personal influence with the Prince of Orange. Correspondence flourished between these two during the year 1674, but as each was trying to make use of the other without committing himself to anything, neither could extract the slightest satisfaction.1

In domestic politics the Secretary was steering a middle course with much delicacy and caution. By his abandonment of the Declaration of Indulgence and his friendship with Shaftesbury, and, most recently, by his opposition to the last prorogation of Parliament,' which had been resolved to check an agitation begun by Shaftesbury and Ormonde looking to the exclusion of papists from the succession, Arlington had attracted for the third time in his career the hatred of the Duke of York. This was further increased by the Secretary's official severity towards Catholics, practised, no doubt, to convince the world of his orthodoxy.2 York allied himself with two other enemies of the Secretary, the Lord Treasurer, now Earl of Danby, and the Duke of Lauderdale, and all three exerted themselves to ruin himwith the King. The most obvious course for Arlington would have been to associate himself frankly and completely with the Country Party. But that would mean his exclusion from place and from the Courtla possibility that he could not contemplate. He was too old a servant, and too old a courtier to dream of mastery save through the royal favor and weakness. Therefore he preferred to circumvent the Duke by secretly encouraging that aversion to a Catholic successor to the throne, already manifested by Shaftesbury's party. At the same time he promoted the interests of the two men whose pretensions and ambitions were most feared by the Duke of York, namely, the Prince of Orange and the Duke of Monmouth. Arlington argued constantly with the King the expediency of marrying the Princess Mary, York's eldest daughter, to William of Orange, regardless of the opposition of her father who saw in this an effort to strengthen the Prince's position as a possible heir to the throne.4 As for Monmouth, Arlington insinuated himself into the confidence of the vain, weak young man, and made a tool of him.'

1 See the Prince's letters to Arlington of this year, *Original Letters from William III,* 15, 21, 22, 23, 24.

1 Arlington's opposition to the prorogation was reported by Ruvigny. (Arch. Aff. $tr., Angleterre, 111, f. 232, Feb. 26, 1674, N. S., Ruvigny to Pomponne; *ibid.,* 112, ft". 38-39, March 8, 1674, N. S., the same to Louis XIV.)

8 For the Roman Catholic opinion of Arlington at this time, see the letters of William Throckmorton to Coleman (Hist. MSS. Comm., *13th Report,* part VI, pp. 51-66, MSS. of Sir W. Fitzherbert); also Coleman's letter to Father La Chaise, Sept. 29, 1675 *(Mr. Coleman's Two Letters to Monsieur I'Chaise,* 1-18).

4 " Et sur cela on ne double pas qu'il [Arlington] n'aye fait un plan de marier la Princesse Marie au Prince d'Orange, de ruiner cnsuitte Monsieur le Due d'lork et puis apres de gouverner cette Cour par la Hol- lande, ce qui luy sera aussi facile, estant asseure de ne trouver pas d'obstacle du coste du Roy son Maitre." (Arch. Aff. E"tr., Angleterre, 112, f. 149, April 16, 1674, N. S., Ruvigny to Louis XIV.)

" " Arlington makes his Interest amongst the discontented Members of Hous of Comons, and Duke [York] and Lodderdale are his mortal enemies." *(Essex Papers,* I, 228, May 19, 1674, Conway to Essex.) " There is a great feud between York and Monmouth: the whole Court backs Monmouth, and Arlington hath wisely made him head of the party wich wil give him credit now and in Parliament." *(Ibid.,* I, 261, Sept. 29, 1674, William Harbord to Essex.) " The Duke of York told Monmouth, who was with him in the evening, that he feared Arlington. Though he was about to quit the place of Secretary of State, for the white staff, he would still have some part in affairs; and, by his fearful councils, ruin the King's affairs, as he had already done. He knew it was his design toruin the good understanding between them. Monmouth answered, that he could not believe he had such evil intentions, else he would have nothing to do with him. The Duke of York made him suitable returns and parted; conjuring him, at the same time, to have a care of Arlington's practices." (Macpherson, *Original Papers,* I, 73, July 17, 1674.)

The French ambassador's comment on these circumstances and their bearing on foreign affairs is of considerable interest: " It is certain ", he wrote his master, " that the Earl of Arlington is entirely devoted to the interests of the Prince of Orange, not only against those of France, but also against those of his master, who cannot be persuaded of it because, being informed thereof only by the declared enemies of that minister, he cannot believe them in the least when they talk to Arlington's disadvantage. That is why they say nothing more about him to the King, and leave him full liberty to say anything he pleases to his master without any contradiction from them; so that this minister, supported by the Duke of Monmouth who has great influence over the spirit of the King, his father, and by ladies and courtiers who live and breathe solely for money, is in a way to succeed in whatever he undertakes. His declared enemies, who are the Duke of York, the Lord Treasurer, and the Duke of Lauder- dale, know this well, and therefore are obliged to seek friends in Parliament in order not to lack protection in case of necessity. These three persons talk to me every day of the understanding which Arlington has with the rebels in Parliament, and of the correspondence he maintains with the Prince of Orange, with whom, since the peace of England, he keeps Silvius, who is known by all to be the creature of that Prince; and this without order from the King, his master. The trio urge me often to speak of it to the King. But I believethis advice is given out of a desire for vengeance, rather than for the welfare of your Majesty's service."' In September, 1674, Arlington carried out a step he had long been meditating: he resigned the Secretaryship of State which he had held for twelve years, and received instead the white staff of Lord Chamberlain of the Household. The change was at once a relief and a worry to him. He was tired of the drudgery of the secretaryship, which had of late become increasingly burdensome by reason of his failing health. On the other hand, the place of Lord Chamberlain, though of greater dignity, would remove him from daily touch with foreign affairs, of which he did not propose to lose control, and perhaps from that constant intercourse with the King which had been the means of his success.7 He kept the matter under reflection for two years,8 hesitating at the last because Williamson, on whom he had arranged to devolve the secretaryship, now showed signs of defection to the camp of Danby and Lauderdale.' It is possible that he would have been glad to withdraw from the bargain, had he not been too far engaged; certainly his friends were rather surprised when he actually relinquished the signet.

Arch. Aff. $tr., Angleterre, 113, ff. 20-21, Aug. 13, 1674, N. S., Ru- vigny to Louis XIV.

1 In the summer of 1673 Arlington spoke of the proposed change to Colbert, wh0, in his report to Pomponne, made the comment: " . . . ce Ministre espere avec beaucoup de raison que le Roy son Maitre luy con- servera la principale direction des affaires." *(Ibid.,* 107, f. 94, July 10, 1673, N. S.

Williamson, writing to Arlington about the secretaryship on July 10, 1673, refers to "that great goodnesse your Lordship has been pleased to expresse for mee, in the overtures of the last winter to my Lord Chamberlain upon this matter "lwhich dates the beginning of negotiations for the change of place. (State Papers, Archives, 224, p. 171. Copy.)

'*Essex Papers,* I, 236, June 15, 1674, Conway to Essex; *ibid.,* I, 242, July 16, 1674, Francis Godolphin to Essex; Evelyn, *Diary,* July 22, 1674.

If the Duke of York fancied that this change would make Arlington less troublesome to him, he was speedily undeceived. One day in the early autumn, the new Lord Chamberlain ventured to suggest to him that the Dutch ambassador, Odyke, Lady Arlington's brother, was restrained from proposing the marriage of the Princess Mary to the Prince of Orange solely by his fear of the Duke's displeasure. James responded in a fashion that could leave no doubt of his displeasure, and Arlington deemed it wise to say no more to him." But with the King he succeeded better. Yielding to his arguments, Charles agreed to send Arlington to Holland on a secret mission: he was to sound the Prince as to the terms of peace that would content the allies, and to discover the nature and aims of certain intrigues in Scotland, in which William had apparently been dabbling.11 If the Prince seemed disposed to satisfy the King in these matters, a hint might be dropped that an offer for the hand of the Princess Mary would not be unacceptable to the King and the Duke. Out of consideration for his brother, whom he forced to give his consent to this overture, Charles joined the Earl of Ossory with Arlington, and entrusted the more delicate topic to him."

The secret of their going was well kept until the day before the party left London, when the Duke of York confessed mournfully to Ruvigny that he had beenobliged to agree to the match." The ambassador, who had hitherto believed that the purpose of the mission was simply to discuss the conditions of peace, sought out the King to reproach him with a deceit which could not fail to awaken suspicion in the mind of Louis XIV. But Ruvigny's anger was mild compared to that of Lauderdale and Danby, who now learned of the journey for the first time: " The Duke of Lauderdale and the Lord Treasurer are exasperated in the highest degree because their master has kept this journey a secret from them. The latter could not restrain himself from complaining to his master, saying that it was very unkind to good and faithful servants to see that a man who had ill served him, enjoyed his confidence to their prejudice."" Thus assailed, Charles tried to please both parties: he would not renounce the embassy, but. to Arlington's deep disgust, he added Lord Lati- mer, the Treasurer's son, to the party." As Latimer was given no part in the negotiation, the Lord Chamberlain had no difficulty in recognizing that his mission was to report all that went on at the Hague to the Treasurer and his colleagues.1"

10 Arch. Aff. for., Angleterre, 113, f. 102, Sept. 24, 1674, N. S., Ruvigny to Louis XIV.

11 It was supposedlnot without reasonlthat the Prince was in correspondence with a party in Scotland hostile to the Duke of Lauderdale. See Lingard's *History of England,* IX, 254-255, and a confused account by Burnet, *Own Time,* II, 64-65; als0, "A Coppy of Mr. Castares examination, Oct. *3,* '74 ". in the Carte MSS., 222, f. 192.

12 Clarke, *James 11,* I, 501.

The envoys had no written instructions, and in order to convince the world that their journey was entirely unofficial, and purely a family affair, the Countess of Arlington, her daughter, the little Countess of Euston, her brother, Odyke, and her sister, Charlotte of Beverwaert, were of the party. They left London on November 10, and made a tempestuous voyage to Holland. The Prince hastened to the Hague as soon as he heard of their arrival, and, eager to learn the extent of their errand, displayed the utmost affability, supping every night at Odyke's house, where Arlington was lodged. The first conference, at which no one was present save the Prince and Arlington, consisted chiefly of an interchange of compliments and an agreement to explain all grievances that might have interrupted the confidence properly existing between the King of England and his nephew." The Prince consented reluctantly to this " battle " as he called it, or *esclaircissement* as Arlington called it, to which the second conference was devoted. The Earl's rehearsal of the wrongs which had induced his master to enter the war now happily ended for England, was received drily enough, but in the end the Prince professed himself satisfied. Then " in the strain of a governour", as Burnet says," particularly annoying to William, Arlington took him to task for lending countenance to disaffected men in Scotland. The Prince admitted that during the war he might have encouraged any proposals likely to lead to the withdrawal of England from the French alliance, but denied having been drawn into anything of the sort since the Treaty of Westminster. When the interview ended, Arlington was entirely confident of the Prince'sgood-will and docility, and did not realize that he had merely exasperated him.10

18 Mignet, *Negotiations,* IV, 323-324.

"Arch. Aff. $tr., Angleterre, 113, f. 184, Nov. 19, 1674, N. S., Ru- vigny to Louis XIV.

18 *Ibid.,* 113, f. 200, Nov. 22, 1674, N. S., the same to Pomponne. See also Temple's letter to Danby, evidently written in response to a request for information as to the nature of the embassy. (Temple, *Works,* IV, 60-62, Dec. 4, 1674, N. S.)

"Arch. Aff. Etf., Angleterre, 113, f. 200, Nov. 22, 1674, N. S., Ru- vigny to Pomponne.

17 Additional MSS., 32o94, f. 325 *et seq.,* Nov. 14/24, 1674, Arlington to Charles II. (Copy.)

18 *Own Time,* II, 71. The Prince said afterwards to Temple that Arlington was arrogant and insolent, as one who deals with a child. (Temple, *Works,* II, 299.)

That same afternoon Arlington received a visit from the Grand Pensionary of Holland, Fagel, who had in his pocket the project of an offensive and defensive alliance between the United Provinces and England, with the proviso that it should not apply to the current war with France. Arlington was obliged to excuse himself from discussing it for lack of power, but he did not decline all commerce with the idea, which did not displease him. He took a copy of the project home with him to England.20

In a third conference with the Prince, Arlington endeavored to persuade him of the advisability of accepting moderate conditions of peace. William finally agreed to name terms that he thought would be satisfactory to his allies, but they conceded so little to France that Arlington could build no hopes upon them, though he believed they might be used to extract counter-proposals from Ruvigny.21

The Earl of Ossory's negotiation was not so unqualified a success as both he and Arlington had expected. Ossory was an honest, simple-hearted fellow, ill-suited to the diplomacy of that or any other day. He did not understand that there was a necessary connection between his errand and Arlington's, and having no written instructions to guide him, transacted the affair with soldierly directness. The Prince, by accident or design, afforded him an opening by the turn he gave the conversation, and Ossory then told him that his pretension to the Princess's hand would be well received by the King and the Duke of York. But William feared that some trap underlay this offer. He knew that the Duchess of York was with child at the time; if she bore a son, the Princess Mary would no longer be presumptive heir to the crown. He professed all imaginable gratitude for so great an honor and the liveliest desire to avail himself of it at the earliest possible moment, but at present he was so involved in affairs relating to the war, that he could not make the journey to England to assure himself that his person was not displeasing to the Princess. Thus he adjourned the matter so skilfully that Ossory never suspected the evasion, and always insisted that the Prince accepted the proposal with joy.22

M " Wee are, My Lord of Ossory and myselfe the most deceived men in the World, if the Prince bee not in every degree (I ought to say) much more desirous of Your Majesties good will and affection then you can bee of his duty and zeale to your Person, Government and Service." (Additional MSS., 32094, f. 325, Nov. 14/24, 1674, Arlington to Charles II.)

20 There is a copy of the project in the handwriting of Williamson in the Record Office. (Treaty Papers, 48, " Account of the Project as proposed by Holland to Lord Chamberlain 1674 etc.") The King, under the eye of Ruvigny, would have nothing to do with the project, and said Arlington had done wrong to accept it. (Mignet, *Negotiations,* IV, 327.)

21 The Prince suggested as the basis of a treaty that France restore Franche Comte to Spain, and exchange Charleroi, Ath, and Oudenarde for Aire and St. Omer. Maestricht should be handed over to France after the demolition of its fortifications. (Additional MSS., 32094, ff. 329-331, Nov. 24-27, 1674, Arlington to Charles II.) Conditions such as these were certain to be regarded as insulting by Louis XIV.

But the King and his brother understood the meaning of William's reply without difficulty, and were annoyed that Ossory had gone so far with so little encouragement from the Prince." This rebuff and the meagre results of Arlington's efforts to manage the stubborn, reserved young Dutchman, gave the Treasurer and his friends opportunity to condemn theconduct of the envoys emphatically to the King.24 There was ample time for this, because the return of the party was delayed by contrary winds so long that the ministers began to suspect that there might be some part of the Lord Chamberlain's errand yet concealed from them. " Lord Arlington has not yet returned ", wrote Ruvigny. " It is impossible that his overlong sojourn at the Hague should not give rise to much suspicion. The King has declared to me that if he had been in his place, he would have returned long ago."-" Evidently Charles was aware that he was slipping into the hands of Arlington's enemies. It was not until January 6 that the envoys presented themselves at Whitehall to kiss the King's hand.

22 Carte MSS., 22o, f. 472, Nov. 1674, Ossory to the Duke of York; Carte, *Life of Ormonde,* bk. VII, par. 16o-166. a Mignet, *Negotiations,* IV, 326.

At first Arlington's credit with his master seemed entirely undiminished by his absence and the failure of his negotiation at the Hague. Charles was apathetically trying to keep the power of the rivals at balance, in spite of their mutual hatred, and was carefully impartial in the division of his confidence between the Treasurer and Lauderdale on one side, and Arlington on the other. But it was a difficult program to maintain, for he had nohelp in it from any of the three." Arlington, spoiled by his long supremacy in the King's regard, could ill endure such an arrangement, and his revolt disturbed the equilibrium to his own disadvantage. This began to appear during the session of Parliament which took place in the spring of 1675. In the House of Lords Arlington incurred the displeasure of the King by holding aloof from the Court party, though he was too timid to vote with the opposition led by Shaftesbury.17 In the Commons, where he could act less conspicuously, through his adherents, he promoted the resolution of a second address for the removal of the Duke of Lauderdale, and the introduction of articles of impeachment against Danby. " Tis a tryall of skill between Arlington and Treasurer with the malice of some members to either side to lett King see which of them hath bestinterest", declared one member.28 If this were so, Danby proved to have the best interest, for the impeachment failed, and its sole result was to make the King angrier with Arlington. Charles began to believe that the Chamberlain was in league with a faction of the Commons in favor of refusing supply as long as Danby was Treasurer, and that he no longer cared how the King's business went if he could but work his enemy's ruin.28 This simple conviction accomplished at one blow what the logic and persuasions of a succession of counsellors|Clarendon, Buckingham, Laud- erdale, York, and Danby|had been unable to effect: Arlington fell into disgrace. " Sire ", rejoiced Ru- vigny, " your Majesty will not be able to believe how low the credit of my Lord Arlington has fallen. The King speaks to him very little, and when that Minister says something to him, it is almost ignored ... the King treats him with such complete indifference that my Lord Arlington is greatly dejected by it, and, no longer participating in anything, is clearly in a sort of disgrace . . . The abasement of Lord Arlington is the cause of the elevation of the Lord Treasurer. He has at present the entire confidence of the King." 80

24 " The winde being contrary keeps our frends yet in Holland which will vex them the more when they heere how their actions are descanted upon by such as wish them lost in his Majesties opinion." (Carte MSS., 38, f. 226, Dec. 26, 1674, Sir George Lane to Ormonde.)

28 Arch. Aff. Etr., Angleterre, 115, ff. 20-21, Jan. 10, 1675, N. S., Ruvigny to Pomponne. It is not impossible that Arlington intentionally delayed his departure, hoping to obtain further satisfaction from the Prince of Orange, but he must have known that advantage would be taken of his absence, and his letters to Williamson sound as if he were anxious to return. On the fourth of December, he wrote that the party expected to sail at the beginning of the next week (State Papers, Holland, 197, f. 180) and on the twenty-fifth of that month, he explained that they were still detained by contrary winds: " I must this day wish you a merry Xmas, and that I my selfe were there to take my share of it, for Wee are sufficiently weary of this place." *(Ibid.,* 197, f. 273.)

M " Duke, Treasurer and that party made their braggs that they would resigne Arlington at his Returne; But King is very kinde to him, and tis wonderfull to see him shutt upp in the morning with Arlington severall hours, and the same day as many with Duke, Treasurer and Lodder- dale". *(Essex Papers,* I, 286, Jan. 16, 1674/5, W. Harbord to Essex.)

" but for all Duke, Treasurer, Lodderdale, Ranelagh, and all

that party, I finde that Arlington keeps his post." *(Ibid.,* I, 287, Jan. 19, 1674/5. the same to the same.) " Je crois qu'il n'y a jamais eu une plus forte haine que celle qui est entre ces trois Ministres ", wrote Ruvigny of Danby, Lauderdale, and Arlington. (Arch. Aff. Etr., Angle- terre, 115, f. 51, Jan. 21, 1675, to Louis XIV.)

" When a motion to thank the King for the speech from the throne was contested in the House of Lords, Arlington tried to carry water on both shoulders by proposing a modified vote of thanks. But the compromise was rejected, and a vote of thanks in the usual form was finally carried. " Sa Majeste Britanique m'a paru assez mal satisfaite de la proposition du temperament, ne l'imputant toutes fois qu'a la timidite naturellc de son Ministre." *(Ibid.,* 115, f. 204, April 25, 1675, N. S., Ruvigny to Pom- ponne.) If the King expressed his displeasure to Arlington, it is not surprising that he did not participate in the most exciting contest of the session over the bill imposing a new test, amounting to an oath of passive obedience, on all persons in public employment. The names of all peers active on one side or the other are to be found in an anonymous pamphlet attributed to Shaftesbury, *Letter from a Person of Quality to his Friend in the Country,* London, 1675 *(State Tracts).* Arlington's name is not mentioned at all.

Seeing no prospect of supply, Charles prorogued Parliament on the ninth of June, and tried to establish lif not peacelat least a truce among the ministers. His irritation at Arlington had somewhat evaporated, and he was again anxious to reconcile him with the now all-powerful Danby. Therefore he appealed to Sir William Temple, whom he supposed to be onfriendly terms with both men, to persuade them to lay aside their quarrel, explaining that it had done great harm in Parliament. Temple, though he now despised Arlington as much as he had once admired him, obediently made the attempt. Danby agreed readily to a reconciliation, being convinced that he had little to fear from the Lord Chamberlain. But Arlington could not trust the disinterestedness of Temple whom he looked upon as the Treasurer's man, and so answered him only with reproaches of ingratitude and disloyalty, which that gentleman was not one to endure patiently, and so the mediation ended.81

"*Essex Papers,* I, 319, April 17, 1675, W. Harbord to Essex.

28 Charles expressed this opinion to Temple, after the prorogation in June, 1675. (Temple, *Works,* II, 316.)

80Arch. Aff. for., Angleterre, 116, ff. 46-47, May *23,* 1675, N. S., Ru- vigny to Louis XIV.

Furious with all the world, Arlington now withdrew to the seclusion of Euston, where he spent the summer of 1675 drearily enough. But this period of rustication, sulking, and gout yielded to a more reasonable frame of mind when he returned to town in the first week of October. Though he found himself out of affairs, he claimed once more his place at Court, and dispensed the princely hospitality of Arlington House n to his friends, gathering at his board all the lions whose roar could be heard in London. He made friends with the newly arrived Spanish ambassador, and entertained the " pushing, talking, pressing " Van Beuningen who was once more the representative of the States. " He would join the Devil to ruin an enemy whom he cannot endure", exclaimed Ruvigny." The King received Arlington with easy kindness, but treated him ratheras an old friend and servant than as a minister, a role to which the proud man could not resign himself. " It seems that his sojourn of three months in the country has somewhat disconcerted him, and that he returns to a Court which he no longer understands ... I know well that the members of the Council 2 are working to deprive him of the confidence of their master, and that such a thing may come about in appearance. But I am not sure what the real outcome will be, when there is so much tenderness for a minister who does not lack industry, and who is a good courtier."8! Thus Ru- vigny, and later in the autumn he assured the Marquis de Pomponne: " I shall not fail to observe the conduct of my Lord Arlington, who hurls himself at all doors in the effort to re-enter affairs." M

81 Temple, *Works,* II, 316-317.

82 Arlington House had been recently built to replace Goring House, destroyed by fire in 1674. In 1702 the widowed Countess of Arlington sold the place to John Sheffield, marquis of Buckingham, who tore down the house and erected the present Buckingham Palace on the site. (Wheatley, *London Past and Present,* II, 130, 566.)

88 Arch. Aff. $tr., Angleterre, 117, f. 57, Nov. 4, 1675, N. S., Ruvigny to Pomponne.

One of the doors which the Lord Chamberlain attempted was the King's weakness for beautiful women, on which Arlington had experimented in past years. Knowing that Louise de la Kerouaille, duchess of Portsmouth, would always use her influence to continue his exclusion from power, Arlington tried to effect a change of mis- tresses by encouraging the beautiful Duchess of Mazarin to come to England." But, thoughCharles welcomed the adventurous lady to his Court and enjoyed her society, the power of the Duchess of Portsmouth was not impaired.

84 Ruvigny says *conseil,* but it is probably the Cabinet, or Committee of Foreign Affairs, that he has in mind.

86 Arch. Aff. Etr., Angleterre, 117, f. 29, Oct. 14, 1675, N. S., Ruvigny to Pomponne.

"*Ibid.,* 117, f. 92, Nov. 21, 1675, N. S., the same to the same.

87 Arlington's participation in this intrigue rests mainly on the testimony of Ruvi- gny, who says that Arlington's ambitious friend, Ralph Montagu, who was also in the

Duchess of Portsmouth's disfavor, rode ten miles out of London to meet the Duchess of Mazarin. " Ce qui est vray est que Montaigu agit de son chef, et que si quelqu'un est de sa confidence, c'est Mylord Arlington, qui n'est pas mieux que luy dans les bonnes graces de la favorite, et qui peut estre voudroient bien tous deux ensemble se servir d'un si beau moyen pour la disgracier." *(Ibid.,* 117, f. 132, Jan. 2, 1676, N. S., Ruvigny to Pomponne.) On Feb. 27, N. S., Ruvigny wroteagain that Arlington was promoting the fortunes of the new beauty. *(Ibid.,* 117, f. 204.) Evelyn, supping at the Lord Chamberlain's on Sept. 6 of this year, met the Duchess of Mazarin there. *(Diary,* Sept. 6, 1676.)

Another opportunity promised fair in the autumn of 1677, when the Prince of Orange made a long-deferred visit to England. He had written a very friendly letter to Arlington informing him of his coming, and assuring him of his regard." In the mind of the recipient this conjured up a pleasant prospect of basking in the confidence of the popular Prince, and when William joined the Court at Newmarket in October, the Lord Chamberlain essayed to establish a sort of proprietorship over him. But the Prince observedland perhaps had long knownlwho was first minister of England, and he wooed Danby with a graciousness that was wormwood to Arlington, and nectar to Sir William Temple looking on." The Prince was, to be sure, very kind to the unhappy man, and with the King and the Duke of York honored him by passing a night at Huston Hall. He even interested himself in trying to end the old feud between Arlington and the Treasurer, but, although Danby again showed willingness, Arlington clung stubbornly to his grudge and would not be placated." He was very bitter because the Prince'smarriage to the Duke of York's daughter, which he had tried to bring about three years ago, was suddenly resolved while William was in London without consulting, or even informing him.41

88 " I hope to have the Honour of seeing you there, and to dispel those Impressions, as my Lord Ossory tells me, some People have made upon you, That I was not so much your Friend and Servant as I always have been. It will not be long before I shall have an Opportunity to assure you to the contrary by word of mouth, desiring you to continue me still in your friendship." *(Original Letters from King William III,* 53, Sept. 20, 1677, N. S.)

88 Temple, *Works,* II, 431.

40 Hist. MSS. Comm., *MSS. of the Marquis of Ormonde,* new series, IV, 385, Nov. 13, 1677, Sir Robert Southwell to Ormonde.

During the year 1678, Arlington's influence at Court reached lowest ebb. The Duchess of Cleveland, who had been two years in France with her sons, considered the moment had come when the match between the young Duke of Grafton and Arlington's daughter might easily be broken off, and she returned to England for that purpose, though, as one observer said of Arlington, " he is so little in favor that it is believed that might be done at the distance she keeps." " When her Grace went back to France again in June, she was happy in the belief that all was arranged to her satisfaction.8 The marriage service had, of course, been performed, but the children were so young at the time that it was but a formal betrothal.

It is not surprising that this was the year when Arlington's Whigism was most rampant. He was grown, writes Temple, " out of all credit and confidence with the

King, the Duke, and Prince of Orange; and thereby forced to support himself by intrigues with the persons most discontented against my Lord Treasurer's Ministry, whose greatness he so much envied ". This means that he acted with Shaftesbury's party through the stirring sessions of Parliament that took place in this year, and that he watched with joy the impeachment of Danby on the charge of criminal correspondence withFrance, and may have helped his friend Montagu to plan it. But the association with this party was purely for the sake of ruining the Treasurer, and bespoke no approval of the political uses to which Shaftesbury turned the pretended Popish Plot, or of the attempt to exclude from the succession the Duke of York whom he seems now to have preferred to the Prince of Orange." When in January, 1679, Charles was finally obliged to dismiss his unpopular Treasurer, Arlington fell away from the Country Party, and never afterwards interested himself in its designs, though the continuance of his friendship with Shaftesbury caused him to be looked upon as of the same political persuasion."

41 Temple, *Works,* IV, 337, Nov. 1677, Sir William Temple to his father, Sir John Temple.

a Cal. St. P., Dom., 1677-1678, p. 694.

" Hist. MSS. Comm., *MSS. of the Marquis of Bath,* II, 162, June 4, 1678, Henry Savile to the Earl of Rochester.

Temple, *Works,* II, 492.

The fall of Danby did not throw the control of affairs into Arlington's hands as the latter had hoped; indeed, he had no more power than before, but he could bear it now that his enemy was in worse case. The King was kind to him again, and in November, 1679, gratified the dearest wish of his heart by commanding the remarriage of the Duke of Graf ton to the Lady Isabella Bennet. She was still but a child-bride, being but twelve years old. Her devoted admirer, Sir John Evelyn, was no more reconciled to the match than he had been seven years ago: " A sudden and unexpectedthing ", he wrote, " when everybody believed the first marriage would have come to nothing; but, the measure being determined, I was privately invited by my Lady, her mother, to be present. I confess I could give her little joy, and so I plainly told her, but she said the King would have it so, and there was no going back. This sweetest, hopefullest, most beautiful child, and most virtuous too, was sacrificed to a boy that had been rudely bred, without anything to encourage them but his Majesty's pleasure. I pray the sweet child find it to her advantage, who, if my augury deceive me not, will in few years be such a paragon, as were fit to make the wife of the greatest Prince in Europe!... My love to my Lord Arlington's family and the sweet child made me behold all this with regret, though as the Duke of Grafton affects the sea, to which I find his father intends to use him, he may emerge a plain, useful and robust officer; and, were he polished, a tolerable person; for he is exceeding handsome, by far surpassing any of the King's other natural issue." "

45 York had quarreled with Danby in 1675 over the latter's design to obtain money from Parliament by showing great severity towards Catholics. Since then James had treated Arlington with more amiability, though he trusted him no more than before. (See *Essex Papers,* I, 289, Jan. 23, 1674/5. W. Harbord to Essex; Burnet, *Own Time,* II, 73.) The Earl of Ailesbury, who had a personal reason for disliking Arlington, and

says much against him, still admits: "... to do him justice, I believe he then stood firm to his Royal Highness as to the succession." *(Memoirs, I,* 4I-)

48 The Earl of Dartmouth, in his notes to Burnet's *Own Time,* says of Arlington that he always professed himself of the Whig party. *(Own Time,* I, 181, footnote I.)

This satisfied Arlington's ambition, and thereafter he contented himself with the dignity of his place and a nominal participation in the King's counsels. " Hitherto ", wrote Sir Robert Southwell to Ormonde, " my Lord Chamberlain makes no progress, and while he has still enemies in power he is very well contented that they will let him alone with his staff." K In years he was not an old man, but like many others whose lives were spent in the Court of the Restoration, he was early worn out. He was more interested in hiscollection of pictures, in the hawks that Ormonde sent him from Ireland, in the milk diet as a cure for the gout, than in all the worries and disputes that absorbed the Council. He spent as much time as he could in the quiet of Euston, and took pleasure in adorning and perfecting his estate that it might descend in order and beauty to the Duchess of Grafton. His tenants were well cared for; his servants contented. In place of the decayed church he had found on the estate, he sub stituted one of stone, because, as he told Evelyn, " his heart smote him that, after he had bestowed so much on his magnificent palace there, he should see God's House in the ruine it lay in ".' He could not wholly divest himself of his manner of patronage even when considering the case of the Almighty God. His debts worried him a little, but not greatly. When he was too gouty to hunt or hawk with his guests, or the time hung heavy on his hands, he had Milton's nephew, Edward Phillips, read to him in the great library at Euston.'0

47 Evelyn, *Diary,* Nov. *6,* 1679.

Hist. MSS. Comm., *MSS. of the Marquis of Ormonde,* new series, IV, 5o4, April 19, 1679, Sir Robert Southwell to Ormonde.

Arlington's neutrality in the political struggle for the exclusion of the Duke of York from the succession, gave him a peculiar position among the disputants in the latter years of Charles's reign. It was in the garden of Arlington House that the Duke of Monmouth took leave of his father when he was sent abroad." The Prince of Orange spent two nights under the Lord Chamberlain's roof when he came to England in 1681.82 The following year, when the Duke of York returned from his exile in Scotland, it was at Arlington Housethat he found the King and Queen awaiting him." A story was current that when Parliament met at Oxford in 1681, and an exclusion bill was again brought into the House, the King called Shaftesbury to him, and proposed that the Earl with two of his party join him in a conference, at which the King would likewise have two advisers, for the purpose of discovering whether some compromise acceptable to both might not be evolved. " My Lord Shaftesbury accepted the motion and desired to know the place which the King would needs refer to him, who thereupon said that he thought no place fitter than my Lord Chamberlain's lodgings. The King asked why there above all other places, and was answered, first, that it was the most indifferent place in the world, because my Lord Chamberlain was neither good Protestant nor good Catholic; and next, because there was the best wine, which was the only good thing that could be had from their meeting." "

40 Evelyn, *Diary,* Sept. 9, 1677. 80 *Ibid.,* Sept. 18, 1677.

51 Hist. MSS. Comm., *Jth Report,* p. 475, MSS. of Sir H. Verney, Bart., Sept. 29, 1679, John Verney to Sir R. Verney.

82 *Id., MSS. of the Marquis of Ormonde,* new series, VI, 113, July 30, 1681, R. Mulys to I .

When, later in the same year, Shaftesbury found himself a prisoner in the Tower, it was to Arlington that he turned as his " particular friend " to present a petition for his liberation and permission to betake himself to his plantation in Carolina. To the surprise of the Court, Arlington undertook this office: " The politicians of the coffee-houses discourse variously of this matter and those who love my Lord Chamberlain fear this may be his ruin, and will subject him to the revenge of the Duke of York and Ministers, without

"Id., MSS. of the Duke of Buccleuch, I, 337, May 27, 1682, Lord Hunsdon to the Duke of Albemarle.

M *Id., MSS. of the Marquis of Ormonde,* new series, VI, 6-7, March 25, 1681, Col. Edward Cookc to Ormonde.

whose knowledge he did it." TM But, perhaps because the petition was refused, James cherished no resentment.

The last five years of Arlington's life were serene, old-man's years. In 1680 the Earl of Ossory died, a loss that touched Arlington as no death before had ever touched him. In 1683, a son and heir was born to the Duchess of Grafton, " which Lord Arlington is so joy'd with that some says he will smother itt with kisses "." In 1685 occurred the King's death, a shock and sorrow to his old servant, who did not long survive him. James II had at once confirmed to Arlington the white staff of Lord Chamberlain,87 and he seems to have participated in the ceremonies of the coronation. In the journals of the House of Lords, it is recorded that the Earl of Arlington took the Oaths of Supremacy and Allegiance, and subscribed to the Declaration onMay 23." He attended the debates regularly until the Houses adjourned on July *2,* shortly after which he fell ill at Arlington House.

"i Hist. MSS. Comm., *MSS. of the Marquis of Ormonde,* new series, VI, 188, Oct. 11, 1681, Earl of Longford to Ormonde. See als0, Christie, *Life of Shaftesbury,* II, 419; Macpberson, *Original Papers,* I, 128-129.

" Hist. MSS. Comm., *nth Report,* part V, p. 81, MSS. of the Duke of Rutland, Nov. 6, 1683, G. Lady Chaworth to her brother, the Earl of Rutland. This child, Charles, the only issue of the marriage, became the second Duke of Grafton, from whom the present Duke is directly descended. The first Duke of Grafton, who seems to have been no more admirable than Evelyn fancied him, was among the first of the English nobility to join the Prince of Orange in 1688. He died in 1690, and his widow married again in 1698, Sir Thomas Hanmer. As Countess of Arlington in her own right, she was present at the coronation of George I. (Cokayne, *Complete Peerage,* Arlington title.) She seems to have been a person of rare virtue and sweetness, according to the following eulogy by her cousin, John Hervey, Lord Bristol: " Thursday, the beautiful Duchess of Grafton dyed at London; in justice to whose memory I can strictly averr, that in above fourty years time that I had the honour and happiness of her acquaintance, I never heard her say anything of any absent person, which, had they been present, they could have been in the least offended at." (Quoted from Lord Bristol's Diary, Feb. *7, 1723,* in the *Little Saxham Parish Registers,* 176.)

87 Evelyn, *Diary,* Feb. 17, 1685.

When he knew that there was no hope of recovery, he begged those around him to fetch a priest, and when they hesitated in astonishment, he repeated his wish, but, with a touch of his old caution, added: " Yet I will not have it knowne untill I am dead." So the priest was brought; the Earl confessed his sins as he knew them and was absolved. That same night, July 25, he died.89

The news of his conversion produced the sensation which Arlington had been glad to escape from the world without witnessing. The old rumor of his being at heart a Catholic had almost died out, and he had taken the Test with business-like regularity in the reign of Charles as well as in the present. Public opinion, with unbecoming flippancy, declared that he died a Roman Catholic to make his court to King James.'0 The King admitted to Pepys that, as to Arlington's inclinations, " he had known them long wavering, but from fear of losing his place, he did not think it convenient to declare himself." " Roger North is perhaps nearest the truth when he surmises that Arlington became terrified in the hour of deathlfor dying, as North says, is no Court trickland longed for the visible, palpable symbols of forgiveness and reconciliation which the Church of Rome affords.02 And yet, because he was a mancapable of living in entire detachment from his own beliefs and principles, the old story that had its origin at Fuentarabia may be right after all. Arlington's conscience could have accommodated itself easily to the necessity of bowing in the House of Rimmon, though for a lifetime.

Lords' Journal, May 23, 1685.

n Autobiography of Sir John Bramston, 204.

M Burnet, *Own Time,* I, 181, footnote 1 (by the Earl of Dartmouth.)

n Pepys repeated this to Evelyn, who records it in his diary, Oct. 2, 1685.

2 North, *Examen,* 29.

14

SECTION 14

BIBLIOGRAPHY.
PRINTED MATERIALS.

Ailesbury, see Bruce, Thomas.

Arlington, see Bebington, T.

Bate, F., *The Declaration of Indulgence. 1672. A Study in the Rise of Organised Dissent,* London, 1908. Explains the circumstances and results of the Declaration of 1662, penned by Bennet.

Beatson, R., *A Political Index to the Histories of Great Britain and Ireland,* 3 vols., London, 1806. Chiefly useful to this study for its discussion of the office of Secretary of State.

Bebington, T., *The Right Honourable the Earl of Arlington's Letters to Sir W. Temple, Bart.* (vol. I), *and to the several Ambassadors to Spain* (vol. II), 2 vols., London, 1701. Cited as *Arlington's Letters.* Purely official letters, and very uncommunicative, but of value in connection with Dutch and Spanish affairs.

Birch, Thomas, *The Court and Times of James the First,* 2 vols., London, 1848. Contains letters referring to Arlington's grandfather, Sir John Bennet.

Blok, P. J., *History of the People of the Netherlands,* translated by Ruth Putnam and O. A. Bierstadt, 5 vols., New York and London, 1898-1912. Of value for the study of England's relations with the Dutch.

Boase, C. W., *Oxford* (Historic Towns Series), London, 1887.

Bramston, Sir John, Autobiography of, edited by Lord Braybrooke (Camden Society), London, 1845. Contains an account of the circumstances of Arlington's death.

Brown, Thomas, *Miscellanea Aulica, or a Collection of State Treatises, never before publish'd,* London, 1702. Contains a great deal of information about Bennet's career previous to the Restoration, in letters addressed to him by Charles II and by Abraham Cowley; also some letters from Bennet to the Duke of Ormonde after the former became Secretary of State, chiefly about Irish affairs, and not very useful for this study.

[Bruce], Thomas, Earl of Ailesbury, Memoirs of, edited by H. H. Gibbs (Roxburghe Club), 2 vols., Westminster, 1890. Ailesbury had a personal grudge against Arlington, and is not a very reliable witness in his respect.

Burghclere, see Gardner, Winifred.

Burnet, Gilbert, *History of my Own Time,* edited by Osmund Airy, 2 vols., Oxford, 1897-1900. Useful more for its observations on Arlington's character and conduct, than for its facts, which are considerably jumbled.

Carte, Thomas, *The Life of James Duke of Ormonde . . . with an Appendix and a Collection of Letters, serving to verify the most material facts in the said History,* 6 vols., Oxford, 1851. Useful as to Arlington's relations with the Duke of Ormonde and the Earl of Ossory.

A Collection of Original Letters and Papers Concerning

the Affairs of England, from the Year 1641 to 1660, Found among the Duke of Ormonde's Papers, 2 vols., London, 1739. Contains a very little information about Bennet.

Cartwright, Julia (Mrs. Ady), *Madame, A Life of Henrietta, Daughter of Charles I, and Duchess of Orleans,* London, 1894. Contains letters from Charles II and one from Arlington to the Duchess of Orleans, which help to explain Arlington's conduct in 1669-1670.

[Charles II], *His Majesties Declaration to All His loving Subjects, Dec. 26, 1662.* Printed by John Bill and Christopher Barker, London, 1662. This is the Declaration of (prospective) Indulgence written by Bennet. It represents his political theories at that date.

Christie, W. D., *A Life of Anthony Ashley Cooper, First Earl of Shaftesbury, 2* vols., London, 1871. Valuable for the period of the Cabal, but written in a spirit very partial to Shaftesbury.

Clarendon, The Life of Edward, Earl of, in which is included a Continuation of his History of the Grand Rebellion, 2 vols., Oxford, 1857. Clarendon has much to say of Ben- net, particularly between the years 1660-1667, but he is too embittered to be a good witness.

Clarendon, State Papers collected by Edward, Earl of, 3 vols., Oxford, 1767-1786. Contains several letters written by Bennet from Spain previous to the Restoration. In the Supplement to vol. Ill is Clarendon's " Character of Sir Henry Bennet", very hostile to the subject.

Clarendon State Papers, Calendar of the, edited by O. Ogle, W. H. Bliss, and W. D. Macray, under the direction of H. O. Coxe, 3 vols., Oxford, 1872-1876. The Calendar has progressed no further than 1657, but affords some information about Bennet during his secretaryship to the Duke of York.

Clarke, J. S., *The Life of James II, 2* vols., London, 1816. The Duke of York had a long acquaintance with Bennet, but he is prejudiced, not only by his dislike of Bennet's personality, but also by his own narrow and bigoted nature.

Cobbett, William, *Parliamentary History of England from the Norman Conquest in 1066 to the Year 1803,* 36 vols., London, 1806-1820. The fourth volume is the only one used in the preparation of this essay.

Cokayne, G. E., *Complete Peerage,* London, 1910.

Mr. Coleman's Two Letters to Monsieur l'Chaise, London, 1678. Testifies to the detestation in which Roman Catholics held Arlington.

Coronae Carolinae Quadratura, sive Perpetuandi Imperii Carolini ex Quarto Pignore Felititer Suscepto, Oxford, 1638. Oxford verse, including a poem written by Bennet when a student in the University.

Courtenay, T. P., *Memoirs of the Life, Works and Correspondence of Sir William Temple, Bart.,* 2 vols., London, 1836. Particularly valuable for Arlington's connection with the conception of the Triple Alliance.

Dalrymple, Sir John, *Memoirs of Great Britain and Ireland,* 2 vols., with a third containing the Appendix, Edinburgh, 1771-1788. The Appendix consists of letters from the several French ambassadors in England to the French Court, and some of the letters of Charles II to the Duchess of Orleans. This publication has been largely superseded by Mignet's ampler one, but the two do not cover precisely the same ground.

Death Repeal'd by a Thankful Memoriall Sent from Christ- Church in Oxford, Celebrating the Noble Deserts of the Right Honourable Paule, Late Lord Vis-Count Bayning of Sudbury, etc., Oxford, 1638. Oxford verse, including a poem written by Bennet when a student in the University.

Dictionary of National Biography, The.

Essex Papers, 1672-1679, edited by Osmund Airy (Camden Society), London, 1890. These are intelligence letters written to the Earl of Essex, lord lieutenant of Ireland, by various correspondents. They contain much valuable information about factions at Court and in the ministry in the later years of Arlington's secretaryship.

D'Estrades, Lettrcs, Memoires et Negotiations de Monsieur le Comte, 9 vols., London, 1743. D'Estrades was Louis XIV's ambassador in England in 1660-1662, and his despatches reflect Bennet's rise to power.

Evelyn, Sir John, Diary and Correspondence of, edited by William Bray, 4 vols., London, 1850-1852. Evelyn was one of Arlington's few warm friends. He knew nothing of his political conduct, but a good deal of his social qualities.

Flos Britannicus Veris Novissimi Filiola Carolo et Mariae Nata XVII Martii, Anno 1636, Oxford, 1637. Oxford verse, including a poem written by Bennet when a student in the University.

Forneron, H., *Louise de Keroualle, Duchesse de Portsmouth,* Paris, 1886. Contains the story of Arlington's promotion of this favorite.

Foster, Joseph, *Alumni Oxonienses, 1500-1714,* Oxford, 1891. Contains the main facts of Bennet's life, and of the lives of several of his kindred.

Register of Admissions to Gray's Inn, 1521-1881 (Collectanea Genealogica), London, 1883. Miscellaneous information about Bennet's kindred, several of whom were members of Gray's Inn.

Foxcroft, H. C, *The Life and Letters of Sir George Savile, Bart., First Marquis of Halifax,* 2 vols., London, 1898. Contains a thorough account of the mission of Buckingham and Arlington to Holland in 1672.

Fruin, Robert, *Verspreide Geschriften,* edited by P. J. Blok, P. L. Muller, and S. Muller, 10 vols., the Hague, 1900-1905. In vol. IV, p. 338, is an article entitled " Willem III en zijn geheime Onderhandelingen met Karel II van Engeland in 1672 ", which supplements the English material on this subject in the Record Office at London.

Gardiner, Samuel Rawson, *History of the Great Civil War, 1642-1649,* 4 vols., London, 1893. Used for the background of Bennet's life during the War.

Gardner, Winifred, Lady Burghclere, *George Villiers, Second Duke of Buckingham, 1628-1687,* London, 1903. This book avoids politics as much as possible, and so has little value for this study.

Grammont, see Hamilton.

Green, M. A. E., *Letters of Queen Henrietta Maria,* London, 1857. Bennet is alluded to only twice in these letters.

Grey, Anchitell, *Debates of the House of Commons, from the Year 1667 to the Year 1694,* 10 vols., London, 1769. Besides furnishing an abstract of the proceedings of the House of Commons, the Debates contain much information about Arlington personally and politically.

Hamilton, A., *Memoirs of the Court of Charles II by Count Grammont,* edited by Sir Walter Scott (Bohn edition), London, 1891. Contains a somewhat malicious sketch of Arlington.

Hatton, Correspondence of the Family of, A. D. 1601-1704, edited by E. ,M. Thompson (Camden Society), 2 vols., London, 1878. These letters afford some miscellaneous information about Arlington from men who knew him well.

Historical Manuscripts Commission. *5th Report,* MSS. of the Duke of Sutherland. *7th Report,* MSS. of Sir H. Verney, Bart. *nth Report,* MSS. of the Duke of Leeds. *I2th Report,* MSS. of the Duke of Rutland. *I3th Report,* MSS. of Sir W. Fitzherbert, Bart.; MSS. of

Lieut.-Gen. Lyttelton-Annesley. *I5th Report,* MSS. of J. E. Hodgkin.*Report on the MSS. of the Duke of Buccleuch and Queens-*
berry, preserved at Montagu House, Whitehall, 3 vols.
Calendar of the MSS. of the Marquis of Ormonde, pre-
served at Kilkenny Castle, new series, 7 vols.
Calendar of the MSS. of the Marquis of Bath, preserved
at Longleat, 3 vols.

A series of letters to Arlington from Ralph Montagu when he was ambassador to France, which are printed with the .Montagu House Papers, are of some assistance to this study. The Ormonde MSS. are full of information about Arlington, and particularly valuable for the latter part of his life. The other Reports above mentioned contain but a few miscellaneous facts available for this study.

Hop, Cornells, and Vivien, Nicholaas, *Notulen gehouden ter Staten-Vergadering van Holland (1671-1675),* edited by N. Japikse, Amsterdam, 1903. Supplements the English accounts of the mission of Buckingham and Arlington to Holland in 1672.

Horti Carolini Rosa Altera, Oxford, 1640. Oxford verse, including a poem written by Bennet when a student in the University.

Japikse, N., *De Verwikkelingen tusschen de Republiek en Engeland van 1660-1665,* Leiden, 1900. A comprehensive study of Anglo-Dutch relations previous to the outbreak of the war in 1665.

Journal of the House of Commons.

Journal of the House of Lords.

Jusserand, J. J., *A French Ambassador at the Court of Charles the Second,* London, 1892. This book, which is based on the despatches of the Count de Comenge, deals with the society, rather than with the politics, of the English Court, and so is of little value for this study.

Kennet, White, *A Complete History of England,* vol. Ill, London, 1706. Contains a muddled story about Bennet at Fuentarabia.

A Register and Chronicle, Ecclesiastical and Civil, from

the Restoration of King Charles II, London, 1728. Of very slight value for this study.

Killigrew, Thomas, *The Prisoners and Claratilla, Two Tragae-Comedies,* London, 1641. Contains a prefatory poem by Bennet.

Lefevre-Pontalis, A., *John de Witt ...* or *Twenty Years of a Parliamentary Republic,* translated by S. E. and A. Stephenson, 2 vols., London, 1885. Contributes to an understanding of Anglo-Dutch relations during Arlington's secretaryship.

Lingard, John, *The History of England from the First Invasion by the Romans to the Accession of William and Mary in 1688,* 10 vols., London, 1849. Used for the general background of the reign of Charles II.

Lister, T. H., *Life and Administration of Edward, First Earl of Clarendon,* 3 vols., London, 1837-1838. In the third volume several important letters from Bennet to Ormonde, taken from the Carte MSS., are printed.

Little, Francis, *A Monument of Christian Munificence,* edited by C. D. Cobham, Oxford and London, 1871. Affords a little information about Bennet's family.

Little Saxham Parish Registers, 1559-1850, edited by S. H. A. H., Woodbridge, 1901. The entry of Bennet's baptism is given together with much information about his mother's family.

Longin, E., *Un Diplomate Franc-Comtois, Frangois de Lisola,* Dole, 1900. Explains the position of the Imperial envoy at the time of the formation of the Triple Alliance.

Lysons, Daniel, *An Historical Account of those Parishes which are not described in the Environs of London,* London, 1800. Contains information about the parish of Harlington, and about the Bennets' connection with it.

Macpherson, James, *Original Papers Containing the Secret History of Great Britain from the Restoration to the Accession of Hannover,* 2 vols., London, 1775. The first volume contains *Extracts from the Life of James II as Written by Himself,* in which Arlington is frequently mentioned.

Madan, Falconer, *Oxford Books, a Bibliography of Printed Works Relating to the University and City of Oxford or Printed or Published there,* vol. II, Oxford, 1912. Through this book I was able to find the poems written by Bennet while he was a student in the University.

Magalotti, Lorenzo, *Travels of Cosmo the Third, Grand Duke of Tuscany, through England, during the Reign of King Charles the Second (1669),* London, 1821. Arlington was one of the Duke's entertainers, and is several times mentioned in this account.

Marvell, Andrew, The Complete Works of, edited by A. B. Grosart, 4 vols., London, 1875. Marvell was a political opponent of Arlington, and is always very savage in his criticisms of the Secretary of State.

Mavidal, J., *Memoires du Marquis de Pomponne, Ministre et Secretaire d'Etat au Departement des Affaires Etran- geres,* Paris, 1860. Not of very much importance for this study.

Mazarin, Lettres du Cardinal, ou Von voit le Secret de la Negotiation de la Paix des Pirenees, 2 vols., Amsterdam, 1745. Contains a little interesting information about Bennet when he was at Fuentarabia.

Mignet, F. A. M., *Negotiations relatives a la Succession d'Es- pagne sous Louis XIV,* 4 vols., Paris, 1835-1842. Many of the despatches of the French ambassadors in England are printed in this work, and furnish very important information about Arlington, particularly in connection with foreign affairs.

Miscellanea Aulica, see Brown, Thomas.

Miscellanea Genealogica et Heraldica, edited by J. J. Howard, new series, vol. Ill, London, 1880. Affords some information about the family of Bennet's mother.

Musarum Oxoniensium Charistcria pro Serenissima Regina Maria Recens e Nixus Laboriosi Discrimine recepta, Oxford, 1838. Oxford verse, including a poem written by Bennet when a student in the University.

Nicholas Papers, The, edited by G. F. Warner (Camden Society), 3 vols., London, 1886-1897. Throws some light on Bennet's career previous to the Restoration.

North, Roger, *Examen, or an Enquiry into the Credit and Veracity of a Pretended Complete History,* London, 1740. Of very slight value for a biography of Arlington.

Parliament, Return of the Names of every Member returned to, 1213-1885, 4 vols., London, 1878-1891.

Pepys, Samuel, The Diary of, edited by H. B. Wheatley, 9 vols., London, 1904. Contains much social and political gossip about Arlington and the other ministers of his time.

Perwich, William, English Agent in Paris, The Dispatches of, 1669-1677, edited by M. B. Curran (Royal Historical Society), London, 1903. Of very slight use for this biography.

Pontalis, see Lefevre-Pontalis.

Pribram, A. F., *Franz Paul, Freiherr von Lisola, 1613-1674, und die Politik seiner Zeit,* Leipzig, 1894. Enlightening for the negotiations preceding the formation of the Triple Alliance.

IIPOTEAEIA *Anglo-Batava, Pan plusquam Virgineo Gulielmo Arausii et Mariae Britanniarum Academia Oxoniensi Procurante,* Oxford, 1641. Oxford verse, including a poem written by Bennet when a student in the University.

Remembrancia, Analytical Index to the Series of Records known as the, Preserved among the Archives of the City of London. A. D. 1579-1664, London, 1878. Furnishes some facts about Bennet's family.

Shaw, William A., *The Knights of England,* 2 vols., London, 1906.

Sheffield, John, *The Works of John Sheffield, Earl of Mulgrave, Marquis of Normanby, and Duke of Buckingham,* 2 vols., London, 1740. Contains a favorable sketch of Bennet's life and character.

State Papers, Domestic, Calendar of the, 1660-1685. Exceptionally informative about Bennet because of his office of Secretary of State.

State Tracts, Being a Collection of Several Treatises relating to the Government Privately Printed in the Reign of King Charles II, London, 1693. Political pamphlets offering some interesting criticisms of the government.

Symonds, Richard, Diary of the marches kept by the Royal Army during the Great Civil War; kept by, edited by C. E. Long (Camden Society), London, 1859. Affords information regarding the skirmish at Andover in which Bennet participated.

Taafe, Memoirs of the Family of (privately printed), Vienna, 1856. Contains the correspondence of Arlington with the Earl of Carlingford, English envoy at Vienna. Of value for an understanding of foreign affairs in 1665-1666.

Temple, Sir William, Bart., The Works of, 4 vols., London, 1814. Essential to an understanding of Arlington's diplomacy. The memoirs are very bitter in tone where he is concerned.

Thornbury, Walter, *Old London and New,* 6 vols., London, 1873-1878.

Thurloe, John, Esq., A Collection of the State Papers of, published by Thomas Birch, 7 vols., London, 1742. Contains a few letters from Bennet to Charles II, written during the Exile.

Treasury Books, Calendar of the, 1660-1685. Of minor importance for this study.

Villiers, George, *The Works of His Grace, George Villiers, Duke of Buckingham,* 2 vols., London, 1775. Contains a satiric poem about Arlington.

Walker, Sir Edward, *Historical Discourses upon Several Occasions,* London, 1705. Contains an account of the skirmish at Andover in which Bennet participated.

Welch, Joseph, *A List of Scholars of St. Peter's College, Westminster,* London, 1788. Incomplete for the period when Bennet was a scholar.

Wheatley, H. B., *London Past and Present,* 3 vols., London, 1891.

Wicquefort, Abraham de, *Histoire des Provinces-Unies des Pats Bas, depuis le parfait Etablissement de cet Etat par la Paix de Munster,* edited by M. L. Ed. Lenting and C. A. Chais Van Buren, 4 vols., Amsterdam, 1861-1874. Affords reliable and valuable information about the embassy of Buckingham and Arlington to the Hague in 1672.

[William III], *Original Letters from King William III, then Prince of Orange, to King Charles II, Lord Arlington,* etc., London, 1704. Enlightening as to Arlington's relations with the Prince, but otherwise of no particular value.

Williamson, Sir Joseph, Letters addressed to, while Plenipotentiary at the Congress of Cologne in 1673 and 1674, edited by W. D. Christie (Camden Society), 2 vols., London, 1874. These are intelligence letters giving Williamson all the English news. Of much value for the story of the attempted impeachment of Arlington.

Wood, Anthony a, *Athenae Oxonienses, to which are added The Fasti, or Annals of the said University,* edited by Philip Bliss, 4 vols., London, 1813-1820. The Fasti contain a sketch of Arlington's career.

The History and Antiquities of the Colleges and Halls

in the University of Oxford, edited and continued to the present time by John Gutch, Oxford, 1786. Used in connection with Bennet's University career.

The History and Antiquities of the University of Ox-

ford, edited by John Gutch, 2 vols., Oxford, 1792-1796. Used in connection with Bennet's University career.
Woolsey, T. D., *Introduction to the Study of International Law,* New York, 1879. Explains the practice of belligerent powers in regard to neutral commerce in the seventeenth century.

PERIODICAL LITERATURE.

Digby, H. M., " George Digby, Earl of Bristol", the *Ancestor,* XI, 71. A brief sketch of the career of Bennet's first patron.

Hora Siccama, J., " Sir Gabriel de Sylvius ", *Revue d'Histoire Diplomatique,* XIV, 598. A biography, including an account of Sylvius's connection with Arlington and with Buat.

Hughes, Charles, " Nicholas Faunt's Discourse touching the Office of Principal Secretary of Estate, etc., 1592", *English Historical Review,* XX, 499. A description of the duties of the Secretary of State in the time of Elizabeth.

Japikse, N., and Del Court, W., " Brieven van Sylvius en Buat", *Bijdragen en Mededeelingen van het Historisch Genoot- schap,* XXVII, 536. Contains the letters written to Arlington in regard to Buat's negotiation with the Orange party in 1666.

UNPUBLISHED MATERIALS.

Archives des Affaires Etrangeres, Paris. Correspondance Po- litique, Angleterre, 75-117. The despatches of the French ambassadors give so minute and careful an account of all that went on both in politics and in Court intrigue, that their value cannot well be overrated. Much of this material has already been published by Dalrymple and Mignet, but much is still unprinted that is of importance for this reign.

Bodleian Library, Oxford.

Ashmole MSS., 807. Contains an account of the speeches of Buckingham in the House of Commons in 1674.

Carte MSS. These include a great many letters from Arlington to the Duke of Ormonde, the most intimate he ever wrote.

Clarendon MSS. Include a practically complete series of letters written by Bennet to Hyde during the former's sojourn in Spain.

Rawlinson MSS., A. 429; A. 40. Afford some information about "Bennet's family.

British Museum, London.

Additional ,MSS., 18981; 22920; 25123; 28045; 32o4; 34342. Letters containing miscellaneous information about Arlington.

Egerton MSS., 812. Copies of the despatches of the French ambassadors in England during the year 1665.

Egerton MSS., 2543. Copy of the patent which was to have created Bennet Lord Cheney.

Parish Registers of Harlington, Middlesex, containing entries of births and deaths in the Bennet family.

Public Record Office, London.

State Papers, Domestic, Interregnum, 497; A. *12;* A. *22;*

A. 61; A. 155. These MSS. furnish some information

about Rennet's father. State Papers, Domestic, Charles II, 235, f. 140. A letter from

Lord Conway to Sir J. Finch about Arlington.

State Papers, Domestic, Charles II, 231, Williamson's Diary.

State Papers, Domestic, Charles II, 319 A. Williamson's

Diary.

State Papers, Foreign.

Archives, 100-101; 221-224. Contain copies of several let- ters from Arlington to the English ambassadors at Cologne.

Flanders, 12. Contains the despatches of Bennet's grandfather, Sir John Bennet, written in the course of his embassy to Flanders in 1617.

France, 115-149. Letters from the English ambassadors in France to the Secretaries of State, intelligence letters, and a few memoranda of French negotiations at London.

Holland, 163-219. Letters from the English ambassadors at the Hague to the Secretaries of State. Miscellaneous papers.

Spain, 43-71. Letters from the English ambassadors at Madrid to the Secretaries of State. Miscellaneous papers.

Foreign Entry Books, 176-180. Minutes, mostly by Williamson, of the deliberations of the Committee of Foreign Affairs. Of great value in determining the opinions of the various Ministers on matters of foreign and domestic policy, particularly during the years 1668-1674.

Treaty Papers, 48. Sundry memoranda in regard to negotiations with the Dutch.

Privy Council Office, Whitehall. Registers of the Privy Council, 1660-1685. Meagre in information and of no particular value for this study.

SECTION 15

INDEX.

Lightning Source UK Ltd.
Milton Keynes UK
05 March 2010

150982UK00002B/109/P

9 780217 482103